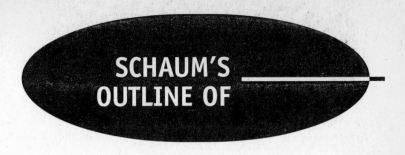

SCHAUM'S
OUTLINE OF

BASIC BUSINESS MATHEMATICS

EUGENE DON, M.S., Ph.D.

Department of Mathematics
Queens College (CUNY)

JOEL LERNER, M.S., P.D.

Retired Professor of Business
Sullivan County Community College (SUNY)

Schaum's Outline Series

McGRAW-HILL

New York   San Francisco   Washington, D.C.   Auckland   Bogotá   Caracas   Lisbon
London   Madrid   Mexico City   Milan   Montreal   New Delhi
San Juan   Singapore   Sydney   Tokyo   Toronto

EUGENE DON received his B.S. from Queens College, M.S. from Columbia University, and Ph.D. in Applied Mathematics and Statistics from the State University of New York at Stony Brook. He has been a member of the Faculty of Mathematics at Queens College of the City University of New York for over 30 years, where he teaches a variety of mathematics and business mathematics courses. He has also taught courses in business at other schools in New York State. His area of research is numerical analysis and he is interested in the application of computers to solving mathematics problems.

JOEL LERNER is a retired Professor and former Chairman of the Business Division at Sullivan County Community College, Loch Sheldrake, New York. He received his B.S. from New York University and his M.S. and P.D. from Columbia University. He has coauthored the Schaum's Outlines of *Principles of Accounting I and II* and *Business Mathematics* and is the sole author of *Bookeeping and Accounting* and McGraw-Hill's publication of *Financial Planning for the Utterly Confused*, now in its fifth edition. Professor Lerner is also a financial lecturer to several Fortune 500 firms, has produced his own TV and radio series for 15 years, and addresses thousands of people annually on finances.

Schaum's Outline of
BASIC BUSINESS MATHEMATICS

Copyright © 2000 by The McGraw-Hill Companies, Inc. All rights reserved. Printed in the United States of America. Except as permitted under the United States Copyright Act of 1976, no part of this publication may be reproduced or distributed in any form or by any means, or stored in a data base or retrieval system, without the prior written permission of the publisher.

1 2 3 4 5 6 7 8 9 10 11 12 13 14 15 16 17 18 19 20 PRS PRS 9 0 9 8 7 6 5 4 3 2 1 0 9

ISBN 0-07-038182-8

Sponsoring Editor: Barbara Gilson
Production Supervisor: Modestine Cameron
Editing Supervisor: Paul R. Sobel
Project Supervision: Keyword Publishing Services Ltd.

Library of Congress Cataloging-in-Publication Data

Don, Eugene.
   Basic business mathematics / Eugene Don, Joel Lerner.
      p.   cm. — (Schaum's outline series)
   Includes index.
   ISBN 0-07-038182-8
   1. Business mathematics.   I. Lerner, Joel J.   II. Title.
III. Series.
HF5691.D66   1999
650'.01'513—dc21   99-29346
                                                CIP

McGraw-Hill

A Division of The McGraw-Hill Companies

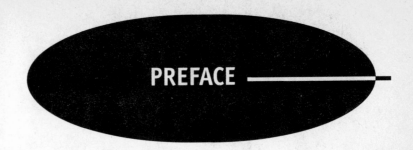

PREFACE

This book brings to the study of business mathematics the same solved-problems approach which has proved so successful in other volumes of the Schaum's Outline Series. *Schaum's Outline of Basic Business Mathematics* is organized around the practical application of mathematical concepts used in the financial world. The work that is presented in the following pages will provide students with

1. Concise definitions and explanations in easily understood terms with illustrative examples
2. Fully worked-out solutions to a large range of problems (against which students can check their own solutions)
3. Supplementary problems

The primary purpose of this book is to increase the student's competency in the mathematical computation of practical business problems. However, the student need not fear the mathematics involved. It is presented here in an easy-to-understand, readable way, and if the student is willing to expend a little time and effort, he or she will be rewarded with basic knowledge of the field of business mathematics.

EUGENE DON
JOEL LERNER

CONTENTS

Preface   iii

CHAPTER 1   **Review of Arithmetic**   **1**
              1.1   Whole Numbers   1
              1.2   Fractions   5
              1.3   Order of Operations   10
              1.4   Decimals   11
              1.5   Using an Electronic Calculator   15
              1.6   A Little Basic Algebra   17

CHAPTER 2   **Ratio, Proportion, and Percent**   **25**
              2.1   Ratio   25
              2.2   Proportion   28
              2.3   Percent   31
              2.4   Problems of Increase and Decrease   35

CHAPTER 3   **Payroll**   **41**
              3.1   Gross Pay   41
              3.2   Hourly Rate and Hours Worked   43
              3.3   Overtime   45
              3.4   Salary   49
              3.5   Commission   50
              3.6   Net Pay   54

CHAPTER 4   **Depreciation**   **68**
              4.1   Depreciation and Salvage Value   68
              4.2   Straight-Line Method   68
              4.3   Units of Production   75
              4.4   Double Declining Balance Method   82
              4.5   Sum-of-the-Years'-Digits Method   91
              4.6   Summary   99

CHAPTER 5   **Interest and Discount**   **105**
              5.1   Simple Interest   105
              5.2   Calculating Due Dates   107
              5.3   Methods for Computing Simple Interest   112
              5.4   Promissory Notes and Bank Discount   114

CHAPTER 6   **Annuities and their Applications**   **123**
                     6.1 Annuities   123
                     6.2 Sinking Funds   132
                     6.3 Amortization   137
                     6.4 Capital Budgeting   141

CHAPTER 7   **Stocks and Bonds**   **150**
                     7.1 Stocks and Dividends   150
                     7.2 Bonds   157

CHAPTER 8   **Buying**   **171**
                     8.1 Trade Discounts   171
                     8.2 Chain Discounts   174
                     8.3 Cash Discounts   177
                     8.4 Partial Payments   181

CHAPTER 9   **Selling**   **186**
                     9.1 Markup in General   186
                     9.2 Percent Markup   187
                     9.3 Selling Price as the Base   187
                     9.4 Cost as the Base   190
                     9.5 Markup Conversions   194
                     9.6 Inventory   196

CHAPTER 10   **Insurance**   **202**
                     10.1 The Need for Insurance   202
                     10.2 Insurance Premiums   202
                     10.3 Property Insurance   205
                     10.4 Major Medical Insurance   208
                     10.5 Life Insurance   210
                     10.6 Automobile Insurance   213

CHAPTER 11   **Introduction to Statistics**   **222**
                     11.1 Ungrouped Data   222
                     11.2 The Mean   222
                     11.3 The Median   224
                     11.4 The Mode   227
                     11.5 The Standard Deviation   228
                     11.6 Grouped Data   234

Index   **245**

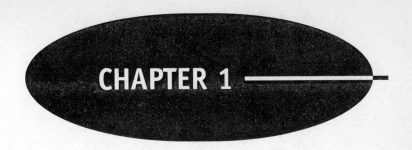

CHAPTER 1

Review of Arithmetic

1.1 WHOLE NUMBERS

Our number system, the decimal or base 10 system, uses the digits 0 through 9 to represent numerical values. A *whole number* is a string of digits representing, from right to left, how many ones, tens, hundreds, thousands, ten thousands, and so on are included within the number. Commas are often used to separate groups of three digits for visual clarity.

EXAMPLE 1

The number 247 represents 2 hundreds, 4 tens, and 7 ones.

$$
\begin{array}{ccc}
\text{hundreds} & \text{tens} & \text{ones} \\
2 & 4 & 7
\end{array}
$$

EXAMPLE 2

The number 1,547,689 represents 1 million, 5 hundred thousands, 4 ten thousands, 7 thousands, 6 hundreds, 8 tens, and 9 ones.

$$
\begin{array}{ccccccc}
\text{millions} & \text{hundred thousands} & \text{ten thousands} & \text{thousands} & \text{hundreds} & \text{tens} & \text{ones} \\
1, & 5 & 4 & 7, & 6 & 8 & 9
\end{array}
$$

Whole numbers are added by adding digits in corresponding columns and "carrying" if necessary. The result of an addition is called the *sum*. Addition is most conveniently done in a vertical format and columns are added from right to left.

EXAMPLE 3

To add 125, 231, and 122 we list the numbers vertically. We add the ones: $5 + 1 + 2 = 8$, the tens: $2 + 3 + 2 = 7$, and the hundreds: $1 + 2 + 1 = 4$.

$$
\begin{array}{r}
125 \\
231 \\
\underline{122} \\
478
\end{array}
$$

EXAMPLE 4

To add 287, 168, and 271, we add the ones: $7 + 8 + 1 = 16$ (write 6 and carry 1 to the tens column), the tens: $1 + 8 + 6 + 7 = 22$ (write 2 and carry 2 to the hundreds column), and the hundreds: $2 + 2 + 1 + 2 = 7$.

$$
\begin{array}{r}
2\,1 \\
287 \\
168 \\
\underline{271} \\
726
\end{array}
$$

EXAMPLE 5

Find the sum of 1,367, 4,672, 1,258, and 2,116.

$$
\begin{array}{r}
1\,2\,2 \\
1{,}367 \\
4{,}672 \\
1{,}258 \\
\underline{2{,}116} \\
9{,}413
\end{array}
$$

Whole numbers are subtracted by subtracting digits in corresponding columns and "borrowing" or "exchanging" if necessary. The result of a subtraction is called the *difference*.

EXAMPLE 6

To subtract 237 from 579 we list the numbers vertically with the larger number on top. We subtract the ones: $9 - 7 = 2$, then the tens: $7 - 3 = 4$, and finally the hundreds: $5 - 2 = 3$. In this example exchanging is not necessary.

$$
\begin{array}{r}
579 \\
-237 \\
\hline
342
\end{array}
$$

EXAMPLE 7

Subtract 257 from 492. Since 7 cannot be subtracted from 1, we exchange 1 ten for 10 ones, giving a total of 12 ones. 7 is then subtracted from 12: $12 - 7 = 5$ and the 9 in the tens column is reduced to 8. Then 5 is subtracted from 8: $8 - 5 = 3$ and finally, in the hundreds column, 2 is subtracted from 4: $4 - 2 = 2$.

$$
\begin{array}{r}
8\,12 \\
4\,\cancel{9}\cancel{2} \\
-257 \\
\hline
235
\end{array}
$$

EXAMPLE 8

Find the difference between 2,257 and 1,189. Here, two exchanges are necessary. Since 9 cannot be subtracted from 7, 1 ten is exchanged for 10 ones, giving 17 in the ones column. 9 is subtracted from 17: $17 - 9 = 8$. Since 8 cannot be subtracted from 4, one hundred is exchanged for 10 tens giving 14 in the tens column. Then 8 is subtracted from 14: $14 - 8 = 6$.

$$
\begin{array}{r}
1\,14 \\
4\,17 \\
2{,}\cancel{2}\cancel{5}\cancel{7} \\
-1{,}189 \\
\hline
1{,}068
\end{array}
$$

To multiply two numbers, multiply the first number (multiplicand) by each digit of the second number (multiplier). Then add. The result is called the *product*. The symbol for multiplication is either · or ×.

EXAMPLE 9

Multiply 54 by 23. Since the "2" in the number 23 really represents 20 its product with 54 is really 1,080. The rightmost "0" may be omitted and the 108 shifted one column to the left.

$$
\begin{array}{r}
54 \\
\times 23 \\
\hline
\end{array}
$$

$$
\begin{array}{rcl}
54 \times 3 = 162 & \rightarrow & 162 \\
54 \times 2 = 108 & \rightarrow & 108 \\
\hline
& & 1{,}242
\end{array}
$$

EXAMPLE 10

Multiply 112 by 245.

$$
\begin{array}{r}
112 \\
\times 245 \\
\hline
\end{array}
$$

$$
\begin{array}{rcl}
112 \times 5 = 560 & \rightarrow & 560 \\
112 \times 4 = 448 & \rightarrow & 448 \\
112 \times 2 = 224 & \rightarrow & 224 \\
\hline
& & 27{,}440
\end{array}
$$

The process of division is the most complicated of the four basic arithmetic operations. We divide the *dividend* (the number to be divided) by the *divisor* (the number you are dividing by) and the result is called the *quotient*. The next example illustrates the process of "long division."

EXAMPLE 11

Divide 345 by 15. We write the problem using the standard division symbol: $\overline{)}$. First we compare the two-digit divisor, 15, with the first two digits of the dividend, 345. Since 15 goes into 34 twice ($15 \times 2 = 30$ but 15×3 is too large), we put the first digit of the quotient, 2, in the position shown.

$$
\begin{array}{r}
2 \\
15\overline{)345}
\end{array}
$$

Next, multiply the partial quotient, 2, by the divisor 15 to get 30. Then subtract, bringing down the next rightmost digit.

$$
\begin{array}{r}
2 \\
15\overline{)345} \\
30 \\
\hline
45
\end{array}
$$

Finally, divide 15 into 45. Since 15 goes into 45 three times, we put 3 as the next digit of the quotient and multiply by the divisor, 15. Subtract to get a remainder of 0.

$$
\begin{array}{r}
23 \\
15\overline{)345} \\
30 \\
\hline
45 \\
45 \\
\hline
0
\end{array}
$$

EXAMPLE 12

Divide 6,247 by 23. In this example, the final subtraction gives 14. Since this number is less than the divisor, 23, the process ends with a remainder of 14.

$$
\begin{array}{r}
271 \\
23\overline{)6,247} \\
\end{array}
$$

$\underline{46}$	← $23 \times 2 = 46$
164	← subtract; bring down the 4
$\underline{161}$	← $23 \times 7 = 161$
37	← subtract; bring down the 7
$\underline{23}$	← $23 \times 1 = 23$
14	← subtract; this is the remainder

This answer is often represented as 271 R 14.

In algebra, exponents are used to represent repetitive multiplication by the same number.

$$ a^n = \underbrace{a \cdot a \cdot a \cdot \ldots \cdot a}_{n} $$

This is usually read "*a* to the power *n*."

EXAMPLE 13

(*a*) $2^4 = 2 \cdot 2 \cdot 2 \cdot 2 = 16$ (*b*) $3^5 = 3 \cdot 3 \cdot 3 \cdot 3 \cdot 3 = 243$

A *prime* is a positive integer which can only be divided by itself and 1. Examples of primes are 2, 3, 5, 7, 11, 13, 17, 19, 23, ... (For technical reasons, 1 is not prime.) Every whole number which is not prime can be written as a product of primes. This is called its *prime factorization*. A given number has only one prime factorization except for the order in which the primes are written.

The prime factorization of a number can be determined by successively factoring into smaller numbers until only primes remain. Exponents offer a convenient way to represent prime factors.

EXAMPLE 14

Find the prime factorizations of (*a*) 180, (*b*) 504.

(*a*) $\begin{aligned}
180 &= 18 \cdot 10 \\
&= 6 \cdot 3 \cdot 5 \cdot 2 \\
&= 2 \cdot 3 \cdot 3 \cdot 5 \cdot 2 \\
&= 2^2 \cdot 3^2 \cdot 5
\end{aligned}$ (*b*) $\begin{aligned}
504 &= 2 \cdot 252 \\
&= 2 \cdot 2 \cdot 126 \\
&= 2 \cdot 2 \cdot 2 \cdot 63 \\
&= 2 \cdot 2 \cdot 2 \cdot 21 \cdot 3 \\
&= 2 \cdot 2 \cdot 2 \cdot 7 \cdot 3 \cdot 3 \\
&= 2^3 \cdot 3^2 \cdot 7
\end{aligned}$

SOLVED PROBLEMS

1.1   Explain the significance of each of the digits in the number 23,456.

SOLUTION

The "2" represents 2 ten-thousands, the "3" represents 3 thousands, the "4" represents 4 hundreds, the "5" represents 5 tens, and "6" represents 6 ones.

1.2   Add 194, 638, and 211.

SOLUTION

$$
\begin{array}{r}
{}^{11} \\
194 \\
638 \\
\underline{211} \\
1{,}043
\end{array}
$$

1.3   Subtract 672 from 913.

SOLUTION

$$
\begin{array}{r}
{}^{8\,11} \\
9\!\!\!/13 \\
\underline{-672} \\
241
\end{array}
$$

1.4   Multiply 431 by 25.

SOLUTION

$$
\begin{array}{r}
431 \\
\underline{\times 25} \\
2{,}155 \\
\underline{8\,62} \\
10{,}775
\end{array}
$$

1.5   Divide 2,842 by 58.

SOLUTION

$$
\begin{array}{r}
49 \\
58\overline{)2{,}842} \\
\underline{232} \\
522 \\
\underline{522} \\
0
\end{array}
$$

1.6   Determine the prime factorization of 360.

SOLUTION

$$360 = 36 \cdot 10 = 6 \cdot 6 \cdot 2 \cdot 5 = 2 \cdot 3 \cdot 2 \cdot 3 \cdot 2 \cdot 5 = 2^3 \cdot 3^2 \cdot 5$$

1.2 FRACTIONS

Fractions are used to represent quantities which cannot be represented as whole numbers. A fraction is written in the form $\frac{a}{b}$ or a/b. a is called the *numerator* and b is the *denominator*. The denominator of a fraction can never be 0.

A quantity can be written as a fraction many different ways. For example, 1/2, 2/4, and 3/6 all represent the same value. The essential feature of fractions, which will be used extensively, is the following "fundamental principle":

> The value of a fraction is unchanged if its numerator and denominator are multiplied or divided by the same nonzero number.

EXAMPLE 15

Express the fraction 2/5 three equivalent ways. If we multiply the numerator and denominator by 2, 3, and 7 the fraction becomes, respectively, 4/10, 6/15, and 14/35. Any nonzero numbers may be used as multipliers.

EXAMPLE 16

Simplify the appearance of 21/35 without changing its value. Since the numerator and denominator are both divisible by 7, the fraction can be reduced to 3/5.

A fraction is *reduced to lowest terms* if its numerator and denominator cannot be divided by the same whole number.

EXAMPLE 17

Reduce 154/182 to lowest terms. Since both numerator and denominator are even, they can both be divided by 2. Applying the fundamental principle gives 77/91. Both 77 and 91 are divided by 7 to yield 11/13. Since the numerator and denominator cannot be divided by the same whole number, the fraction is reduced to lowest terms.

As a check to see if two fractions have the same value, we can use the following principle which is sometimes called *cross-multiplication*:

$$\frac{a}{b} = \frac{c}{d} \text{ if and only if } a \times d = b \times c$$

EXAMPLE 18

Check that 154/182 = 11/13. $154 \times 13 = 2,002$ and $182 \times 11 = 2,002$. Therefore the fractions are equal. (Note that there is no particular significance to the number 2,002, only that you get the same value two different ways.)

If two or more fractions have the same denominator we say that they have a *common denominator*. To add or subtract fractions with a common denominator, simply add or subtract their numerators and keep the common denominator.

EXAMPLE 19

Combine as a single fraction: $2/13 + 5/13 - 3/13$. Since the fractions have a common denominator, 13, we add and subtract the numerators: $2 + 5 - 3 = 4$. The answer is 4/13.

EXAMPLE 20

Combine as a single fraction: $1/20 + 3/20 - 7/20 + 17/20$. Since $1 + 3 - 7 + 17 = 14$, the answer is 14/20, which can be reduced to 7/10.

To combine fractions with different denominators, we must convert each fraction into an equivalent fraction with a common denominator. If the denominators have no common factors, i.e., they cannot both be divided by the same whole number, the common denominator is the product of the two denominators.

EXAMPLE 21

To add $2/3 + 3/5$ we first have to find a common denominator. In this problem the common denominator is $5 \times 3 = 15$. By the fundamental principle, $2/3 = 10/15$ and $3/5 = 9/15$ so $2/3 + 3/5 = 10/15 + 9/15 = 19/15$.

We can obtain a common denominator by multiplying the individual denominators, but this often leads to large numbers which are difficult to work with. It is sometimes possible to obtain a smaller common denominator which will work more efficiently. The smallest possible common denominator is called the *least common denominator* (LCD).

EXAMPLE 22

Add $5/24 + 7/36$.

To determine the LCD, obtain the prime factorizations of the denominators: 24 and 36. Then compute the highest power (exponent) of each prime and multiply.

For this example, $24 = 2^3 \cdot 3^1$ and $36 = 2^2 \cdot 3^2$. The highest power of 2 is 2^3 and the highest power of 3 is 3^2. Thus our LCD is $2^3 \cdot 3^2 = 72$. Since $5/24 = 15/72$ and $7/36 = 14/72$ by the fundamental principle, $5/24 + 7/36 = 15/72 + 14/72 = 29/72$.

EXAMPLE 23

Combine as a single fraction: $5/12 + 11/18 - 7/15 - 1/10$.

$$12 = 2^2 \cdot 3^1 \qquad 15 = 3^1 \cdot 5^1 \qquad \frac{5}{12} = \frac{75}{180} \qquad \frac{7}{15} = \frac{84}{180}$$

$$18 = 2^1 \cdot 3^2 \qquad 10 = 2^1 \cdot 5^1 \qquad \frac{11}{18} = \frac{110}{180} \qquad \frac{1}{10} = \frac{18}{180}$$

The LCD is $2^2 \cdot 3^2 \cdot 5^1 = 180$

$$\frac{75}{180} + \frac{110}{180} - \frac{84}{180} - \frac{18}{180} = \frac{83}{180}$$

To multiply two or more fractions, multiply their numerators and multiply their denominators. Then reduce, if possible.

EXAMPLE 24

Multiply $3/5$ by $6/7$:

$$\frac{3}{5} \times \frac{6}{7} = \frac{3 \times 6}{5 \times 7} = \frac{18}{35}$$

EXAMPLE 25

Multiply $2/9$, $3/4$, and $1/2$:

$$\frac{2}{9} \times \frac{3}{4} \times \frac{1}{2} = \frac{6}{72} = \frac{1}{12}$$

To divide two fractions, invert the second fraction and multiply.

EXAMPLE 26

Divide 3/5 by 6/7.
First, $3/5 \div 6/7$ is rewritten as $3/5 \times 7/6$. Multiplication yields $21/30 = 7/10$.

A *mixed number* is a combination of whole number and fraction. The number $3\frac{2}{5}$ is an example of a mixed number. To convert a mixed number to a fraction, multiply the whole number by the denominator of the fraction, add the numerator, and place that result over the original denominator.

EXAMPLE 27

Convert $3\frac{2}{5}$ to a fraction: $3 \times 5 + 2 = 17$, so the fraction is 17/5.

An *improper fraction* is a fraction whose numerator is larger than its denominator. To convert an improper fraction to a mixed number, divide numerator by denominator. This determines the whole number part. The remainder, if not 0, is placed over the denominator to determine the fractional part of the mixed number.

EXAMPLE 28

Convert 67/12 to a mixed number. If you divide 67 by 12 the quotient is 5 with remainder 7. Thus the mixed number is $5\frac{7}{12}$.

SOLVED PROBLEMS

1.7   Express the fraction 5/7 three equivalent ways.

SOLUTION

If we multiply the numerator and denominator by the same number, the value of the fraction does not change. Multiply, for example, by 2, 3, and 4:

$$\frac{5}{7} \times \frac{2}{2} = \frac{10}{14} \qquad \frac{5}{7} \times \frac{3}{3} = \frac{15}{21} \qquad \frac{5}{7} \times \frac{4}{4} = \frac{20}{28}$$

1.8   Reduce $\dfrac{1,575}{2,205}$ to lowest terms.

SOLUTION

$$\frac{1,575}{2,205} = \frac{315}{441} \qquad \leftarrow \text{divide by 5}$$

$$= \frac{105}{147} \qquad \leftarrow \text{divide by 3}$$

$$= \frac{35}{49} \qquad \leftarrow \text{divide by 3 again}$$

$$= \frac{5}{7} \qquad \leftarrow \text{divide by 7}$$

1.9   Check that $\dfrac{1,575}{2,205} = \dfrac{5}{7}$.

SOLUTION

$$1,575 \times 7 = 11,025 \qquad 2,205 \times 5 = 11,025$$

Since we get the same number, 11,025, both ways, the fractions are equivalent.

1.10   Combine as a single fraction: $1/11 - 3/11 + 5/11 - 2/11$.

SOLUTION

Since the denominators are the same, we combine the numerators and place the result over the denominator: $(1 - 3 + 5 - 2)/11 = 1/11$.

1.11   Add $5/12 + 7/18$.

SOLUTION

The LCD is 36: $5/12 = 15/36$ and $7/18 = 14/36$, so $5/12 + 7/18 = 15/36 + 14/36 = 29/36$.

1.12   Combine as a single fraction: $1/5 + 1/3 - 1/7$.

SOLUTION

Since the denominators are all primes, the LCD is simply $5 \times 3 \times 7 = 105$. Now, $1/5 = 21/105$, $1/3 = 35/105$, and $1/7 = 15/105$, so $1/5 + 1/3 - 1/7 = 21/105 + 35/105 - 15/105 = (21 + 35 - 15)/105 = 41/105$.

1.13   Combine as a single fraction: $5/12 + 7/18 - 3/20$.

SOLUTION

To determine the LCD, factor each denominator into primes. $12 = 2^2 \cdot 3^1$, $18 = 2^1 \cdot 3^2$, and $20 = 2^2 \cdot 5^1$. Take the highest exponent of each prime factor and multiply to get LCD $= 2^2 \cdot 3^2 \cdot 5^1 = 180$.

Next, convert each fraction to an equivalent fraction having a common denominator of 180. $5/12 = 75/180$, $7/18 = 70/180$, and $3/20 = 27/180$. Now add: $75/180 + 70/180 - 27/180 = 118/180$. This can be reduced to $59/90$ by dividing numerator and denominator by 2.

1.14   Multiply 4/7 by 5/8.

SOLUTION

$$4/7 \times 5/8 = 20/56$$

which can be reduced to 5/14.

1.15   Divide 3/11 by 6/7.

SOLUTION

$$\frac{3}{11} \div \frac{6}{7} = \frac{3}{11} \times \frac{7}{6} = \frac{21}{66} = \frac{7}{22}$$

1.16   Convert the mixed number $5\frac{2}{3}$ to a fraction.

SOLUTION

$$5 \times 3 + 2 = 17; \quad 5\frac{2}{3} = \frac{17}{3}$$

1.17   Convert the fraction 23/5 to a mixed number.

SOLUTION

Divide 23 by 5 to get a quotient of 4 with a remainder of 3. $23/5 = 4\frac{3}{5}$.

1.3 ORDER OF OPERATIONS

When two or more operations are involved in the same expression, they are performed in the following order:

$$\text{Powers (exponents)}$$
$$\text{Multiplication and division}$$
$$\text{Addition and subtraction}$$

Within each level, operations are performed left to right. If any modifications are to be made to this scheme, they are indicated by parentheses. Calculations within parentheses are always performed first.

EXAMPLE 29

Compute (a) $2 + 3 \cdot 5$, (b) $3 + 2^3 \cdot 5$, (c) $(2 + 3) \cdot 5$, (d) $(3 + 2)^2 \cdot 7$.

(a) $2 + 3 \cdot 5 = 2 + 15 = 17$

(b) $3 + 2^3 \cdot 5 = 3 + 8 \cdot 5 = 3 + 40 = 43$

(c) $(2 + 3) \cdot 5 = 5 \cdot 5 = 25$

(d) $(3 + 2)^2 \cdot 7 = 5^2 \cdot 7 = 25 \cdot 7 = 175$

This ordering scheme applies to fractions in a similar manner.

EXAMPLE 30

Compute (a) $2/3 + 3/4 \cdot 1/3$ and (b) $(2/3 + 3/4) \cdot 1/3$.

(a) $\dfrac{2}{3} + \dfrac{3}{4} \cdot \dfrac{1}{3} = \dfrac{2}{3} + \dfrac{3}{12}$

$\qquad\quad = \dfrac{8}{12} + \dfrac{3}{12}$

$\qquad\quad = \dfrac{11}{12}$

(b) $\left(\dfrac{2}{3} + \dfrac{3}{4}\right) \cdot \dfrac{1}{3} = \dfrac{17}{12} \cdot \dfrac{1}{3}$

$\qquad\qquad\quad = \dfrac{17}{36}$

SOLVED PROBLEMS

1.18 Explain the difference between $5 + 7 \cdot 3$ and $(5 + 7) \cdot 3$ and compute their values.

SOLUTION

In the expression $5 + 7 \cdot 3$ the multiplication is performed first to give 21. Then 5 is added to give an answer of 26. In the expression $(5 + 7) \cdot 3$ the parentheses indicate that the addition is to be performed first and the sum, 12, is then multiplied by 3. The result is 36.

1.19 Compute the value of $2 + 3 \cdot 5^2$.

SOLUTION

The exponent is evaluated first to give 25. Then 3 is multiplied by 25 to give 75. Finally 2 is added to give 77 as the answer.

1.20 Compute the value of $(3 + 2^3) \cdot 5$.

SOLUTION

All operations inside parentheses are performed first. The exponent is evaluated first and then the addition is performed. This gives a value of 11 $(3 + 2^3 = 3 + 8)$. This is then multiplied by 5 to give an answer of 55.

1.21 Compute the value of $\frac{1}{2} + \frac{1}{3} \cdot \frac{1}{4}$.

SOLUTION

Multiplication is the first operation considered, followed by addition:

$$\frac{1}{3} \cdot \frac{1}{4} = \frac{1}{12}. \qquad \frac{1}{2} + \frac{1}{12} = \frac{6}{12} + \frac{1}{12} = \frac{7}{12}$$

1.22 Compute the value of $\left(\frac{1}{2} + \frac{1}{3}\right) \cdot \frac{1}{4}$.

SOLUTION

The addition inside the parentheses is performed first: $1/2 + 1/3 = 3/6 + 2/6 = 5/6$.
This result is then multiplied by 1/4: $5/6 \cdot 1/4 = 5/24$.

1.4 DECIMALS

Decimals allow us to represent fractions with the convenience of whole-number representation. A decimal number consists of two strings of digits separated by a decimal point. The number 123.456 is an example of a decimal number.

Digits to the left of the decimal point represent the "whole" part of the number while digits to the right of the decimal point represent the fractional part according to the following scheme:

$$
\begin{array}{ccccccc}
\text{hundreds} & \text{tens} & \text{ones} & . & \text{tenths} & \text{hundredths} & \text{thousandths} \\
1 & 2 & 3 & . & 4 & 5 & 6
\end{array}
$$

The value of 123.456 is 1 hundred + 2 tens + 3 ones + 4 tenths + 5 hundredths + 6 thousandths

$$= 100 + 20 + 3 + \frac{4}{10} + \frac{5}{100} + \frac{6}{1{,}000}$$

Decimal positions further to the right would be ten thousandths, hundred thousandths, and so on.

Decimals are added and subtracted in a manner similar to whole numbers except that one must be very careful to line up the decimal points vertically. Zeros can be placed to the right of the decimal portion of the number for convenience. Thus 1.23, 1.230, 1.2300, and 1.230000 all have the same value.

EXAMPLE 31

Add 12.4, 13.12, and 1.765:

$$
\begin{array}{r}
12.400 \\
13.120 \\
1.765 \\
\hline
27.285
\end{array}
$$

← 0s have been added to
← the right of the decimal

EXAMPLE 32

Subtract 1.732 from 5.69:

$$
\begin{array}{r}
5.690 \\
-1.732 \\
\hline
3.958
\end{array}
$$

← a 0 has been added to the right of the decimal

Multiplication of decimals is similar to multiplication of whole numbers except that the number of decimal places in the product is equal to the sum of the numbers of decimal places in the numbers multiplied. Always count from the right when inserting the decimal point.

EXAMPLE 33

Multiply 1.742 by 2.13:

$$
\begin{array}{r}
1.742 \\
\times 2.13 \\
\hline
5,226 \\
1,742 \\
3,484 \\
\hline
3.71046
\end{array}
$$

← Disregard the decimals and multiply
   as if they were whole numbers.

← Since 1.742 has 3 decimal places and 2.13 has 2
   decimal places, the product has 5 decimal places.

To divide a decimal number by a whole number, divide as you would divide whole numbers and line up the decimal point in the quotient with the decimal point in the dividend.

EXAMPLE 34

Divide 18.75 by 15:

Decimal point lined up →
$$
\begin{array}{r}
1.25 \\
15\overline{)18.75} \\
\underline{15} \\
375 \\
\underline{300} \\
75 \\
\underline{75} \\
0
\end{array}
$$

To divide a decimal number by another decimal number, move both decimal points the same number of positions to the right until the divisor becomes a whole number. You may have to append zeros to the dividend.

EXAMPLE 35

Divide 19.5 by 3.75: $3.75\overline{)19.5}$ becomes $375\overline{)1,950}$ when the decimal point is moved 2 places to the right:

$$
\begin{array}{r}
5.2 \\
375\overline{)1,950} \\
1,875 \\
\hline
750 \\
750 \\
\hline
0
\end{array}
$$

Decimals may be converted to fractions by representing the digits, without the decimal point, by an appropriate power of 10 (10, 100, 1,000, etc.). Fractions may be converted to decimal form by performing a long division.

EXAMPLE 36

Convert 0.36 to a fraction:

$$0.36 = \frac{36}{100} = \frac{9}{25}$$

EXAMPLE 37

Convert 1.25 to a fraction:

$$1.25 = \frac{125}{100} = \frac{5}{4}$$

EXAMPLE 38

Convert 15/16 to a decimal:

$$
\begin{array}{r}
0.9375 \\
16\overline{)15.0000} \\
144 \\
\hline
60 \\
48 \\
\hline
120 \\
112 \\
\hline
80 \\
80 \\
\hline
0
\end{array}
$$

We perform a division, dividing 15 by 16. For convenience, extra 0s are appended to the right of the decimal in the dividend.

SOLVED PROBLEMS

1.23   Add 11.2, 12.35, and 13.423.

   SOLUTION

$$
\begin{array}{r}
11.200 \\
12.350 \\
13.423 \\
\hline
36.973
\end{array}
$$

1.24   Subtract 6.235 from 8.7.

SOLUTION

$$
\begin{array}{r}
8.700 \\
-6.235 \\
\hline
2.465
\end{array}
$$

1.25   Multiply 34.15 by 2.9.

SOLUTION

$$
\begin{array}{r}
34.15 \\
\times 2.9 \\
\hline
30735 \\
6830 \\
\hline
99.035
\end{array}
$$

← Ignore the decimal point until the end.

← Count 3 decimal places from the right.

1.26   Divide 138.7 by 19.

SOLUTION

$$
\begin{array}{r}
7.3 \\
19{\overline{)138.7}} \\
133 \\
\hline
57 \\
57 \\
\hline
0
\end{array}
$$

← line up the decimal points

← $7 \times 19 = 133$

← $3 \times 19 = 57$

1.27   Divide 109.53 by 4.5.

SOLUTION

First multiply both numbers by 10 to make the divisor a whole number:

$$
\begin{array}{r}
24.34 \\
45{\overline{)1,095.30}} \\
90 \\
\hline
195 \\
180 \\
\hline
153 \\
135 \\
\hline
180 \\
180 \\
\hline
0
\end{array}
$$

← append a 0

1.28   Convert 0.125 to a fraction.

SOLUTION

$$
0.125 = \frac{125}{1,000} = \frac{25}{200} = \frac{5}{40} = \frac{1}{8}
$$

1.29   Convert 7/8 to a decimal.

SOLUTION

$$\begin{array}{r} 0.875 \\ 8)\overline{7.000} \\ \underline{64} \\ 60 \\ \underline{56} \\ 40 \\ \underline{40} \\ 0 \end{array} \qquad \frac{7}{8} = 0.875$$

1.5   USING AN ELECTRONIC CALCULATOR

Electronic calculators provide the ability to do complex calculations quickly and efficiently and with less error than hand calculations. Because they are so inexpensive, they are widely used and have become a basic tool in mathematics.

Students studying business mathematics should purchase a calculator with a power function. This will make problems involving compound interest much easier to deal with.

Although many different models are available, with many advanced options and features, their basic operations work in a very similar manner. Consult your owner's manual for a description of more advanced features.

EXAMPLE 39

To add $23.178 + 16.624$ we enter the numbers separated by the $\boxed{+}$ key. The answer is displayed by pressing the $\boxed{=}$ key.

Enter	Press	Display	
23.178	$\boxed{+}$	23.178	
16.624	$\boxed{=}$	39.802	← answer

EXAMPLE 40

Add 16.75 to 12.7 and then subtract 8.572:

Enter	Press	Display	
16.75	$\boxed{+}$	16.75	
12.7	$\boxed{-}$	29.45	
8.572	$\boxed{=}$	20.878	← answer

EXAMPLE 41

Multiply 12.34 by 7.23:

Enter	Press	Display	
12.34	$\boxed{\times}$	12.34	
7.23	$\boxed{=}$	89.2182	← answer

EXAMPLE 42

Divide 193.8 by 15.2:

Enter	Press	Display	
193.8	$\boxed{\div}$	193.8	
15.2	$\boxed{=}$	12.75	← answer

EXAMPLE 43

Raise 1.2 to the fifth power (i.e., 1.2^5):

Enter	Press	Display
1.2	y^x	1.2
5	$=$	2.48832 ← answer

In algebra, multiplication and division are always performed before addition and subtraction. Therefore the value of the expression $2 + 3 \times 7$ is 23. If we want to do the addition first, we use parentheses to change the order of operations. Thus $(2 + 3) \times 7$ has a value of 35. If your calculator does not have parentheses, you can evaluate the expression, but you have to be careful to compute the addition, press the $=$ key, then do the multiplication and press the $=$ key again.

EXAMPLE 44

(a) Calculate the value of $(23.6 + 5.2) \times 2.7$ using parentheses:

Enter	Press	Display
	$($	0
23.6	$+$	23.6
5.2	$)$	28.8
	$\times$	28.8
2.7	$=$	77.76 ← answer

(b) Calculate the value of $(23.6 + 5.2) \times 2.7$ without using parentheses:

Enter	Press	Display
23.6	$+$	23.6
5.2	$=$	28.8
	$\times$	28.8
2.7	$=$	77.76 ← answer

SOLVED PROBLEMS

1.30   Add 26.2, 17.3, and 65.9.

SOLUTION

Enter	Press	Display
26.2	$+$	26.2
17.3	$+$	43.5
65.9	$=$	109.4 ← answer

1.31   Multiply 27.68 by 16.27 and then add 37.585 to the sum.

SOLUTION

Enter	Press	Display
27.68	$\times$	27.68
16.27	$+$	450.3536
37.585	$=$	487.9386 ← answer

1.32   Divide 34.925 by 12.7 and then subtract 1.22.

      SOLUTION

Enter	Press	Display
34.925	$\div$	34.925
12.7	$-$	2.75
1.22	$=$	1.53 ← answer

1.33   Add 12.2 to 25.9 and multiply the sum by 3.

      SOLUTION

    (*a*)   The standard order of operations require that multiplication be performed first. Since we wish to perform addition before multiplication, parentheses may be used.

Enter	Press	Display
	(	0
12.2	+	12.2
25.9	)	38.1
	$\times$	38.1
3	$=$	114.3 ← answer

    (*b*)   This problem may also be done without using parentheses:

Enter	Press	Display
12.2	+	12.2
25.9	$=$	38.1
	$\times$	38.1
3	$=$	114.3 ← answer

1.34   Compute the value of 1.05^{20}.

      SOLUTION

Enter	Press	Display
1.05	y^x	1.05
20	$=$	2.6532977 ← answer

1.6   A LITTLE BASIC ALGEBRA

In algebra, symbols, called *variables*, are used to represent numbers whose values are unknown. This enables us to work with them even though we don't yet know what their values are.

EXAMPLE 45

If p represents the price, in dollars, of a commodity, and we wish to increase its price by 3 dollars, its new price is represented as $p + 3$.

EXAMPLE 46

The cost of manufacturing a computer is c dollars. What is the cost of manufacturing 10 computers?

We multiply the cost of one computer by 10. Hence the cost becomes $10c$. Note that $10c$ is the same as $10 \times c$. In algebra, if a symbol is omitted, multiplication is assumed.

Equations are used to represent equality between two quantities. If the cost c of an item is the same as its selling price p, we write $c = p$ to represent that fact.

The phrase *more than* denotes addition, *less than* indicates subtraction, and the word *is* usually denotes equality.

EXAMPLE 47

Express the sentence "3 more than p is 7 less than c" as an equation.

We translate phrase by phrase. The word *is* becomes the center of the equation and is represented by $=$. 3 more than p becomes $p + 3$ and 7 less than c becomes $c - 7$. The resulting equation is

$$p + 3 = c - 7$$

EXAMPLE 48

Express "5 more than a is 3 more than b" as an equation:

$$a + 5 = b + 3$$

If an equation involves an unknown variable, we can determine the value of that variable by using the following simple principle:

> If you perform any arithmetic operation to one side of an equation, and perform the <u>same</u> operation to the other side, the equation remains valid.

By performing the right combination of operations, the values of unknown variables can be determined.

EXAMPLE 49

Solve for x: $2x + 3 = 13$.

To get to x, we first subtract 3 from both sides of the equation:

$$2x + 3 - 3 = 13 - 3$$
$$2x = 10$$

Next we divide both sides of the equation by 2:

$$\frac{2x}{2} = \frac{10}{2} \qquad \leftarrow 2x \text{ divided by 2 is } x$$
$$x = 5$$

The value of the unknown variable x is 5.

EXAMPLE 50

Solve for x: $\frac{x}{12} = \frac{1}{3}$.

We can cross-multiply to get $3x = 12$. Then divide both sides of the equation by 3 and $x = 4$.

EXAMPLE 51

Solve for y: $\frac{(y - 2)}{3} = 6$.

First multiply both sides of the equation by 3. It is helpful to think of 3 as 3/1:

$$\frac{y - 2}{3} \times \frac{3}{1} = 6 \times 3$$
$$y - 2 = 18$$

Now add 2 to both sides:

$$y = 20$$

We can solve simple word problems by first putting the problem into the form of an equation and then solving the equation algebraically.

EXAMPLE 52

Ryan orders three TV sets and leaves a $50 deposit. If the balance due is $1,225, how much is each television set?

We represent the cost of a television set by x. The three sets will cost $3x$ dollars. Since he left a $50 deposit, the balance remaining on the purchase is $3x - 50$ dollars. Thus $3x - 50 = 1,225$.

$$3x - 50 = 1,225$$
$$3x = 1,275 \quad \leftarrow \text{add 50 to both sides}$$
$$x = 425 \quad \leftarrow \text{divide both sides by 3}$$

Each set costs $425.

SOLVED PROBLEMS

1.35 If a refrigerator costs x dollars and goes on sale for $50 off, how much will it cost to purchase?

SOLUTION

$x - 50$ dollars.

1.36 Express the sentence "12 more than x is 5 less than y" as an equation.

SOLUTION

$x + 12 = y - 5$.

1.37 Solve for x: $5x - 7 = 33$.

SOLUTION

$$5x - 7 = 33$$
$$5x - 7 + 7 = 33 + 7 \quad \leftarrow \text{add 7 to both sides}$$
$$5x = 40$$
$$\frac{5x}{5} = \frac{40}{5} \quad \leftarrow \text{divide both sides by 5}$$
$$x = 8$$

1.38 Solve for y: $2y/3 = 16$.

SOLUTION

$$2y = 48 \quad \leftarrow \text{multiply both sides by 3}$$
$$y = 24 \quad \leftarrow \text{divide both sides by 2}$$

1.39   Solve for b: $b/14 = 3/7$.

SOLUTION

Cross-multiply to get $7b = 42$. Then divide both sides by 7. $b = 6$.

1.40   Solve for w: $(2w - 3)/9 = 3$.

SOLUTION

$$2w - 3 = 27 \quad \leftarrow \text{multiply both sides by 9}$$
$$2w = 30 \quad \leftarrow \text{add 3 to both sides}$$
$$w = 15 \quad \leftarrow \text{divide both sides by 2}$$

1.41   Bill orders five VCRs and two TV sets for a total cost of $1,260. Each television set costs $390. How much is one VCR?

SOLUTION

Let v represent the cost of one VCR. Since two TV sets cost $780 ($2 \times 390 = 780$), we have the equation $5v + 780 = 1,260$. Now solve for v:

$$5v + 780 = 1,260$$
$$5v = 480 \quad \leftarrow \text{subtract 780}$$
$$v = 96 \quad \leftarrow \text{divide by 5}$$

Supplementary Problems

1.42   How many hundreds, tens, and ones are represented by the number 659?

1.43   How many millions, hundred thousands, ten thousands, thousands, hundreds, tens, and ones are represented by the number 7,684,713?

1.44   Add the numbers 579 and 317.

1.45   Find the sum of 1,582, 2,359, and 3,456.

1.46   Subtract 782 from 953.

1.47   Add 5,392 to 7,683 and then subtract 8,567.

1.48   Multiply 29 by 57.

1.49   Find the product of 173 and 62.

1.50   Divide 3,526 by 43.

1.51   Find the quotient of 1,170 and 45.

1.52   Find the remainder if 257 is divided by 19.

1.53   Which of the following numbers is *not* prime: 13, 17, 23, 37, 57?

1.54 Find the prime factorization of 2,520.

1.55 Express the fraction 3/4 three different ways.

1.56 Reduce each of the following fractions to lowest terms:

(a) $\dfrac{75}{100}$, (b) $\dfrac{80}{120}$, (c) $\dfrac{65}{85}$.

1.57 Which of the following fractions is *not* equivalent to 2/3?

$\dfrac{26}{39}, \dfrac{74}{111}, \dfrac{100}{150}, \dfrac{38}{59}, \dfrac{110}{165}$.

1.58 Combine as a single fraction and then simplify:

$\dfrac{5}{99} + \dfrac{7}{99} + \dfrac{10}{99}$.

1.59 Combine as a single fraction and then simplify:

$\dfrac{13}{76} + \dfrac{15}{76} - \dfrac{11}{76} + \dfrac{21}{76}$.

1.60 Express the fraction 7/9 as an equivalent fraction whose denominator is 72.

1.61 Find the LCD of the fractions 5/21 and 7/35. Then add the fractions together.

1.62 Find the LCD of the fractions 5/99 and 1/24. Then subtract the second from the first.

1.63 Combine as a single fraction: $2/3 + 3/4 - 1/8$.

1.64 Combine as a single fraction: $3/10 + 2/15 - 1/35$.

1.65 Multiply 5/7 by 14/35 and reduce.

1.66 Multiply 3/5, 2/9, and 5/8. Be sure to reduce.

1.67 Convert $5\frac{2}{7}$ to a fraction.

1.68 Convert 72/11 to a mixed number.

1.69 Evaluate (a) $3 + 4 \cdot 6$ (b) $(3 + 4) \cdot 6$

1.70 Evaluate (a) $5 + 3^2 \cdot 6$ (b) $(5 + 3)^2 \cdot 6$

1.71 Evaluate (a) $\dfrac{5}{6} + \dfrac{2}{3} \cdot \dfrac{1}{5}$ (b) $\left(\dfrac{5}{6} + \dfrac{2}{3}\right) \cdot \dfrac{1}{5}$

1.72 Add: $2.76 + 3.52 + 6.79$.

1.73 Add: $3.1 + 5.12 + 2.73$.

1.74 Subtract 5.311 from 7.512.

1.75 Subtract 2.753 from 5.611.

1.76 Multiply 3.41 by 2.123.

1.77 Multiply 6.21 by the sum of 1.23 and 2.34.

1.78 Add 6.21 to the product of 1.23 and 2.34.

1.79 Divide 164.7 by 13.5.

1.80 Divide 14.875 by 1.25.

1.81 Convert to a fraction: (a) 0.75, (b) 0.625, (c) 0.45.

1.82 Convert to a decimal: (a) 33/100, (b) 7/8, (c) 11/32.

1.83 Use a calculator to compute the answers to the following problems: (a) $17.23 + 5.367$, (b) $19.1 - 6.57$, (c) 19.6×11.25, (d) $15.2 + 12.6 - 11.1$, (e) $12.75 \div 1.25$, (f) 5.2^3.

1.84 Use a calculator to compute the answers to the following problems: (a) $1.25 + 2.67 \times 3.47$, (b) $(1.25 + 2.67) \times 3.47$, (c) $7.5 \div 1.25 \times 3.4$, (d) $7.5 \div (1.25 \times 3.4)$.

1.85 Compute each of the following using your calculator (round to four decimal places):

$$(a) \quad 200\left[\frac{(1.075)^{10} - 1}{0.075}\right] \qquad (b) \quad 200\left[\frac{1 - \dfrac{1}{(1.075)^{10}}}{0.075}\right] \qquad (c) \quad \frac{200 \times 1.075}{1 - \dfrac{1}{(1.075)^{10}}}$$

1.86 If p represents the price (in dollars) of a new car and the manufacturer gives a $2,000 rebate, express the actual cost of the car in terms of p.

1.87 If an apple costs a cents and a banana costs b cents, express the cost of five apples and seven bananas in terms of a and b.

1.88 Express the sentence "5 more than x is 9 less than twice y" as an equation.

1.89 Solve for x: $3x + 5 = 38$.

1.90 Solve for x: $(x/15) = 1/5$.

1.91 Solve for x: $(2x - 3)/7 = 5$.

1.92 Peter buys three tacos from Taco City. He gives the waiter $5.00 and gets $2.15 change. How much is one taco?

1.93 Walter orders eight chairs for his dining-room table. He leaves a $75 deposit. If the balance due is $845, how much is each chair?

1.94 Samuel goes to the store and buys five videotapes and seven rolls of film. He pays $30.95. If each videotape costs $3.25, how much is a roll of film?

Answers to Supplementary Problems

1.42 6 hundreds, 5 tens, and 9 ones

1.43 7 millions, 6 hundred thousands, 8 ten thousands, 4 thousands, 7 hundreds, 1 ten, and 3 ones

1.44 896

1.45 7,397

1.46 171

1.47 4,508

1.48 1,653

1.49 10,726

1.50 82

1.51 26

1.52 10

1.53 57 is *not* prime; $57 = 19 \times 3$

1.54 $2^2 \cdot 3^2 \cdot 5 \cdot 7$

1.55 6/8, 9/12, and 15/20

1.56 (*a*) 3/4, (*b*) 2/3, (*c*) 13/17

1.57 38/59

1.58 2/9

1.59 1/2

1.60 56/72

1.61 The LCD is 105; 46/105

1.62 The LCD is 792; 73/792

1.63 31/24

1.64 85/210 = 17/42

1.65 2/7

1.66 1/12

1.67 37/7

1.68 $6\frac{6}{11}$

1.69 (*a*) 27, (*b*) 42

1.70 (*a*) 59, (*b*) 384

1.71 (*a*) 29/30, (*b*) 3/10

1.72 13.07

1.73 10.95

1.74 2.201

1.75 2.858

1.76 7.23943

1.77 22.1697

1.78 9.0882

1.79 12.2

1.80 11.9

1.81 (*a*) 3/4, (*b*) 5/8, (*c*) 9/20

1.82 (*a*) 0.33, (*b*) 0.875, (*c*) 0.34375

1.83 (*a*) 22.597, (*b*) 12.53, (*c*) 220.5, (*d*) 16.7, (*e*) 10.2, (*f*) 140.608

1.84 (*a*) 10.5149, (*b*) 13.6024, (*c*) 20.4, (*d*) 1.764705882

1.85 (*a*) 2,829.4175, (*b*) 1,372.8162, (*c*) 417.6330

1.86 $p - 2,000$ dollars

1.87 $5a + 7b$

1.88 $x + 5 = 2y - 9$

1.89 $x = 11$

1.90 $x = 3$

1.91 $x = 19$

1.92 $0.95

1.93 $115

1.94 $2.10

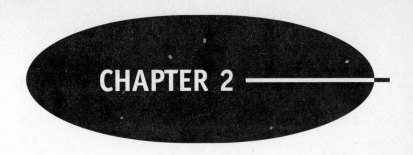

CHAPTER 2

Ratio, Proportion, and Percent

2.1 RATIO

A *ratio* is a way of comparing two or more quantities. If we have five red balls and three green balls, we say that the ratio of red balls to green balls is 5 to 3. Often this is abbreviated 5:3. If, in addition, we have two blue balls, we can express the ratio of red to green to blue as 5:3:2.

If units are involved, they are excluded from the ratio. However, it is important that all quantities in a given problem be represented using identical units of measure.

EXAMPLE 1

Find the ratio of weights of 2 lb of flour to 9 oz of sugar.
Since 2 lb of flour contain 32 oz, we express the ratio as 32:9.

If only two quantities are to be compared, the ratio may be conveniently represented as a fraction. For example, a ratio of 4:6 may be written as 4/6. It is often convenient to simplify the ratio by reducing its fractional value to 2/3, as discussed in Chap. 1.

EXAMPLE 2

Determine the ratio of 1 hour to 25 minutes.
Since 1 hour contains 60 minutes, we can write the ratio as 60:25 or, as a fraction, 60/25. Since 60/25 = 12/5 the ratio may be expressed 12:5. Since 12/5 = 2.4, we can also express the ratio as 2.4:1.

In finance, it is common to allocate funds according to a specific ratio. This can be conveniently done by dividing the total amount into "parts."

EXAMPLE 3

Suppose that $80,000 is to be allocated for advertising, research, and investment in the ratio 8:5:3. How much money will be allocated for each?
Since 8 + 5 + 3 = 16, we divide $80,000 into 16 parts of $5,000 (80,000 ÷ 16 = 5,000). Advertising gets 8 parts, $40,000, research gets 5 parts, $25,000, and investment gets 3 parts, $15,000. Note that the sum of the allocations must equal the original $80,000.

Since ratios behave like fractions, we can use the results of Chap. 1 to analyze them. For example, we know that $5:3 = 10:6$ because $5/3 = 10/6$.

EXAMPLE 4

Determine x, given $x:3 = 4:5$.
We write this in fractional form: $\frac{x}{3} = \frac{4}{5}$. Cross-multiply to get $5x = 12$. Then divide both sides of the equation by 5 and $x = 2.4$.

EXAMPLE 5

How many pounds of peanuts should be added to 50 lb of cashews if their weight ratio is to be 3:2?
Let x be the number of pounds of peanuts to be added. It follows that $x:50 = 3:2$. In fractional form this is written $\frac{x}{50} = \frac{3}{2}$. Cross-multiply to get $2x = 150$. Dividing by 2 yields $x = 75$ lb of peanuts.

SOLVED PROBLEMS

2.1   Reduce the ratios (*a*) 250:75, (*b*) 69:15, (*c*) 1.2 to 3.6.

SOLUTION

(*a*) $\dfrac{250}{75} = \dfrac{10}{3}$ (divide by 25), so the reduced ratio is 10:3.

(*b*) $\dfrac{69}{15} = \dfrac{23}{5}$ (divide by 3), so the reduced ratio is 23:5.

(*c*) $\dfrac{1.2}{3.6} = \dfrac{12}{36} = \dfrac{1}{3}$,   so the reduced ratio is 1:3.

2.2   Find the ratio of lengths 3 ft to 6 in.

SOLUTION

Since 3 ft = 36 in, the ratio must be expressed 36:6 or 6:1.

2.3   Determine the ratio of weights 3 lb to 24 oz.

SOLUTION

Since 3 lb = 48 oz, the ratio is 48:24 or 2:1.

2.4   A business spends $180,000 on advertising, $120,000 on research and development, and $150,000 on office rent. Find the ratios between these expenses.

SOLUTION

$$180,000:150,000:120,000 = 18:15:12 \quad \text{(divide by 10,000)}$$
$$= 6:5:4 \quad \text{(divide by 3)}$$

2.5   Allocate $1,500 in the ratio 3:2.

SOLUTION

 3 + 2 = 5, so divide $1,500 into 5 parts of $300 each:

$$300 \times 3 = 900$$
$$300 \times 2 = 600$$

so the allocations are $900 and $600.

2.6   Allocate $11,250 in the ratio 3:5:7.

SOLUTION

 3 + 5 + 7 = 15, so divide 11,250 by 15 to get 750:

$$750 \times 3 = 2,250$$
$$750 \times 5 = 3,750$$
$$750 \times 7 = 5,250$$

so the allocations are $2,250, $3,750, and $5,250.

2.7   A $14,000 grant is to be divided between Harvard and Yale in the ratio 4:3. How much money should each university receive?

SOLUTION

 4 + 3 = 7 so the $14,000 is divided into 7 parts of $2,000 each. Harvard gets 4 parts, $8,000 and Yale gets 3 parts, $6,000.

2.8   The order in which a race horse crosses the finish line determines how much money his owner will win. If a purse of $9,000 is divided among the win, place, and show horses in the ratio 3:2:1, how much will each horse earn?

SOLUTION

 3 + 2 + 1 = 6, so the purse of $9,000 is divided into 6 parts of $1,500 each (9,000 ÷ 6 = $1,500). The winner receives 3 parts, $4,500, the place horse receives 2 parts, $3,000, and the horse that shows receives 1 part, $1,500.

2.9   Solve for x: $x:5 = 18:30$.

SOLUTION

We first express the ratio in terms of fractions:

$$\frac{x}{5} = \frac{18}{30}$$

Then we cross-multiply to obtain $30x = 90$. Finally, divide both sides of the equation by 30 and we get $x = 3$.

2.10   A pancake recipe calls for 2 cups of milk for every 75 pancakes made. How many cups of milk are needed to make 525 pancakes?

SOLUTION

Represent the number of cups of milk required by x. Then $2:75 = x:525$. In terms of fractions, this reads $\frac{2}{75} = \frac{x}{525}$. Cross-multiply to get $75x = 1,050$. Finally, divide by 75 and we get $x = 14$ cups of milk.

2.11 The ratio of carnations to daisies in a floral display is required to be $7:5$. How many carnations are needed if 300 daisies will be used?

SOLUTION

Let x represent the number of carnations needed. The problem requires that $x:300 = 7:5$. Expressing this ratio as a fraction gives $\frac{x}{300} = \frac{7}{5}$. It follows that $5x = 2,100$ so $x = 420$.

2.12 On an investment of $50,000 Joe Brown receives $65,000 after one year. If Joe Green invested $80,000 in the same venture, how much should he be receiving?

SOLUTION

The amount received after one year is proportional to the amount invested. Let x represent the amount of money Mr. Green will receive. For convenience, we shall represent all numbers as thousands of dollars:

$$50:65 = 80:x$$

$$\frac{50}{65} = \frac{80}{x}$$

$$50x = 80 \times 65 \qquad \leftarrow \text{cross-multiply}$$

$$50x = 5,200$$

$$x = 104 \qquad \leftarrow \text{divide by 50}$$

Mr. Green will receive $104,000.

2.2 PROPORTION

In algebra, unknown quantities are represented by letters, such as x and y, called *variables*. The value of one variable is often related to the values of others. Two very special relationships occur often:

y is said to be *directly proportional* to x if their relationship is expressed in the form $y = kx$.

y is said to be *inversely proportional* to x if their relationship is expressed in the form $y = k/x$.

In each case, k is a number whose value is constant; k is called the constant of proportionality. Note that in a *direct* proportion y gets larger as x gets larger while in an *inverse* proportion, as x gets larger y gets smaller.

The constant of proportionality can be easily determined if values of x and y are given.

EXAMPLE 6

(*a*) Determine the value of k assuming that x and y are directly proportional and $y = 15$ when $x = 3$. Since, for direct proportions, $y = kx$, we simply substitute the appropriate values of x and y:

$$15 = k \times 3$$

To solve, divide both sides of the equation by 3 to get $k = 5$.

(*b*) Determine the value of k given that x and y are inversely proportional and $y = 15$ when $x = 3$.
For inverse proportions, $y = k/x$. Substitution yields $15 = k/3$. This time we multiply both sides by 3 to get $k = 45$.

Once we have determined the value of k, we can use the equation to solve problems.

EXAMPLE 7

The amount of money Jim earns is directly proportional to the number of hours he works. If he works 40 hours, he will make \$200. How much will he earn if he works 55 hours?
Let A represent the amount of money earned and h the number of hours worked. Then $A = kh$ represents the relationship between A and h. Since $A = 200$ when $h = 40$, the equation becomes $200 = k \times 40$ so, upon division by 40, $k = 5$. The equation now becomes $A = 5h$. Letting $h = 55$, we see that $A = \$275$.

A direct proportion can often be solved by setting up a ratio in the form of a fraction. If y is directly proportional to x, and y_1 and y_2 correspond, respectively, to x_1 and x_2, then

$$\frac{y_1}{y_2} = \frac{x_1}{x_2}$$

Note that the numerator (denominator) of the fraction on the left corresponds to the numerator (denominator) of the fraction on the right.

EXAMPLE 8

Solve example 7 using a ratio expressed as a fraction.
Let A represent the amount of money earned if Jim works 55 hours:

$$\frac{A}{200} = \frac{55}{40}$$

If we cross-multiply, we get $40A = 11{,}000$ from which it follows (by dividing by 40) that $A = \$275$.

EXAMPLE 9

It takes 72 hours for five workers to paint an office building. If the number of hours worked is inversely proportional to the number of workers, how many hours should it take six workers to paint the building?
Let H be the number of hours to paint the building and n the number of workers. Since H is inversely proportional to n, $H = k/n$. Since $H = 72$ when $n = 5$, $72 = k/5$, and multiplication by 5 yields $k = 360$. We now have $H = 360/n$. If $n = 6$, $H = 360/6 = 60$ hours.

An inverse proportion can also be solved by setting up a ratio in the form of a fraction. If y is inversely proportional to x, and y_1 and y_2 correspond, respectively, to x_1 and x_2, then

$$\frac{y_1}{y_2} = \frac{x_2}{x_1}$$

Note that the *numerator* of the fraction on the left corresponds to the *denominator* of the fraction on the right.

EXAMPLE 10

Solve example 9 using a ratio expressed as a fraction.
Let H represent the number of hours it would take six workers to complete the job.

$$\frac{H}{72} = \frac{5}{6}$$

Cross-multiplying, we get $6H = 360$, from which it follows that $H = 60$ hours.

SOLVED PROBLEMS

2.13 Determine the constant of proportionality, k, given y directly proportional to x and $y = 200$ when $x = 40$.

SOLUTION

   Since y is inversely proportional to x, $y = kx$. Since $y = 200$ when $x = 40$, we have, on substitution, $200 = k \times 40$. Therefore $k = 5$.

2.14 Determine the constant of proportionality, k, given y inversely proportional to x and $y = 20$ when $x = 3$.

SOLUTION

   Since y is inversely proportional to x, $y = k/x$. Since $y = 20$ when $x = 3$, $20 = k/3$. Multiplication by 3 gives $k = 60$.

2.15 The number of gallons of gasoline consumed by an automobile is directly proportional to the number of miles driven. If the car can travel 133 mi on 7 gal of gasoline, how many gallons will be consumed on a 228 mi trip?

SOLUTION

   Let x represent the number of miles driven and let y represent the number of gallons of gasoline used. Since y is directly proportional to x, $y = kx$. When $x = 133$, $y = 7$ so $7 = k \times 133$. Divide both sides of the equation by 133 and $k = 7/133 = 1/19$. Now we have $y = (1/19)x$. When $x = 228$, $y = (1/19) \times 228 = 12$ gal of gasoline.

2.16 Solve problem 2.15 using a ratio expressed as a fraction.

SOLUTION

   Let y be the number of gallons of gasoline needed. Since the number of gallons is directly proportional to the number of miles driven, we write $\frac{y}{228} = \frac{7}{133}$. Cross-multiplying gives $133y = 1,596$, from which it follows that $y = 12$ gal.

2.17 It takes four workers a total of 15 days to frame a house. How many days would it take six workers to complete the project?

SOLUTION

   Let x represent the number of days to frame the house and n the number of workers. Since x is inversely proportional to n, $x = k/n$. Since $x = 15$ when $n = 4$, $15 = k/4$, so $k = 60$. The equation of inverse proportionality now becomes $x = 60/n$, and when $n = 6$, $x = 10$. It would take six workers 10 days to frame the house.

2.18 Solve problem 2.17 using a ratio expressed as a fraction.

SOLUTION

   Let x represent the number of days to frame the house. x is inversely proportional to the number of workers on the job. Therefore $x/15 = 4/6$. Note that the 15 in the denominator on the left, which represents the number of hours to complete the job, corresponds to the 4 on the left, representing the number of workers. It follows that $6x = 60$, and $x = 10$.

2.3 PERCENT

The term *percent*, represented by the symbol %, is a mathematical term meaning one hundredth. Thus, for example, 50% = 50 hundredths = 50/100 = 0.50 and 37% = 37 hundredths = 37/100 =0.37.

EXAMPLE 11

(*a*) Express 24% as a fraction and simplify:

$$24\% = \frac{24}{100} = \frac{6}{25}$$

(*b*) Express 7/20 as a percent:

$$\frac{7}{20} = \frac{35}{100} = 35\%$$

To convert a percent to a decimal, simply drop the % symbol and move the decimal point two places to the left (divide by 100). If necessary, extra 0s can be inserted. To convert a decimal to a percent, move the decimal point two places to the right (multiply by 100) and add the % symbol.

EXAMPLE 12

(*a*) Express 3.7% as a decimal:

3.7% = 0.037 (decimal point moved two places to the left; 0 is inserted to the left of the 3)

(*b*) Express 0.375 as a percent:

0.375 = 37.5% (decimal point moved two places to the right, % symbol added)

EXAMPLE 13

Express 3/8 as a percent.
First convert 3/8 to a decimal by division:

$$\frac{0.375}{8)\overline{3.000}}$$

Then convert 0.375 to a percent by moving the decimal point two places to the right: 3/8 = 37.5%.

When the word *of* is used in connection with percents, it refers to multiplication. To solve problems, simply replace "of" by the symbol $\times$ and multiply.

EXAMPLE 14

Compute 15% of 60:

$$15\% \text{ of } 60 = 0.15 \times 60 = 9$$

$$\begin{array}{r} 60 \\ \times 0.15 \\ \hline 300 \\ 60 \\ \hline 9.00 \end{array}$$

EXAMPLE 15

20% of what number is 40?
Let x = the number to be found. 20% of that number is $20\% \times x = 0.20 \times x$:

$$0.20x = 40$$
$$x = 200$$

EXAMPLE 16

B&G Jewelry store is having a special sale. All ladies' jewelry is 35% off. What is the saving on a lady's ring which sells ordinarily for $350? What is the sale price?

$$35\% \text{ of } 350 = 0.35 \times 350 = \$122.50$$

The saving is $122.50. The sale price of the ring is $350.00 − $122.50 = $227.50.

EXAMPLE 17

An art dealer buys a rare painting for $150,000 and resells it one year later for $175,500. Express her profit as a percentage of the original price paid for the painting.

Her profit is $175,500 − $150,000 = $25,500. The ratio of profit to the original price paid is 25,500/150,000 = 17/100 (divide by 1,500). Expressed as a percentage, her profit is 17%.

One common application of percents is the computation of sales tax. The amount of purchase is multiplied by the sales tax rate (usually expressed as a percent) to compute the tax to be collected. In other words,

$$\text{Tax amount} = \text{Purchase price} \times \text{tax rate}$$

This equation can be expressed in two equivalent forms:

and

$$\text{Purchase price} = \frac{\text{tax amount}}{\text{tax rate}}$$

$$\text{Tax rate} = \frac{\text{tax amount}}{\text{purchase price}}$$

EXAMPLE 18

How much tax will be collected on a purchase of $350 if the tax rate is 5%?

$$\text{Tax amount} = \text{purchase price} \times \text{tax rate}$$
$$= 350 \times 5\%$$
$$= 350 \times .05$$
$$= \$17.50$$

EXAMPLE 19

There is an 8% tax on all purchases made in a certain Western city. How much of a purchase was made if the tax was $6.08?

$$\text{Purchase price} = \frac{\text{tax amount}}{\text{tax rate}}$$
$$= \frac{6.08}{8\%}$$
$$= \frac{6.08}{0.08}$$
$$= \frac{608}{8}$$
$$= \$76$$

EXAMPLE 20

What is the tax rate if there is a tax of $42.50 on a $500 purchase?

$$\text{Tax rate} = \frac{\text{tax amount}}{\text{purchase price}}$$

$$= \frac{42.50}{500}$$

$$= 0.085$$

$$= 8.5\%$$

EXAMPLE 21

If there is a 6% sales tax on all purchases and a certain item purchased costs $795, what was the pretax price of the item purchased?

Since tax $= 0.06 \times$ price, it follows that price $+ 0.06 \times$ price $= 795$. This is the same as $1.06 \times$ price $= 795$. Divide by 1.06 to get price $= 795/1.06 = \$750$.

SOLVED PROBLEMS

2.19   Express 36% as a fraction and simplify.

   SOLUTION

$$36\% = \frac{36}{100} = \frac{9}{25}$$

2.20   Express 3/5 as a percent.

   SOLUTION

$$\frac{3}{5} = \frac{60}{100} = 60\%$$

2.21   (a)   Express 68.5% as a decimal.

   (b)   Express 0.035 as a percent.

   SOLUTION

   (a) $68.5\% = 0.685$ (move the decimal point 2 places to the left)

   (b) $0.035 = 3.5\%$ (move the decimal point 2 places to the right)

2.22   Express 5/16 as a percent.

   SOLUTION

$$\begin{array}{r} .3125 \\ 16\overline{)5.0000}, \end{array} \qquad 0.3125 = 31.25\%$$

2.23   Compute 32% of $120.

   SOLUTION

   32% of $120 = 0.32 \times 120 = 38.4$. The amount of money is $38.40.

2.24 Because of a surplus in inventory, the price of light bulbs is being reduced from 40 cents to 32 cents apiece.

(a) What percentage of the *original price* is the reduction?

(b) What percentage of the *sale price* is the reduction?

SOLUTION

The reduction is 8 cents.

(a) $\dfrac{8}{40} = \dfrac{1}{5} = 0.20 = 20\%$ (b) $\dfrac{8}{32} = \dfrac{1}{4} = 0.25 = 25\%$

2.25 How much tax will be collected on a purchase of a new automobile valued at $20,000 if the tax rate is $8\frac{1}{4}\%$?

SOLUTION

$8\frac{1}{4}\% = 8.25\% = 0.0825$ Tax amount = purchase price × tax rate = $0.0825 \times 20{,}000 = \$1{,}650$

2.26 How much tax will be collected on a luxury item costing $12,750 if the rate is 7% on the first $10,000 and 10% on the amount over $10,000?

SOLUTION

On the first $10,000:

$$\text{Tax amount} = \text{purchase price} \times \text{tax rate}$$
$$= \$10{,}000 \times 0.07$$
$$= \$700$$

On the amount over $10,000:

$$\text{Tax amount} = \text{purchase price} \times \text{tax rate}$$
$$= \$2{,}750 \times 0.10$$
$$= \$275$$

Adding:

Total tax = $700 + $275 = $975

2.27 If the state sales tax is 6%, and a merchant charged $54.00 tax on a purchase, how much was the item purchased?

SOLUTION

$$\text{Purchase price} = \frac{\text{tax amount}}{\text{tax rate}}$$
$$= \frac{54}{6\%}$$
$$= \frac{54}{0.06}$$
$$= \$900$$

2.28   What is the local tax rate if tax of $4.95 is collected on a purchase of $90.00?

SOLUTION

$$\text{Tax rate} = \frac{\text{tax amount}}{\text{purchase price}}$$

$$= \frac{4.95}{90.00}$$

$$= 0.055$$

$$= 5.5\%$$

2.4   PROBLEMS OF INCREASE AND DECREASE

If a quantity increases or decreases, the amount of change is often represented as a percentage of the *original* quantity. Thus, if an inventory of 100 radios increases by 25%, the new quantity is 125.

EXAMPLE 22

Don's appliance store ordinarily stocks 250 assorted appliances. On June 1, Don noticed that his inventory increased by 12%. How many appliances did Don have in stock on June 1?

Since 12% of 250 = 0.12 × 250 = 30 appliances, Don had 280 (250 + 30) appliances in stock.

EXAMPLE 23

A well-known department store sells a certain brand of perfume for $90 an ounce. During a 2-week promotion they reduced the price by 15%. What was the sale price of the perfume?

Since 15% of 90 = 0.15 × $90 = 13.50, the sale price was 90 − 13.50 = $76.50 per ounce.

EXAMPLE 24

The price of a new automobile, including an $8\frac{1}{2}\%$ sales tax, is $16,531.06. What is the price of the car before tax?

Let x be the price of the car before sales tax is added. The tax itself is $0.085x$ ($8\frac{1}{2}\% \times x$). Therefore

$$x + 0.085x = 16{,}531.06$$
$$1.085x = 16{,}531.06$$

Divide both sides of the equation by 1.085 to get $x = \$15{,}236$.

SOLVED PROBLEMS

2.29   How much is 27% more than $500?

SOLUTION

The increase is 27% of 500 = 0.27 × 500 = $135. The new value is 500 + 135 = $635.

2.30   If a price of $80 is increased by 140%, how much will the new price be?

SOLUTION

The price increase = 140% of 80 = 1.40 × 80 = $112. The new price is $80 + $112 = $192.

2.31   What number is 30% less than 210?

SOLUTION

30% of 210 = 0.30 × 210 = 63. The new number is 63 less than 210 = 210 − 63 = 147.

2.32 If the number 100 is increased by 10% and then that number is decreased by 10%, do we get the original 100 back?

SOLUTION

No! 10% of $100 = 0.10 \times 100 = 10$. Adding this to 100, we get 110. Now take 10% of 110. $0.10 \times 110 = 11$. Subtracting this from 110 gives 99.

2.33 How much will a $650 stereo system cost if its price is increased by 15%?

SOLUTION

15% of $650 = 0.15 \times 650 = \$97.50$. The new price is $650 + \$97.50 = \$747.50$.

2.34 A $750 fur jacket goes on sale at a discount of 20%. What is the sale price of the jacket?

SOLUTION

20% of $750 = 0.20 \times 750 = \$150$. The sale price is $750 - \$150 = \$600$.

2.35 A gallon of paint now costs $11.80, but there will be a 15% increase in price tomorrow. How much will the actual price increase be? What will the new price of a gallon of paint be?

SOLUTION

15% of $11.80 = 0.15 \times 11.80 = 1.77$. The increase is $1.77. The new price will be $11.80 + \$1.77 = \$13.57$.

2.36 A diamond necklace costs $10,272, including a 7% sales tax. How much was the necklace before tax?

SOLUTION

Let x = price of the necklace before tax. The tax is $7\% \times x$.

$$x + 0.07x = 10{,}272$$
$$1.07x = 10{,}272$$
$$x = 9{,}600 \qquad \leftarrow \text{divide by } 1.07$$

The price before tax is $9,600.

2.37 The price of a tennis racket is $126 after a 10% reduction is taken. How much was the racket before the reduction was taken?

SOLUTION

Let x = the price of the racket before the reduction.

$$x - 0.10x = 126$$
$$0.9x = 126$$
$$x = 140$$

The racket costs $140 before the reduction is taken.

Supplementary Problems

2.38 Find the ratio of 3 weeks to 6 days.

2.39 Find the ratio of 12 yd to 9 ft.

2.40 Distribute $18,000 in the ratio 5:7.

2.41 A stock dividend is distributed among shareholders in the ratio of shares held. If Tom, Robert, and Sally have 500, 350, and 200 shares, respectively, and their combined dividend is $5,250, how much of the dividend does each receive?

2.42 $500,000 is to be allocated by a small computer company for equipment, advertising, and salaries in the ratio 3:2:5. How much money is allocated for each?

2.43 A family budget allocates money for food, housing, and entertainment in the ratio 4:9:1. If the total amount of money allocated for these expenses is $22,750, how much is to be spent on each item?

2.44 Three physicians invested $150,000, $200,000, and $250,000, respectively, in a medical practice. Their profit for the year was $1,200,000. If they divide the profits in the same ratio as their investments, how much does each receive?

2.45 Determine the value of x if $x:27 = 4:3$.

2.46 Determine the value of y if $5:y = 20:3$.

2.47 How many pounds of hard candies should be mixed with 30 lb of soft candies if their weight ratio is to be 3:2?

2.48 If a car can travel 150 mi on 8 gal of gas, how many gallons will be needed for a 675 mi trip?

2.49 The property tax in a small town is $17 per $100 of assessed valuation. How much is a house assessed for if its property tax is $2,975?

2.50 A philanthropist gives $140,000 to the heart foundation and the cancer society in the ratio 4:3. How much money does each charity receive?

2.51 The contestants in a boxing-match will receive prizes in the ratio 7:4; the winner gets the larger amount. If the total amount to be given out is $550,000 how much will each boxer receive?

2.52 A cookie recipe uses 2 teaspoons of butter for every 50 cookies made. How many teaspoons of butter will be needed if Lindsay wishes to make 225 cookies for a cookie sale?

2.53 The ratio of red balloons to blue balloons in a balloon display is 5:3. How many balloons of each color are present in a display consisting of 360 balloons?

2.54 y is *directly* proportional to x. $y = 30$ when $x = 5$.

   (a) Find the constant of proportionality.
   (b) Determine the value of y when $x = 15$.

2.55 y is *inversely* proportional to x. $y = 30$ when $x = 5$.

   (a) Find the constant of proportionality.
   (b) Determine the value of y when $x = 15$.

2.56   The amount of commission Bruce Sawyer, a salesman, receives is directly proportional to his sales. If Bruce receives $3,200 when he sells $50,000 worth of merchandise, how much will he receive if his sales for the month are $70,000?

2.57   The amount of money Joan earns is directly proportional to the number of hours she works. One week she worked 35 hours and earned $245. How much will she earn if she works 50 hours the following week?

2.58   It takes 20 workers a total of 30 days to pave a highway. How many days would it take 15 workers to do the same job?

2.59   Express as a fraction and simplify: (*a*) 1.25%, (*b*) 12.5%, (*c*) 125%.

2.60   Express as a percentage: (*a*) 9/50, (*b*) 11/20, (*c*) 8/25.

2.61   Express as a decimal: (*a*) 59%, (*b*) 5.9%, (*c*) 0.59%.

2.62   Compute (*a*) 18% of 90, (*b*) 30% of 600.

2.63   (*a*) 30% of what number is 18? (*b*) 45% of what number is 135?

2.64   How much tax will be collected on the purchase of a $450 TV set if the sales tax rate is 7%?

2.65   How much tax will be collected on a new car costing $25,100 if the sales tax rate is 8%?

2.66   How much tax is charged on a $2,700 item if the tax rate is 5% on the first $2,000 and 7% on the amount over $2,000?

2.67   How much tax is charged on a $37,000 automobile if the basic tax rate is $7\frac{1}{2}$% on the first $30,000 and 11% on the excess?

2.68   Suppose that the income tax rate is 20% on the first $30,000 of income, 15% on all income above $30,000 but not exceeding $50,000, and 10% on income above $50,000. How much tax will Bob have to pay if his income was $72,300?

2.69   There is a 7% sales tax on all purchases made in Eastport. If $17.50 tax was charged, how much did the item originally cost?

2.70   If the total price of a cordless telephone, including $7\frac{1}{2}$% sales tax, is $103.20

   (*a*)   What was the pretax price of the phone?
   (*b*)   How much tax was charged on the phone?

2.71   To rent a car for one day with unlimited mileage, you must pay a $2.00 highway tax and a 12% tax on the rental. If it costs $52.40 to rent a car, what was the base price of the rental?

2.72   If there is an $8\frac{1}{4}$% sales tax on new automobiles and a new Cadillac costs a total of $34,640 including tax, what was the pretax price of the automobile?

2.73   What is the tax rate if the tax on a $750 computer is $52.50?

2.74   To buy a $3,000 fur coat, a customer has to pay $3,255 including taxes. What is the tax rate in the town where the coat was purchased?

2.75   What number is 30% less than 90?

2.76   The retail price of a dress is 115% of wholesale. What is the retail price of a dress which wholesales for $140?

2.77   If the number 1000 is increased by 20% and then that number is decreased by 20%, what number do we get?

2.78   David's swimming-pool holds 50,000 gal of water. Because of a leak, the number of gallons decreased by 12%. How many gallons of water are left in the pool?

2.79   Sales for the year 2000 were $150 million, an increase of 20% over 1999 sales. What were the 1999 sales?

2.80   The wholesale price of milk is $2.80 a gallon. What will the new price be if the farmers impose a 5% increase in the price?

2.81   How much will a $175 VCR cost if it goes on sale for "15% off."

2.82   The price of a fax machine is $250 after a 20% reduction is taken. What was the price of the machine before the reduction?

Answers to Supplementary Problems

2.38   7:2

2.39   4:1

2.40 $7,500 and $10,500

2.41   Tom, $2,500; Robert, $1,750; Sally, $1,000

2.42   Equipment $150,000, advertising $100,000, salaries $250,000

2.43   food $6,500, housing $14,625, entertainment $1,625

2.44 $300,000, $400,000, and $500,000

2.45 $x = 36$

2.46 $y = \frac{3}{4}$

2.47   45

2.48   36 gal

2.49 $505.75

2.50 $80,000 to the heart foundation and $60,000 to the cancer society

2.51   Winner, $350,000; loser, $200,000

2.52   9 teaspoons

2.53   225 red and 135 blue

2.54 (a) $k = 6$, (b) $y = 90$

2.55　 (*a*) $k = 150$, (*b*) $y = 10$

2.56　 $4,480

2.57　 $350

2.58　 40 days

2.59　 (*a*) 1/80, (*b*) 1/8, (*c*) 5/4

2.60　 (*a*) 18%, (*b*) 55%, (*c*) 32%

2.61　 (*a*) 0.59, (*b*) 0.059, (*c*) 0.0059

2.62　 (*a*) 16.2, (*b*) 180

2.63　 (*a*) 60, (*b*) 300

2.64　 $31.50

2.65　 $2,008

2.66　 $149

2.67　 $3,020

2.68　 $11,230

2.69　 $250

2.70　 (*a*) $96, (*b*) $7.20

2.71　 $45

2.72　 $32,000

2.73　 7%

2.74　 $8\frac{1}{2}$%

2.75　 63

2.76　 $161

2.77　 960

2.78　 44,000 gal

2.79　 $125 million

2.80　 $2.94 per gallon

2.81　 $148.75

2.82　 $312.50

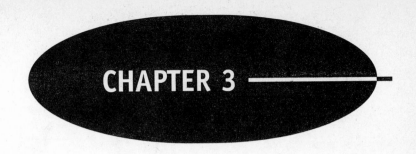

CHAPTER 3

Payroll

3.1 GROSS PAY

Gross pay is the total amount of money—before any deductions—that an employer will pay and is generally determined through negotiations between the employer and the employee. The employer, however, must conform with all applicable federal and state laws (minimum wage, and so on).

Gross pay for wage earners is generally computed by using an individual time card.

Time Card

Name _____	Pay rate/hour _____	
Week ended _____		
	Time in	Time out	Hours
Monday	_____	_____	_____
Tuesday	_____	_____	_____
Wednesday	_____	_____	_____
Thursday	_____	_____	_____
Friday	_____	_____	_____
Approved _____	Total hours for week _____	

EXAMPLE 1

Marcia Braunstein's weekly time card is shown below.

Time Card

Name Marcia Braunstein	Pay rate/hour $10.00	
Week ended 11/1/99		
	Time in	Time out	Hours
Monday	8:00 a.m.	4:00 p.m.	8
Tuesday	8:00 a.m.	4:00 p.m.	8
Wednesday	8:00 a.m.	3:00 p.m.	7
Thursday	8:00 a.m.	2:00 p.m.	6
Friday	8:00 a.m.	4:00 p.m.	8
Approved *Joel Lerner*	Total hours for week 37	

From the time card, we can compute the gross pay as follows:

$$\text{Hours worked} \times \text{hourly rate} = \text{gross pay}$$
$$37\,\text{h} \times \$10/\text{h} = \$370.00$$

SOLVED PROBLEMS

3.1   David Rasnick worked $36\frac{1}{2}$ hours last week at an hourly rate of $8.00. Find his gross pay.

SOLUTION

$$\text{Hours worked} \times \text{hourly rate} = \text{gross pay}$$
$$36.5 \times \$8.00 = \$292$$

3.2   For the week ending June 5, Carol Berg worked 40 hours at an hourly rate of $6.70. Determine her gross pay for the week.

SOLUTION

$$\text{Hours worked} \times \text{hourly rate} = \text{gross pay}$$
$$40 \times \$6.70 = \$268$$

3.3   Find, to the nearest cent, the gross pay of an employee who worked $26\frac{1}{4}$ hours at an hourly rate of $8.50.

SOLUTION

$$\text{Hours worked} \times \text{hourly rate} = \text{gross pay}$$
$$26.25 \times \$8.50 = \$223.13$$

3.4   For the following employees of Honeywell Advertising Company, determine the total hours worked and the gross pay, to the nearest cent.

Name	Mon.	Tues.	Wed.	Thurs.	Fri.	Hourly Rate
M. Bury	$7\frac{1}{2}$	$7\frac{1}{2}$	$7\frac{1}{2}$	$7\frac{1}{2}$	$7\frac{1}{2}$	$8.50
J. Cahn	7	5	$2\frac{1}{2}$	8	6	$7.20
P. Gallagher	8	8	8	8	8	$10.00
S. Klein	8	$3\frac{1}{4}$	8	4	0	$8.20
H. Walter	$6\frac{3}{4}$	5	4	3	$7\frac{1}{4}$	$6.70

SOLUTION

Name	Total Hours	$\times$	Hourly Rate	=	Gross Pay
M. Bury	37.5	$\times$	$8.50	=	$218.76
J. Cahn	28.5	$\times$	$7.20	=	$205.20
P. Gallagher	40	$\times$	$10.00	=	$400.00
S. Klein	23.25	$\times$	$8.20	=	$190.66
H. Walter	26	$\times$	$6.70	=	$174.20

3.2   HOURLY RATE AND HOURS WORKED

We can rewrite the formula for gross pay to solve for hours worked or hourly rate:

$$\text{Hours worked} \times \text{hourly rate} = \text{gross pay}$$

$$\text{Hourly rate} = \frac{\text{gross pay}}{\text{hours worked}} \qquad \text{Hours worked} = \frac{\text{gross pay}}{\text{hourly rate}}$$

EXAMPLE 2

Marlene's gross pay is $27 for 3 hours of work. What is her hourly rate?

$$\text{Hourly rate} = \frac{\text{gross pay}}{\text{hours worked}}$$

$$= \frac{\$27}{3} = \$9$$

EXAMPLE 3

Ivan's gross pay is $24 and his hourly rate is $6. How many hours has he worked?

$$\text{Hours worked} = \frac{\text{gross pay}}{\text{hourly rate}}$$

$$= \frac{\$24}{\$6/h} = 4\ h$$

SOLVED PROBLEMS

3.5   John Notin received $308 gross pay for 28 hours worked. What is his hourly rate?

SOLUTION

$$\text{Hourly rate} = \frac{\text{gross pay}}{\text{hours worked}}$$

$$= \frac{\$308}{28} = \$11$$

3.6   If Thelma Drew worked $37\frac{1}{2}$ hours and received $300 gross pay, what is her hourly rate?

SOLUTION

$$\text{Hourly rate} = \frac{\text{gross pay}}{\text{hours worked}}$$

$$= \frac{\$300}{37.5} = \$8$$

3.7   An employee received $452 gross pay and worked 40 hours. What is this employee's hourly rate?

SOLUTION

$$\text{Hourly rate} = \frac{\text{gross pay}}{\text{hours worked}}$$

$$= \frac{\$452}{40} = \$11.30$$

3.8   If Fred Saltzman received \$262.50 as his gross pay and worked 35 hours, what is his hourly rate?

SOLUTION

$$\text{Hourly rate} = \frac{\text{gross pay}}{\text{hours worked}}$$

$$= \frac{\$262.50}{35} = \$7.50$$

3.9   Given the gross pay and the hours worked, find the hourly rate for the following:

	Gross Pay	Hours Worked
(a)	\$396.00	36
(b)	\$211.60	23
(c)	\$234.50	35
(d)	\$440.20	$35\frac{1}{2}$
(e)	\$212.50	25
(f)	\$304.50	$26\frac{1}{4}$
(g)	\$506.40	40
(h)	\$234.50	$33\frac{1}{2}$

SOLUTION

	Gross Pay	÷	Hours Worked	=	Hourly Rate
(a)	\$396.00	÷	36	=	\$11.00
(b)	\$211.60	÷	23	=	\$ 9.20
(c)	\$234.50	÷	35	=	\$ 6.70
(d)	\$440.20	÷	35.5	=	\$12.40
(e)	\$212.50	÷	25	=	\$ 8.50
(f)	\$304.50	÷	26.25	=	\$11.60
(g)	\$506.40	÷	40	=	\$12.66
(h)	\$234.50	÷	33.5	=	\$ 7.00

3.10   Determine the total hours worked by Caren Don if her hourly rate is \$8.80 and her gross pay is \$88.

SOLUTION

$$\text{Hours worked} = \frac{\text{gross pay}}{\text{hourly rate}}$$

$$= \frac{\$88.00}{\$8.80/h} = 10$$

3.11   If an employee received \$300 gross pay at an hourly rate of \$7.50, how many hours did he work?

SOLUTION

$$\text{Hours worked} = \frac{\text{gross pay}}{\text{hourly rate}}$$

$$= \frac{\$300}{\$7.50/h} = 40$$

3.12 Patti Green works as a painter for Maplewood Painting Company. Her gross pay for last week was $205.20 and her hourly rate is $7.20. Calculate her total hours worked.

SOLUTION

$$\text{Hours worked} = \frac{\text{gross pay}}{\text{hourly rate}}$$

$$= \frac{\$205.20}{\$7.20/h} = 28.5$$

3.13 Determine the total hours worked by an employee if the employee's gross pay is $413.96 and hourly rate is $10.48.

SOLUTION

$$\text{Hours worked} = \frac{\text{gross pay}}{\text{hourly rate}}$$

$$= \frac{\$413.96}{\$10.48/h} = 39.5$$

3.14 Determine the hours worked for each of the following part-time employees:

	Gross Pay	Hourly Rate
(a)	$ 77.00	$ 7.00
(b)	$199.51	$11.24
(c)	$175.20	$ 8.76
(d)	$172.38	$ 6.76
(e)	$359.04	$10.88
(f)	$266.00	$ 7.60
(g)	$169.56	$ 6.28
(h)	$197.60	$ 9.88

SOLUTION

	Gross Pay	÷	Hourly Rate	=	Hours Worked
(a)	$ 77.00	÷	$ 7.00	=	11
(b)	$199.51	÷	$11.24	=	17.75
(c)	$175.20	÷	$ 8.76	=	20
(d)	$172.38	÷	$ 6.76	=	25.5
(e)	$359.04	÷	$10.88	=	33
(f)	$266.00	÷	$ 7.60	=	35
(g)	$169.56	÷	$ 6.28	=	27
(h)	$197.60	÷	$ 9.88	=	20

3.3 OVERTIME

Overtime generally refers to the hours worked in excess of 8 in 1 day or 40 in 1 week. For example, if John worked 10 hours yesterday he will be paid overtime for 2 hours $(10 - 8 = 2)$. If Mary worked 43 hours last week, she will be paid overtime for 3 hours $(43 - 40 = 3)$.

Overtime pay is usually $1\frac{1}{2}$ times the regular hourly rate. This overtime rate is called time-and-a-half. For example, if your hourly rate is $6, then your overtime rate is $1.5 \times \$6 = \$9$ per hour. Work on Sundays or legal holidays is usually paid for at 2 times the regular hourly rate. This rate is called *double time*. Therefore, for an hourly rate of $6, the overtime rate for work on Sundays or holidays is 2 × $6 = $12/h.

SOLVED PROBLEMS

3.15 Ryan Don's time card shows the following hours worked:

Mon.	Tues.	Wed.	Thurs.	Fri.
$8\frac{3}{4}$	9	7	$7\frac{1}{4}$	10

His hourly rate is $6.50 plus time-and-a-half for any hours worked over 40 per week. Determine (*a*) his total hours worked and (*b*) his gross pay.

SOLUTION

(*a*)   Hours worked = total hours worked
$$8.75 + 9 + 7 + 7.25 + 10 = 42$$

(*b*)   The gross pay in this instance is the sum of Ryan's regular pay and his overtime pay. We determine the regular pay as follows:

$$\text{Regular hours} \times \text{hourly rate} = \text{regular pay}$$
$$40 \times \$6.50 = \$260.00$$

To calculate overtime pay, we must first determine the overtime hours worked and the hourly rate for working overtime.

$$\text{Overtime hours} = 42\,\text{h worked} - 40\,\text{h} = 2\,\text{h}$$
$$\text{Overtime rate} = \$6.50 \times 1.5 = \$9.75$$

The overtime pay then is

$$\text{Overtime hours} \times \text{overtime rate} = \text{overtime pay}$$
$$2 \times \$9.75 = \$19.50$$

Ryan Don's gross pay for the week is

$$\text{Regular pay} + \text{overtime pay} = \text{gross pay}$$
$$\$260.00 + \$19.50 = \$279.50$$

3.16 Heather Borod worked the following hours during the week:

Mon.	Tues.	Wed.	Thurs.	Fri.
8	9	$8\frac{1}{2}$	10	$7\frac{1}{2}$

Calculate her gross pay at an hourly rate of $6.00 plus time-and-a-half for any work hours over 40 per week.

SOLUTION

$$\text{Regular hours} \times \text{hourly rate} = \text{regular pay}$$
$$40 \times \$6 = \$240$$

$$\text{Overtime hours*} \times \text{overtime rate**} = \text{overtime pay}$$
$$2.5 \times \$9 = \$22.50$$

$$\text{Regular pay} + \text{overtime pay} = \text{gross pay}$$
$$\$240 + \$22.50 = \$262.50$$

───────────────

*Overtime hours: $42.5 - 40 = 2.5$
**Overtime rate: $1.5 \times \$6 = \$9$

3.17   On Monday, Wednesday, and Friday, Matthew Cirrus worked 10 hours each day. On Tuesday and Thursday he worked 5 hours each day. His hourly rate is $6.70 plus time-and-a-half for any hours worked in excess of 8 per day. What is his gross pay?

SOLUTION

$$\text{Regular hours*} \times \text{hourly rate} = \text{regular pay}$$
$$34 \times \$6.70 = \$227.80$$

$$\text{Overtime hours**} \times \text{overtime rate}\dagger = \text{overtime pay}$$
$$6 \times \$10.05 = \$60.30$$

$$\text{Regular pay} + \text{overtime pay} = \text{gross pay}$$
$$\$227.80 + \$60.30 = \$288.10$$

───────────────

*Regular hours = total hours − overtime hours
    = (10 h/day × 3 days + 5 h/day × 2 days) − (10 h/day − 8 h/day) × 3 days
    = (30 h + 10 h) − 2 h/day × 3 days = 40 h − 6 h = 34 h
**Overtime hours: (10 h/day − 8 h/day) × 3 days (Mon., Wed., and Fri.)
†Overtime rate: $6.70 × 1.5 = $10.05

3.18   At Bullfrog Corp. the employees are paid an hourly rate of $6.50 plus time-and-a-half for any hours worked over 8 per day. Find the gross pay for René Wren when her time card shows the following:

Mon.	Tues.	Wed.	Thurs.	Fri.
9	$6\frac{1}{2}$	8	10	$7\frac{1}{2}$

SOLUTION

$$\text{Regular hours*} \times \text{hourly rate} = \text{regular pay}$$
$$38 \times \$6.50 = \$247.00$$

$$\text{Overtime hours**} \times \text{overtime rate}\dagger = \text{overtime pay}$$
$$3 \times \$9.75 = \$29.25$$

$$\text{Regular pay} + \text{overtime pay} = \text{gross pay}$$
$$\$247.00 + \$29.25 = \$276.25$$

───────────────

*Regular hours = total hours − overtime hours
    = 41 − 3 = 38
**Overtime hours: 1 (Mon.) + 2 (Thurs.) = 3
†Overtime rate: $6.50 × 1.5 = $9.75

3.19   Sylvia Braufman worked 46 hours last week at an hourly rate of $8.40 plus time-and-a-half for working over 40 hours per week. What is her gross pay?

SOLUTION

$$\text{Regular hours} \times \text{hourly rate} = \text{regular pay}$$
$$40 \times \$8.40 = \$336$$

$$\text{Overtime hours} \times \text{overtime rate*} = \text{overtime pay}$$
$$6 \times \$12.60 = \$75.60$$

$$\text{Regular pay} + \text{overtime pay} = \text{gross pay}$$
$$\$336 + \$75.60 = \$411.60$$

*Overtime rate: $\$8.40 \times 1.5 = \$12.60$

3.20   Calculate the gross pay of Harry Rogers. His time card for the week ending February 11 shows $48\frac{1}{2}$ hours worked. His rate of pay is $11 per hour plus time-and-a-half for any hours over 40.

SOLUTION

$$\text{Regular hours} \times \text{hourly rate} = \text{regular pay}$$
$$40 \times \$11 = \$440$$

$$\text{Overtime hours} \times \text{overtime rate*} = \text{overtime pay}$$
$$8.5 \times \$16.50 = \$140.25$$

$$\text{Regular pay} + \text{overtime pay} = \text{gross pay}$$
$$\$440 + \$140.25 = \$580.25$$

*Overtime rate: $\$11 \times 1.5 = \$16.50$

3.21   Francesca Johnson worked the following hours:

Mon.	Tues.	Wed.	Thurs.	Fri.	Sat.	Sun.
$9\frac{3}{4}$	$10\frac{1}{4}$	$6\frac{1}{2}$	8	$7\frac{1}{2}$	0	5

Find her gross pay if she is paid $6.75 per hour plus time-and-a-half for hours in excess of 40 and double time for any hours worked on Sunday.

SOLUTION

$$\text{Regular hours} \times \text{regular rate} = \text{regular pay}$$
$$40 \times \$6.75 = \$270$$

$$\text{Overtime hours} \times \text{overtime rate*} = \text{overtime pay}$$
$$2 \times \$10.125 = \$20.25$$
$$5 \text{ (Sun.)} \times \$13.50 = \underline{\$67.50}$$
$$\text{Total overtime pay} = \$87.75$$

$$\text{Regular pay} + \text{overtime pay} = \text{gross pay}$$
$$\$270 + \$87.75 = \$357.75$$

*Overtime rates: $\$6.75 \times 1.5 = \$10.125$ for weekdays
$\$6.75 \times 2 = \$13.50$ for Sundays

3.4 SALARY

If instead of being paid on an hourly basis, an employee is paid by the week, the month, or the year, he or she is said to be "on salary."

EXAMPLE 4

Joe's salary is $400 a week. What is his annual salary? Since there are 52 weeks in a year, we multiply $400 by 52.

$$\$400/wk \times 52 \text{ wk/yr} = \$20,800/yr$$

Now assume the reverse situation. You know your annual salary is $20,800, but you want to determine your weekly salary. In this case you divide by 52.

$$\$20,800/yr \div 52 \text{ wk/yr} = \$400/wk$$

EXAMPLE 5

Suppose that your salary is $1,400 per month. What is your annual salary?
A year has 12 months; therefore, to find your annual salary, multiply the monthly salary by 12.

$$\$1,400/mo \times 12 \text{ mo/yr} = \$16,800/yr$$

Similarly, if we know the annual salary, we can divide by 12 to find the monthly salary. Assume that Ruth Appel has an annual salary of $16,800. What is her monthly salary?

$$\$16,800/yr \div 12 \text{ mo/yr} = \$1,400/mo$$

SOLVED PROBLEMS

3.22 P. Bloomfeld is paid $40,000 annually. His pay period is biweekly. What is his salary per pay period?

SOLUTION

To find the salary per pay period, we need to divide the annual pay by the number of pay periods in a year. Note that Bloomfeld gets paid only once every 2 weeks (biweekly) rather than once every week. We must therefore divide the number of weeks in a year by 2 to get the number of pay periods in a year.

$$52 \text{ wk/yr} \div 2 = 26 \text{ pay periods/yr}$$

We can now calculate Bloomfeld's salary per pay period.

$$\text{Annual salary} \div \text{pay periods/yr} = \text{salary/pay period}$$
$$\$40,000 \div 26 = \$1,538.46$$

3.23 Determine the salary per pay period, assuming that an employee receives $25,000 per year and is paid monthly.

SOLUTION

$$\text{Annual salary} \div \text{pay periods/yr} = \text{salary/pay period}$$
$$\$25,000 \div 12 \text{ mo} = \$2,083.33$$

3.24 Mary Cassell's annual salary is $13,000. What is her weekly salary?

SOLUTION

$$\text{Annual salary} \div \text{pay periods/yr} = \text{salary/pay period}$$
$$\$13,000 \div 52 \text{ wk} = \$250$$

3.25 Determine the annual salary of an employee who is paid $897.33 biweekly.

SOLUTION

$$\text{Salary/pay period} \times \text{pay periods/yr} = \text{annual salary}$$
$$\$897.33 \times 26 \text{ wk} = \$23,330.58$$

3.26 Solve the following to the nearest cent:

	Annual Salary	Pay Period	Salary/Pay Period
(a)	$33,333	Biweekly	?
(b)	$10,400	?	$200
(c)	?	Weekly	$325.67
(d)	?	Monthly	$2,593.86
(e)	$47,980	Weekly	?
(f)	$42,312	?	$3,526
(g)	?	Biweekly	$765.43
(h)	$25,198	Monthly	?
(i)	$25,678.90	?	$987.65
(j)	$55,555	Biweekly	?
(k)	?	Weekly	$254.90
(l)	$18,000	?	$1,500

SOLUTION

(a) $33,333 ÷ 26 wk = $1,282.04

If we divide annual salary by the salary per pay period, we get the number of pay periods in a year.

(b) $10,400 ÷ $200/pay period = 52 pay periods/yr

The pay period is *weekly*, since there are 52 wk in a year.

(c) 52 wk × $325.67 = $16,934.84
(d) 12 mo × $2,593.86 = $31,126.32
(e) $47,980 ÷ 52 wk = $922.69
(f) $42,312 ÷ $3,526 = 12 pay periods/yr or monthly
(g) 26 wk × $765.43 = $19.901.18
(h) $25,198 ÷ 12 mo = $2,099.83
(i) $25,678.90 ÷ $987.65 = 26 pay periods/yr or biweekly
(j) $55,555 ÷ 26 wk = $2,136.73
(k) 52 wk × $254.90 = $13,254.80
(l) $18,000 ÷ $1,500 = 12 pay periods/yr or monthly

3.5 COMMISSION

At times it becomes impractical for business owners to assume all the functions of buying and selling. In order to relieve their workload, business owners hire salespeople. The means of paying such employees varies. Some receive a salary (see previous section), others receive a commission on the sales they make, and some are paid through a combination of both salary and commission. A *commission* is a fee paid for a service rendered (such as selling) and is usually expressed as a percentage of the money received by the business.

EXAMPLE 6

Suppose that you are working on a 25% commission basis. This means that your employer gives you 25¢ out of every dollar that you bring into the company through sales. The commission rate multiplied by the sales in dollars equals the amount of commission earned. Your commission on $80 of sales would therefore be

$$\text{Commission rate} \times \text{sales} = \text{commission earned}$$
$$25\% \times \$80 = \$20$$

If the commission is based on a single percent (as in the preceding example), it is called *straight* commission. In *variable* or *sliding scale* commission, two or more percents are used.

EXAMPLE 7

An employer pays 25% commission on sales up to $800 and 10% on the amount of sales above $800. How much does a salesperson earn on a sale of $1,200?

$$\text{Commission rate} \times \text{sales} = \text{commission earned}$$
$$0.25 \times \$800 = \$200$$
$$0.10 \times \$400* = \underline{\quad 40}$$
$$\text{Total earned} = \$240$$

---

*The amount above $800 is $1,200 − $800 = $400

A *draw* is an advance, or sort of loan, against future commissions. An employer may allow a salesperson to draw a regular amount of money each week to help the employee get through "slow" sales periods.

EXAMPLE 8

Suppose that an employee draws $200 at the beginning of a week and earns a commission of $240 by the end of the week. How much of the commission does the employee collect at the end of the week?

$$\text{Commission} - \text{draw} = \text{difference to be paid employee}$$
$$\$240 - \$200 = \$40$$

SOLVED PROBLEMS

3.27 Howard Mush receives a 7% commission from M&M Motor Sales. What is his commission on $12,000 in sales?

SOLUTION

$$\text{Commission rate} \times \text{sales} = \text{commission earned}$$
$$0.07 \times \$12,000 = \$840$$

3.28 Harriet Leidna receives a 6% commission on all her real estate sales. Half her commission goes to her broker. What is Harriet's portion of the commission on $150,000 in sales?

SOLUTION

$$\text{Commission rate} \times \text{sales} = \text{commission earned}$$
$$0.06 \times \$150,000 = \$9,000$$

Harriet gets to keep only half the commission she earns. Therefore, her portion in this instance is

$$\$9,000 \times \frac{1}{2} = \$4,500$$

3.29 During a month's time a furniture salesman receives 4% commission on the first $12,000 in sales, 5% commission on the next $12,000 in sales, and 6% commission on anything over $24,000. What is his commission on $42,000 in sales?

SOLUTION

$$\text{Commission rate} \times \text{sales} = \text{commission earned}$$
$$0.04 \times \$12,000 = \$\ \ 480$$
$$0.05 \times \$12,000 = \ \ \ \ 600$$
$$0.06 \times \$18,000^* = \underline{\ \ 1,080}$$
$$\text{Total commission} = \$2,160$$

$$*\$42,000 - \$24,000 = \$18,000$$

3.30 Slayton Music Company pays its salespeople the following commissions on all sales:

2% on the first $1,000 in sales
5% on the next $1,000 in sales
8% on any sales over $2,000

Commissions are paid monthly. Determine to the nearest cent the commissions earned by the following employees:

Employee	Sales
P. Lacey	$1,569.80
E. Marks	$3,486.00
S. Norris	$2,371.99
F. Pinto	$4,507.27
P. Robinson	$2,597.00
K. Stewart	$1,625.30
C. Valley	$4,375.01
T. Yates	$3,625.54

SOLUTION

Employee		Sales	×	Commission Rate	=	Commission Earned
P. Lacey		$1,000.00	×	0.02	=	$ 20.00
		569.80	×	0.05	=	28.49
	Total sales	$1,569.80		Total commission	=	$ 48.49
E. Marks		$1,000.00	×	0.02	=	$ 20.00
		1,000.00	×	0.05	=	50.00
		1,486.00	×	0.08	=	118.88
	Total sales	$3,486.00		Total commission	=	$188.88
S. Norris		$1,000.00	×	0.02	=	$ 20.00
		1,000.00	×	0.05	=	50.00
		371.99	×	0.08	=	29.76
	Total sales	$2,371.99		Total commission	=	$ 99.76

Employee	Sales	×	Commission Rate	=	Commission Earned
F. Pinto	$1,000.00	×	0.02	=	$ 20.00
	1,000.00	×	0.05	=	50.00
	2,507.27	×	0.08	=	200.58
Total sales	$4,507.27		Total commission	=	$270.58
P. Robinson	$1,000.00	×	0.02	=	$ 20.00
	1,000.00	×	0.05	=	50.00
	597.00	×	0.08	=	47.76
Total sales	$2,597.00		Total commission	=	$117.76
K. Stewart	$1,000.00	×	0.02	=	$ 20.00
	625.30	×	0.05	=	31.27
Total sales	$1,625.30		Total commission	=	$ 51.27
C. Valley	$1,000.00	×	0.02	=	$ 20.00
	1,000.00	×	0.05	=	50.00
	2,375.01	×	0.08	=	190.00
Total sales	$4,375.01		Total commission	=	$260.00
T. Yates	$1,000.00	×	0.02	=	$ 20.00
	1,000.00	×	0.05	=	50.00
	1,625.54	×	0.08	=	130.04
Total sales	$3,625.54		Total commission	=	$200.04

3.31 Dianne Wright receives a weekly salary of $200 *plus* a 4% commission on her total sales for the month. What are her gross monthly earnings if her total sales for the month are $8,400?

SOLUTION

Salary: $200/wk × 4 wk = $ 800
Commission: $8,400 × 0.04 =   336
                       Gross monthly earnings = $1,136

3.32 The employees of Adam & Chase Company receive a weekly salary of $250 *plus* a 5% commission on their first $10,000 in monthly sales and 7% on any monthly sales over $10,000. What are the gross monthly earnings, to the nearest cent, of the following employees:

Name	Sales
B. Eddy	$15,943.87
K. Katz	$ 9,500.69
C. Polster	$35,196.50

SOLUTION

B. Eddy

Salary: $250.00/wk × 4 wk = $1,000.00
Commission: $10,000.00 × 0.05 =   500.00
                                 $5,943.87 × 0.07 =   416.07
                       Gross monthly earnings = $1,916.07

K. Katz

Salary: $250.00/wk × 4 wk = $1,000.00
Commission: $9,500.69 × 0.05 =   475.03
                       Gross monthly earnings = $1,475.03

C. Polster

Salary:	$250.00/wk $\times$ 4 wk = $1,000.00
Commission:	$10,000.00 $\times$ 0.05 = 500.00
	$25,196.50 $\times$ 0.07 = 1,763.76
	Gross monthly earnings = $3,263.76

3.33 Brown's Sportswear Company pays its salespeople a straight commission of $8\frac{1}{2}\%$ on net sales for the month. Each salesperson also receives a draw of $150 per week. James Conway's sales for the month were $9,860. At the end of the month he is paid the difference between the draw and commission. What is owed James Conway?

SOLUTION

Commission:	$9,860 $\times$ 0.085 = $838.10
Draw:	$150/wk $\times$ 4 wk = 600.00
	Owed James Conway at end of mo = $238.10

3.34 Jean Gluck is paid a 7% commission on the first $1,500 in carpet sales, 8% on the next $1,500 and 9% on anything over $3,000 in sales. She also receives a $175 per week draw. To the nearest cent, find the difference between the draw and the commission that Jean receives at the end of the month. Her net sales for the month totaled $9,694.66.

SOLUTION

Commission:	$1,500.00 $\times$ 0.07	= $105.00
	1,500.00 $\times$ 0.08	= 120.00
	6,694.66 $\times$ 0.09	= 602.52
Total sales	$9,694.66 Total commission	= $827.52
Draw:	$175/wk $\times$ 4 wk	= 700.00
	Owed Jean Gluck at end of mo	= $127.52

3.6 NET PAY

A *deduction* is anything that decreases gross pay. For instance, gross pay may be reduced by deductions for union dues or for taxes (either federal, state, or city). *Net pay* is the amount of money that an employee takes home and is equal to gross pay less any deductions.

EXAMPLE 9

If Bob's gross pay is $300 and if his employer deducts $10 for union dues and $30 for taxes, how much does Bob take home?

$$\text{Total deductions: } \$10 + \$30 = \$40$$
$$\text{Gross pay} - \text{total deductions} = \text{take-home or net pay}$$
$$\$300 - \$40 = \$260$$

Deductions required by law are called *mandatory deductions* and include:

Federal Withholding Taxes. Under the federal withholding tax system (commonly known as "pay as you go"), federal income tax is collected in the year in which the income is received, rather than in the following year. Thus, employers must withhold funds for the payment of their employees' federal income taxes that will come due the following year. The amount to be withheld depends upon the number of exemptions the employee is allowed (on Form W-4), the amount of the employee's earnings, and the employee's marital status. An employee is entitled to one personal exemption and one for his or her spouse and each dependent.

Federal Insurance Contributions Act (FICA).   The FICA tax (a combination of social security and Medicare) helps pay for federal programs for old age and disability benefits, Medicare, and insurance benefits to survivors. During working years, money is set aside from an employee's earnings and placed along with all other employees' contributions to the Social Security fund. When the employee's earnings cease because of disability, retirement, or death, money from this fund is made available to his or her dependents, survivors, or to the employee himself or herself. A combined tax rate of 7.65% [6.2% for old-age, survivors, and disability insurance (OASDI), also known by the more popular term "Social Security," and 1.45% for hospital insurance (Medicare)] is imposed on both employer and employee. The OASDI rate (6.2%) applies to wages within the OASDI wage base, which is $72,600 (1999). The Medicare rate (1.45%) applies to all wages with no limit.

EXAMPLE 10

If, in a given payroll period, a total of $85 was withheld from employees' wages for Social Security taxes, the employer must remit $170 to the government. The $170 represents the $85 contribution by the employees plus the employer's matching share.

Wages in excess of $72,600 paid to a worker in one calendar year by one employer are not subject to the social security tax portion of FICA taxes.

EXAMPLE 11

Barbara's earnings prior to this week were $72,000. This week her salary is $500. Her FICA deduction would be $38.25 ($500 × 7.65%). If Barbara had earned $72,400 prior to this pay period, instead of the $72,000, only $200 of this week's $500 salary would be subject to the Social Security tax ($200 × 6.2% = $12.40) but the entire $500 would be subject to Medicare tax ($500 × 1.45 = $6.25) for a total FICA deduction of $18.65.

Note that the withholding of any wages represents, from the employer's viewpoint, a liability, because the employer must pay to the government the amount withheld from the employee.

In addition to taxes, or involuntary deductions, there may be a number of voluntary deductions made for the convenience of the employee, such as group insurance premiums, hospitalization programs, savings plans, retirement payments, union dues, and charitable contributions.

EXAMPLE 12

Harold Eccleston earned $300 for the week. Deductions from his pay were as follows: federal withholding taxes of $50, FICA tax of $23, insurance of $6, and union dues of $10. What is his net pay?

Net pay = gross pay − deductions
= $300 − ($50 + $23 + $6 + $10) = $300 − $89 = $211

SOLVED PROBLEMS

3.35   The federal income tax withheld from B. Sheppard's gross pay is $17.56 and the FICA tax is 7.65%. What is her net pay if her gross earnings for the week ending January 12 are $236.87?

SOLUTION

Gross pay		$236.87
Deductions		
Federal income tax	$17.56	
FICA tax*	18.12	
Total deductions		35.68
Net pay		$201.19

*FICA tax: $236.87 × 0.0765 = $18.12

3.36 If H. Bart has $25 withheld from his gross pay for U.S. savings bonds and also contributes $15 per week directly through his employer to his favorite charitable organization, what is his net pay, to the nearest cent, if his gross pay is $489.55 per week, federal income tax deduction is $33.98, and the FICA tax is 7.65%?

SOLUTION

Gross pay		$489.55
Deductions		
Federal income tax	$33.98	
FICA tax*	37.45	
U.S. savings bonds	25.00	
Charitable organization	15.00	
Total deductions		111.43
Net pay		$378.12

*FICA tax: $489.55 \times 0.0765 = $37.45

3.37 The following deductions were made from S. Sarles' gross pay:

Federal income tax	$35.89
FICA tax	25.50
Life insurance	10.44

If her gross pay is $333.33, what is her net pay?

SOLUTION

Gross pay		$333.33
Deductions		
Federal income tax	$35.89	
FICA tax	25.50	
Life insurance	10.44	
Total deductions		71.83
Net pay		$261.50

3.38 At Schmidt Electric the employees' contribution to the pension plan is 3% of their gross pay. If A. Levinson's gross pay is $543.21, federal income tax withheld is $40.65 and FICA tax is 7.65%, what is his net pay?

SOLUTION

Gross pay		$543.21
Deductions		
Federal income tax	$40.65	
FICA tax*	41.56	
Pension plan**	16.30	
Total deductions		98.51
Net pay		$444.70

*FICA tax: $543.21 \times 0.0765 = $41.56
**Pension plan: $543.21 \times 0.03 = $16.30

3.39 Find the net pay for P. Doyle if her gross pay is $257.34 per week and her deductions are $20.57 in federal income tax per week, $19.69 in FICA tax per week, and $20 in hospitalization insurance per month.

SOLUTION

Gross pay		$257.34
Deductions		
Federal income tax	$20.57	
FICA tax	19.69	
Hospitalization ins.*	5.00	
Total deductions		45.26
Net pay		$212.08

*Hospitalization insurance: $20/mo ÷ 4 wk/mo = $5/wk

3.40 D. Feldman pays $5.75 per week union dues. If his gross pay is $445.98 for the pay period and $23,190.96 for the year to date, his federal income tax withholding is $32.67, and his FICA tax is 7.65%, what is his net pay?

SOLUTION

Gross pay		$445.98
Deductions		
Federal income tax	$32.67	
FICA tax*	34.12	
Union dues	5.75	
Total deductions		72.54
Net pay		$373.44

*FICA tax: $445.98 × 0.0765 = $34.12

3.41 An employee's year-to-date gross pay is $36,799. Her current week's earnings amount to $735.98, her federal income tax withheld is $52.67, and her FICA tax is 7.65%. What is her net pay?

SOLUTION

Gross pay		$735.98
Deductions		
Federal income tax	$52.67	
FICA tax	51.52	
Total deductions		104.19
Net pay		$631.79

3.42 At Lord Enterprise the employees contribute 1% of their gross pay to their favorate charitable organization, 2% toward union dues, 3% toward life insurance, and 4% toward hospitalization insurance. If B. Hill's gross pay is $675, federal income tax withholding is $49.87, and FICA tax is $51.64, what is his net pay?

SOLUTION

Gross pay		$675.00
Deductions		
Federal income tax	$49.87	
FICA tax	51.64	
Charitable organization*	6.75	
Union dues**	13.50	
Life insurance***	20.25	
Hospitalization ins.†	27.00	
Total deductions		169.01
Net pay		$505.99

*Charitable organization: $675.00 × 0.01 = $6.75
**Union dues: $675.00 × 0.02 = $13.50
***Life insurance: $675.00 × 0.03 = $20.25
†Hospitalization insurance: $675.00 × 0.04 = $27.00

3.43 L. Bolt's gross pay so far this year totals $73,000. Her gross pay for the week ending December 27 is $640.75, federal income tax withheld is $50.87, FICA tax is 7.65% and union dues deduction is $7.50. She also has deducted $50 for U.S. savings bonds and $50 for her automatic savings account. Find her net pay.

SOLUTION

Gross pay		$640.75
Deductions		
Federal income tax	$50.87	
FICA tax*	9.29	
Union dues	7.50	
U.S. savings bonds	50.00	
Savings	50.00	
Total deductions		167.66
Net pay		$473.09

*$640.75 × 1.45% (Medicare tax) = $9.29

3.44 Ascertain the net pay for an employee whose gross pay is $256.93 per week, federal income tax withheld is $20.41, FICA tax is 7.65%, hospitalization insurance is $6.70, union dues deduction is $4.60, and life insurance is $5. In addition, the employee has made a loan through his employer whereby the employee agreed to a deduction of $25 per week from his paycheck until said loan is paid.

SOLUTION

Gross pay		$256.93
Deductions		
Federal income tax	$20.41	
FICA tax*	19.66	
Hospitalization ins.	6.70	
Union dues	4.60	
Life insurance	5.00	
Loan	25.00	
Total deductions		81.37
Net pay		$175.56

*FICA tax: $256.93 × 0.0765 = $19.66

3.45 Kaufmann Insulation pays its employees biweekly. In addition to the federal income tax withheld, each employee's deductions are as follows:

FICA tax	7.65%
Union dues	$5.50
Hospitalization ins.	$3.20
Life insurance	$4.20

Each employee also receives a $20 uniform allowance. Given the following gross pay, federal income tax withheld, and year-to-date gross pay for each employee, find the respective net pay to the nearest cent.

Name	Gross Pay	Federal Income Tax Withheld	Year-to-Date Gross Pay
P. Basso	$1,570.90	$111.52	$72,500.00
F. Ericson	1,734.66	121.98	74,000.00
C. Johanson	1,269.70	97.10	25,434.00
G. Markie	1,041.12	77.54	20,822.40

SOLUTION

P. Basso

Gross pay		$1,570.90
Deductions		
Federal income tax	$111.52	
FICA tax*	28.98	
Union dues	5.50	
Hospitalization ins.	3.20	
Life insurance	4.20	
Total deductions		153.40
		1,417.50
Uniform allowance		20.00
Net pay		$1,437.50

*FICA tax: ($72,600 − $72,500) × 6.2% = $100 × 0.062 = $6.20
$1,570.90 × 0.0145% = $22.78

F. Ericson

Gross pay		$1,734.66
Deductions		
Federal income tax	$121.98	
FICA tax*	25.15	
Union dues	5.50	
Hospitalization ins.	3.20	
Life insurance	4.20	
Total deductions		160.03
		$1,574.63
Uniform allowance		20.00
Net pay		$1,594.63

*Social security tax is taken only on the first $72,600 in gross yearly earnings.
Medicare tax $1,734.66 × 0.0145 = $25.15

C. Johanson

Gross pay		$1,269.70
Deductions		
Federal income tax	$97.10	
FICA tax*	97.13	
Union dues	5.50	
Hospitalization ins.	3.20	
Life insurance	4.20	
Total deductions		207.13
		$1,062.57
Uniform allowance		20.00
Net pay		$1,082.57

*FICA tax: $1,269.70 × 0.0765 = $97.13

G. Markie

Gross pay		$1,041.12
Deductions		
Federal income tax	$77.54	
FICA tax*	79.65	
Union dues	5.50	
Hospitalization ins.	3.20	
Life insurance	4.20	
Total deductions		170.09
		$ 871.03
Uniform allowance		20.00
Net pay		$ 891.03

*FICA tax: $1,041.12 × 0.0765 = $79.65

N. Schmitz

Gross pay		$867.24
Deductions		
Federal income tax	$60.96	
FICA tax*	66.37	
Union dues	5.50	
Hospitalization ins.	3.20	
Life insurance	4.20	
Total deductions		140.20
		$727.04
Uniform allowance		20.00
Net pay		$747.04

*FICA tax: $867.24 × 0.0765 = $66.34

3.46 At Pond Computer Systems, the following deductions are made from the employees' pay, in addition to the federal income tax withheld:

Mandatory	(a)	FICA tax	7.65% of gross
	(b)	State tax	5.50% of gross
	(c)	Union dues	2.00% of gross
	(d)	Hospitalization ins.	1.50% of gross
	(e)	Pension	3.00% of gross
Optional	(f)	Life insurance	2.25% of gross
	(g)	Charitable organ.	5.00% of gross
	(h)	Savings	7.00% of gross
	(i)	U.S. savings bonds	$25.00 per paycheck
	(j)	Loan payment	8.00% of gross (if loan outstanding)

Given the gross pay, federal income tax withheld, year-to-date gross pay, and optional deductions, find the net pay to the nearest cent for the following employees:

Name	Gross Pay	Federal Income Tax Withheld	Year-to-Date Gross Pay	Optional Deductions
J. Doyle	$489.76	$35.92	$24,488.00	f, g, i, j
D. Mabey	599.35	43.76	29,967.50	h, i

J. Doyle

Gross pay		$489.76
Deductions		
Federal income tax	$35.92	
FICA tax	37.47	
State tax	26.94	
Union dues	9.80	
Hospitalization ins.	7.35	
Pension	14.69	
Life insurance	11.02	
Charitable organization	24.49	
U.S. savings bonds	25.00	
Loans	39.18	
Total deductions		231.86
Net pay		$257.80

D. Mabey

Gross pay		$599.35
Deductions		
Federal income tax	$43.76	
FICA tax	45.85	
State tax	32.96	
Union dues	11.99	
Hospitalization ins.	8.99	
Pension	17.98	
Savings	41.95	
U.S. savings bonds	25.00	
Total deductions		228.48
Net pay		$370.87

Note that for all deductions except (*i*), the calculation is:

$$\text{Gross pay} \times \text{deduction \%}$$

Supplementary Problems

3.47 Sarah Litt worked $32\frac{1}{2}$ hours last week at an hourly rate of $6.20. Find her gross pay.

3.48 Find the gross pay of an employee who worked $22\frac{3}{4}$ hours at an hourly rate of $6.70.

3.49 Richard Hammer's time card shows the following hours worked:

Mon.	Tues.	Wed.	Thurs.	Fri
$7\frac{1}{2}$	$8\frac{3}{4}$	$9\frac{3}{4}$	6	8

His hourly rate is $7.50 plus time-and-a-half for any hours worked over 40 per week. Determine (*a*) his total hours worked and (*b*) gross pay.

3.50   Determine the total hours worked and the gross pay for the following employees of Tyson Automotive:

	Name	Mon.	Tues.	Wed	Thurs.	Fri.	Hourly Rate
(a)	D. Earle	$6\frac{1}{2}$	8	$7\frac{1}{4}$	5	8	$6.50
(b)	N. McHugh	8	$6\frac{1}{4}$	8	$7\frac{3}{4}$	6	$8.00

3.51   Patricia Gray received $239.25 gross pay for 33 hours worked. What is her hourly rate?

3.52   An employee received $221 gross pay and worked 34 hours. What is the employee's hourly rate?

3.53   Given the gross pay and the hours worked, find the hourly rate for the following:

	Gross Pay	Hours Worked
(a)	$230.00	$28\frac{3}{4}$
(b)	$420.00	$37\frac{1}{2}$
(c)	$270.80	40
(d)	$261.80	34

3.54   Determine the total hours worked by George Townsend if his hourly rate is $8.40 and his gross pay is $302.40.

3.55   Janis Klein works as a carpenter for Johnston Construction Company. Her gross pay for last week was $316.80 and her hourly rate is $9.60. Calculate her total hours worked.

3.56   Given the following information, determine the hours worked.

	Gross Pay	Hourly Rate
(a)	$261.00	$7.25
(b)	$248.00	$8.00
(c)	$327.60	$8.40
(d)	$144.10	$6.55

3.57   An employee worked the following hours during the week:

Mon.	Tues.	Wed.	Thurs.	Fri
10	6	7	11	8

Calculate his gross pay at an hourly rate of $6.40 plus time-and-a-half for any hours over 8 per day.

3.58   On Tuesday and Thursday Margaret Darder worked $9\frac{1}{2}$ hours each day. On Monday, Wednesday, and Friday, she worked 7 hours each day. Her hourly rate is $9.00 plus time-and-a-half for any hours in excess of 8 per day. What is her gross pay?

3.59 Find the gross pay for John Devore if he earns $6.80 per hour, time-and-a-half for any hours over 8 per day, and double time for working on Sundays. His time card for the week ending September 24 is as follows:

Mon.	Tues.	Wed.	Thurs.	Fri.	Sat.	Sun.
0	10	4	$7\frac{1}{2}$	$6\frac{3}{4}$	$9\frac{1}{2}$	5

3.60 The following employees of B&B Concrete, Inc. each receive an hourly rate of $6.20, plus time-and-a-half for hours in excess of 8 per day, and double time for Sundays and holidays. (New Year's Day is designated as a holiday.) Calculate each employee's gross pay.

	Name	1/1 Mon.	1/2 Tues.	1/3 Wed.	1/4 Thurs.	1/5 Fri.	1/6 Sat.	1/7 Sun.
(a)	L. Smith	6	9	0	$7\frac{1}{4}$	0	$7\frac{3}{4}$	5
(b)	K. Young	7	$7\frac{1}{2}$	$8\frac{1}{2}$	0	$9\frac{1}{2}$	0	6

3.61 Calculate the gross pay for Rita Hansen. Her time card for the week ending June 27 shows $51\frac{1}{4}$ hours worked. Her rate of pay is $8.60 per hour plus time-and-a-half for any hours over 40 per week.

3.62 Given the hours worked and hourly rate of pay, find the overtime rate (at time-and-a-half) and gross pay for the following. Overtime is paid for hours worked in excess of 40 per week.

	Hours Worked	Hourly Rate
(a)	$48\frac{1}{2}$	$8.00
(b)	$45\frac{3}{4}$	$6.35
(c)	$54\frac{1}{4}$	$7.50

3.63 For the following employees of Brog Sewing Machine Company, calculate

(a) Regular hours

(b) Regular pay

(c) Overtime hours (hours in excess of 40 per week)

(d) Overtime rate (time-and-a-half)

(e) Overtime pay

(f) Gross pay

Name	Mon.	Tues.	Wed.	Thurs.	Fri.	Sat.	Sun.	Hourly Rate
B. Halper	$7\frac{1}{2}$	8	$9\frac{3}{4}$	$6\frac{1}{4}$	8	0	$2\frac{1}{2}$	$6.50
T. Shaver	$3\frac{1}{2}$	$5\frac{1}{4}$	0	8	$4\frac{3}{4}$	8	$6\frac{3}{4}$	$5.80

3.64 V. Friedman is paid $35,600 annually. Her pay period is biweekly. What are her gross earnings per pay period to the nearest cent?

3.65 An employee receives $17,900 per year and is paid monthly. Determine the gross earnings per pay period to the nearest cent.

3.66 Given the following, find the annual salary for (*a*), the pay period for (*b*), and the gross earnings per pay period for (*c*).

	Annual Salary	Pay Period	Gross Earnings/Pay Period
(*a*)	?	Weekly	$279.88
(*b*)	$17,573.14	?	$675.89
(*c*)	$21,000.00	Monthly	?

3.67 Harry Lober receives a $7\frac{1}{2}\%$ commission on all his real estate sales. Half the commission goes to his broker. Of his commission on $133,300 in sales, how much does Harry get to keep?

3.68 During a month's time an automobile salesperson receives 6% commission on the first $5,000 in sales, 7% commission on the next $5,000 in sales, and 8% commission on anything over $10,000. What is her commission on $36,000 in sales?

3.69 Victor Link receives a biweekly salary of $500 plus a $5\frac{1}{2}\%$ commission on his total sales for the month. What are his gross monthly earnings if his total sales for the month were $3,485?

3.70 Elise Thompson is paid a 5% commission on the first $800 in paint sales, 6% on the next $800, and 7% on anything over $1,600 in sales. She also receives a $150 per week draw. To the nearest cent, find the difference she receives at the end of the week between the draw and the commission. Her net sales for the week totaled $3,600.

3.71 Assuming the federal income tax withheld from C. Thomas' gross pay is $26.94 and the FICA tax is 7.65%, what is his net pay to the nearest cent, if his gross earnings for the week ending January 5 are $345.70?

3.72 At Vallone Computer Company the employees' contribution to the pension plan is $2\frac{1}{2}\%$ of their gross pay. If B. Kinney's gross pay is $467.36, federal income tax withheld is $38.62, and FICA tax is 7.65%, what is her net pay?

3.73 Find the net pay for T. Fagan if his gross pay is $298.76 per week and his deductions are $23.69 federal income tax per week, $22.86 FICA tax per week, and $10 life insurance per month.

3.74 An employee's year-to-date gross pay is $38,670. Her current week's earnings amount to $660.20, her federal income tax withheld is $47.81, and her FICA tax is 7.65%. What is her net pay?

3.75 Bush Inc. pays its employees biweekly. In addition to the federal income tax withheld, each employee's deductions are as follows:

FICA tax	7.65%
Union dues	$8.30
Hospitalization ins.	$6.50
Life insurance	$4.50

Given gross pay, federal income tax withheld, and year-to-date gross pay, find the net pay to the nearest cent for the following employees:

	Name	Gross Pay	Federal Income Tax Withheld	Year-to-Date Gross Pay
(a)	J. Dalby	$1,222.24	$ 90.72	$30,556.00
(b)	B. Hahn	1,895.33	137.60	$28,650.00

Answers to Supplementary Problems

3.47 $201.50

3.48 $152.42

3.49 (a) 40, (b) $280 No overtime

3.50 (a) 34.75 h, $225.88; (b) 36 h, $288

3.51 $7.25/h

3.52 $6.50/h

3.53 (a) $8.00/h, (b) $11.20/h, (c) $6.77/h, (d) $7.70/h

3.54 36

3.55 33

3.56 (a) 36, (b) 31, (c) 39, (d) 22

3.57 $316.80

3.58 $373.50

3.59 $336.60

3.60 (a) $288.30, (b) $325.50

3.61 $489.11

3.62 (a) $12.00/h, $244.23; (b) $9.525/h, $308,77; (c) $11.25/h, $460.31

3.63 B. Halper: (a), 40, (b) $260, (c) 2, (d) $9.75/h, (e) $19.50, (f) $279.50
T. Shaver: (a) 36.25, (b) $210.25, (c) 0, (d) $8.70/h, (e) $0, (f) $210.25

3.64 $1,369.23

3.65 $1,491.67

3.66   (*a*) \$14,553.76, (*b*) 26 pay periods/per year or biweekly, (*c*) \$1,750

3.67   \$4,998.75

3.68   \$2,730

3.69   \$1,191.68

3.70   \$78

3.71   \$292.31

3.72   \$392.99

3.73   \$249.71

3.74   \$561.89

3.75   (*a*) \$1,038.02, (*b*) \$1,612.74

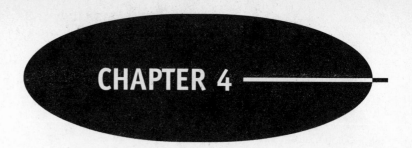

CHAPTER 4

Depreciation

4.1 DEPRECIATION AND SALVAGE VALUE

Although the useful life of equipment (a fixed asset) may be long, it is nonetheless limited. Eventually the equipment will lose all productive worth and will possess only salvage value (scrap value). Accounting demands a period-by-period matching of costs against income. Hence, the cost of a fixed asset (over and above its salvage value) is distributed over the asset's estimated lifetime. This spreading of the cost over the periods which receive benefits is known as *depreciation*.

The depreciable amount of a fixed asset—that is, cost minus salvage value—may be written off in different ways. For example, the amount may be spread evenly over the years affected, as in the straight-line method. The units of production method bases depreciation for each period on the amount of output. Two accelerated methods, the double declining balance method and the sum-of-the-years'-digits method, provide for greater amounts of depreciation in the earlier years.

4.2 STRAIGHT-LINE METHOD

This is the simplest and most widely used depreciation method. Under this method an equal portion of the cost (above salvage value) of the asset is allocated to each period of use. The periodic depreciation charge is expressed as

$$\frac{\text{Cost} - \text{salvage value}}{\text{Estimated life}} = \text{depreciation}$$

EXAMPLE 1

If the cost of a machine is $17,000, its salvage value $2,000, and its estimated useful life 5 yr, the straight-line depreciation is

$$\frac{\$17,000 - \$2,000}{5 \text{ yr}} = \$3,000/\text{yr}$$

The date on which a piece of equipment is bought has an effect on the amount of depreciation taken for the first year. Similarly, if the equipment is later sold, the sale date determines the amount of depreciation taken in the year of sale.

EXAMPLE 2

Suppose that the machine in Example 1 was bought on March 26. Since this date is closer to April 1 than March 1, the depreciation for the first year (ending December 31) is based on April 1 acquisition.

From the yearly depreciation of $3,000 (Example 1), we determine the monthly depreciation as follows:

$$\$3,000/\text{yr} \div 12 \text{ mo/yr} = \$250/\text{mo depreciation}$$

Since April 1 through December 31 encompasses 9 months, we multiply the monthly depreciation by 9 to find the depreciation applicable to the first year.

$$\$250/\text{mo} \times 9 \text{ mo} = \$2,250 \text{ depreciation for 1st year}$$

For the second through the fifth years, the full $3,000 per year depreciation is taken, unless the machine is sold. If the machine is sold *before* the end of a given year, the amount of depreciation applied in that year is calculated on the fraction of the year during which the machine was used, as above.

At any point in time, the *book value* is the cost of the equipment less any depreciation to date.

EXAMPLE 3

If bought on March 26 (Example 2), the end of the first year (December 31) book value of the machine in Example 1 is

$$\text{Book value} = \text{cost} - \text{depreciation}$$
$$= \$17,000 - \$2,250 = \$14,750$$

At the end of the fifth year, the book value of this machine is its salvage value, $2,000.

SOLVED PROBLEMS

4.1   On January 1 Greenwood Industries purchased machinery for $5,000. It is estimated that the machinery will have a useful life of 5 years and a salvage value of $500. Using the straight-line method, determine the depreciation per year.

SOLUTION

$$\frac{\text{Cost} - \text{salvage}}{\text{Estimated life}} = \text{depreciation}$$
$$\frac{\$5,000 - \$500}{5 \text{ yr}} =$$
$$\frac{\$4,500}{5 \text{ yr}} =$$
$$\$900/\text{yr} =$$

4.2   Find the amount of depreciation per year if a fixed asset bought on January 1 for $15,000 has an estimated life of 10 years and a salvage value of $3,000.

SOLUTION

$$\frac{\text{Cost} - \text{salvage}}{\text{Estimated life}} = \text{depreciation}$$
$$\frac{\$15,000 - \$3,000}{10 \text{ yr}} =$$
$$\frac{\$12,000}{10 \text{ yr}} =$$
$$\$1,200/\text{yr} =$$

4.3   If Miller Farms purchased equipment on January 5 for $35,000, calculate the depreciation per year using the straight-line method. The salvage value is $7,000, and the estimated useful life is 10 years.

SOLUTION

$$\frac{\text{Cost} - \text{salvage}}{\text{Estimated life}} = \text{depreciation}$$

$$\frac{\$35,000 - \$7,000}{10 \text{ yr}} =$$

$$\frac{\$28,000}{10 \text{ yr}} =$$

$$\$2,800/\text{yr} =$$

4.4   Harold Enterprises bought office furniture on May 12. The purchase price was $4,000 and the estimated useful life is 5 years. The salvage value is $550. Find the depreciation as of December 31 (same year).

SOLUTION

$$\frac{\text{Cost} - \text{salvage}}{\text{Estimated life}} = \text{depreciation}$$

$$\frac{\$4,000 - \$550}{5 \text{ yr}} =$$

$$\frac{\$3,450}{5 \text{ yr}} =$$

$$\$690/\text{yr} =$$

First-year depreciation:

$$\$690/\text{yr} \div 12 \text{ mo/yr} = \$57.50/\text{mo depreciation}$$
$$\$57.50 \times 8 \text{ mo}^* = \$460 \text{ depreciation as of Dec. 31}$$

---

*May through December = 8 mo

4.5   A delivery truck was purchased by Wade Florists on September 12. The initial cost of the truck was $9,000, but some new parts were needed, totaling $800. Under the straight-line method, what is the depreciation to the nearest cent at the end of the year if the estimated useful life of the truck is 5 years and the salvage value is $1,200?

SOLUTION

$$\frac{\text{Cost} - \text{salvage}}{\text{Estimated life}} = \text{depreciation}$$

$$\frac{\$9,800 - \$1,200}{5 \text{ yr}} =$$

$$\frac{\$8,600}{5 \text{ yr}} =$$

$$\$1,720/\text{yr} =$$

First-year depreciation:

$$\$1,720 \div 12 \text{ mo} = \$143.33/\text{mo}$$
$$\$143.33 \times 4 \text{ mo} = \$573.32 \text{ depreciation at end of yr}$$

4.6   What is the amount of depreciation at the end of the second year, if a piece of equipment was purchased on July 24 for $1,300, its estimated useful life is 8 years, and trade-in value is $100?

SOLUTION

$$\frac{\text{Cost} - \text{salvage}}{\text{Estimated life}} = \text{depreciation}$$

$$\frac{\$1,300 - \$100}{8 \text{ yr}} =$$

$$\frac{\$1,200}{8 \text{ yr}} =$$

$$\$150/\text{yr} =$$

End of second-year depreciation:

$$\$150 \div 12 \text{ mo} = \$12.50/\text{mo}$$

$$\$12.50 \times 5 \text{ mo}^* = \$62.50 \text{ depreciation for 1st yr}$$

$$\$62.50 + \$150 = \$212.50 \text{ depreciation at end of 2d yr}$$

----

*The month of July is not included since July 24 is closer to August 1 than to July 1.

4.7   A dishwasher was purchased by the Check-Inn Restaurant on October 1. The purchase price was $1,200 and the installation cost was $300. The estimate useful life of the dishwasher is 6 years and its salvage value is $300. What is the amount of depreciation to the nearest cent at the end of the fourth year?

SOLUTION

$$\frac{\text{Cost} - \text{salvage}}{\text{Estimated life}} = \text{depreciation}$$

$$\frac{\$1,500 - \$300}{6 \text{ yr}} =$$

$$\frac{\$1,200}{6 \text{ yr}} =$$

$$\$200/\text{yr} =$$

End of fourth-year depreciation:

$$\$200 \div 12 \text{ mo} = \$16.67/\text{mo}$$

$$\$16.67 \times 3 \text{ mo} = \$50.01 \text{ depreciation for 1st yr}$$

$$\$200 \times 3 \text{ yr}^* = \$600 \text{ depreciation for years 2, 3, and 4}$$

$$\$600 + \$50.01 = \$650.01 \text{ depreciation at end of 4th yr}$$

----

*For the second, third, and fourth years the full depreciation of $200 per year is applied.

4.8   If office furniture purchased on January 2 for $8,100 has an estimated useful life of 6 years and a trade-in value of $750, what is the book value at the end of the fifth year?

SOLUTION

$$\frac{\text{Cost} - \text{salvage}}{\text{Estimated life}} = \text{depreciation}$$

$$\frac{\$8,100 - \$750}{6 \text{ yr}} =$$

$$\$7,350/6 \text{ yr} =$$

$$\$1,225/\text{yr} =$$

End of fifth-year depreciation:

$$\$1,225 \times 5 \text{ yr} = \$6,125 \text{ depreciation for 5 yr}$$

Book value at end of fifth year:

$$\text{Cost} - \text{depreciation} = \text{book value}$$
$$\$8,100 - \$6,125 =$$
$$\$1,975 =$$

4.9 Lorino Plumbing and Heating purchased tools on February 18 for $800. The salvage value of the tools is $200, and the estimated life is 10 years. What is the book value at the end of the fourth year?

SOLUTION

$$\frac{\text{Cost} - \text{salvage}}{\text{Estimated life}} = \text{depreciation}$$
$$\$800 - \$200 =$$
$$\frac{\$600}{10 \text{ yr}} =$$
$$\$60/\text{yr} =$$

End of fourth-year depreciation:

$$\$60 \div 12 \text{ mo} = \$5/\text{mo}$$
$$\$5 \times 10 \text{ mo} = \$50 \text{ depreciation for 1st year}$$
$$\$60 \times 3 \text{ yr} = \$180 \text{ depreciation for years 2, 3, and 4}$$
$$\$180 + \$50 = \$230 \text{ depreciation at end of 4th yr}$$

Book value at end of fourth year:

$$\text{Cost} - \text{depreciation} = \text{book value}$$
$$\$800 - \$230 =$$
$$\$570 =$$

4.10 Determine the depreciation rate per year for an estimated useful life of (a) 10 yr, (b) 50 yr, (c) 8 yr, (d) 5 yr, (e) 16 yr, and (f) 20 yr.

SOLUTION

$$\frac{100\%}{\text{Estimated life}} = \text{depreciation rate/yr}$$

(a) $100\% \div 10 \text{ yr} = 10\%$ (d) $100\% \div 5 \text{ yr} = 20\%$

(b) $100\% \div 50 \text{ yr} = 2\%$ (e) $100\% \div 16 \text{ yr} = 6\frac{1}{4}\%$

(c) $100\% \div 8 \text{ yr} = 12\frac{1}{2}\%$ (f) $100\% \div 20 \text{ yr} = 5\%$

4.11 Determine the (a) depreciation rate, (b) yearly depreciation, and (c) book value after 10 years of a building that cost $100,000 on January 7. After its estimated useful life of 25 yr, the salvage value is $20,000.

SOLUTION

$$\frac{100\%}{\text{Estimated life}} = \text{depreciation rate/yr}$$
$$100\% \div 25 \text{ yr} =$$
$$4\% =$$

(b)   We can rewrite the formula from Sec. 4.2 in terms of depreciation rate, as follows:

$$(\text{Cost} - \text{salvage}) \times \text{depreciation rate/yr} = \text{depreciation}$$
$$(\$100,000 - \$20,000) \times 0.04 =$$
$$\$80,000 \times 0.04 =$$
$$\$3,200/\text{yr} =$$

(c)   Book value after 10 yr:

$$\$3,200 \times 10 \text{ yr} = \$32,000 \text{ depreciation for 10 yr}$$
$$\text{Cost} - \text{depreciation} = \text{book value}$$
$$\$100,000 - \$32,000 = \$68,000$$

4.12   Find the annual depreciation for the following:

Purchase Cost	Additional Cost Involved	Estimated Life (Years)	Salvage Value
$120,000	$ 0	30	$30,000
50,000	0	20	10,000
7,000	200	6	1,200
3,000	0	10	0
150,000	0	50	25,000
10,000	500	8	3,500
33,000	900	20	1,300
100,000	0	50	20,000
650	75	3	125
5,400	600	5	1,500

SOLUTION

Cost* − Salvage Value	÷	Estimated Life (Years)	=	Annual Depreciation
($120,000 − $30,000)	÷	30	=	$3,000
($50,000 − $10,000)	÷	20	=	$2,000
($7,200 − $1,200)	÷	6	=	$1,000
($3,000 − $0)	÷	10	=	$300
($150,000 − $25,000)	÷	50	=	$2,500
($10,500 − $3,500)	÷	8	=	$875
($33,900 − $1,300)	÷	20	=	$1,630
($100,000 − $20,000)	÷	50	=	$1,600
($725 − $125)	÷	3	=	$200
($6,000 − $1,500)	÷	5	=	$900

*Purchase cost + additional cost involved

4.13   Prepare a depreciation schedule for a piece of machinery purchased January 10 for $7,700. Transportation costs amounted to $300. The estimated useful life is 10 years, and the machine has a salvage value of $800. The depreciation schedule spans the estimated life of the machine and includes the depreciation rate for each year, the dollar amount of that year's depreciation, the book value, and each year's accumulated depreciation.

SOLUTION

$$\text{Cost} = \text{purchase cost} + \text{any additional cost involved}$$
$$= \$7,700 + \$300 = \$8,000$$

$$\frac{100\%}{\text{Estimated life}} = \text{depreciation rate/yr}$$

$$\frac{100\%}{10 \text{ yr}} =$$

$$10\% =$$

$$(\text{Cost} - \text{salvage}) \times \text{depreciation rate/yr} = \text{annual depreciation}$$
$$(\$8,000 - \$800) \times 0.10 =$$
$$\$7,200 \times 0.10 =$$
$$\$720 =$$

Year	Depreciation Rate (%)	Yearly Depreciation	Book Value	Accumulated Depreciation
0			$8,000	
1	10	$720	7,280	$ 720
2	10	720	6,560	1,440
3	10	720	5,840	2,160
4	10	720	5,120	2,880
5	10	720	4,400	3,600
6	10	720	3,680	4,320
7	10	720	2,960	5,040
8	10	720	2,240	5,760
9	10	720	1,520	6,480
10	10	720	800	7,200

4.14   Marshall Painters bought 15 paint sprayers at a cost of $80 each. The delivery charge for all 15 sprayers was $80, and delivery was on August 16. Each sprayer has an estimated useful life of 8 years and no salvage value. What is the depreciation on December 31 of the sixth year?

SOLUTION

Cost:

$$15 \text{ sprayers} \times \$80 \text{ each} = \$1,200$$
$$\$1,200 + \$80 \text{ (delivery charge)} = \$1,280$$
$$\frac{\text{Cost} - \text{salvage}}{\text{Estimated life}} = \text{depreciation}$$
$$\frac{\$1,280}{8 \text{ yr}} =$$
$$\$160/\text{yr} =$$

Depreciation at end of sixth year:

$$\$160/yr \div 12\,mo/yr = \$13.33/mo$$
$$\$13.33 \times 4\,mo = \$53.32 \text{ depreciation for 1st yr}$$
$$\$160 \times 5\,yr = \$800 \text{ depreciation for years 2–6}$$
$$\$800 + \$53.32 = \$853.32 \text{ depreciation Dec. 31 of 6th yr}$$

4.15　What is the book value at the end of the third year for each of the following:

(a)	Cost	$10,000		(d)	Cost	$900
	Salvage value	$2,000			Salvage value	$0
	Estimated life	5 yr			Estimated life	3 yr
(b)	Cost	$8,500		(e)	Cost	$5,000
	Salvage value	$1,000			Salvage value	$500
	Estimated life	6 yr			Estimated life	9 yr
(c)	Cost	$26,000		(f)	Cost	$750
	Salvage value	$3,000			Salvage value	$50
	Estimated life	10 yr			Estimated life	4 yr

SOLUTION

	Cost − Salvage Value	÷ Estimated Life (Years)	× No. Years	= Depreciation for 3 Years	Cost −	Depreciation for 3 Years	= Book Value
(a)	($10,000 − $2,000) ÷	5	× 3 =	$4,800	$10,000 −	$4,800	= $5,200
(b)	($8,500 − $1,000) ÷	6	× 3 =	$3,750	$8,500 −	$3,750	= $4,750
(c)	($26,000 − $3,000) ÷	10	× 3 =	$6,900	$26,000 −	$6,900	= $19,100
(d)	($900 − $0) ÷	3	× 3 =	$900	$900 −	$900	= $0
(e)	($5,000 − $500) ÷	9	× 3 =	$1,500	$5,000 −	$1,500	= $3,500
(f)	($750 − $50) ÷	4	× 3 =	$525	$750 −	$525	= $225

4.3 UNITS OF PRODUCTION

Where the use of equipment varies substantially from year to year, the units-of-production method is appropriate for determining the depreciation. For example, in some years logging operations may be carried on for 200 days, in other years for 230 days, in still other years for only 160 days, depending on weather conditions. Under this method, depreciation is computed for the appropriate unit of output or production (such as hours, miles, or pounds) by the following formula:

$$\frac{\text{Cost} - \text{salvage}}{\text{Estimated units of production during lifetime}} = \text{unit depreciation}$$

The total number of units used in a year is then multiplied by the unit depreciation to arrive at the depreciation amount for that year. We can express this as

$$\text{Unit depreciation} \times \text{usage} = \text{depreciation}$$

or 　　　$$\frac{\text{Cost} - \text{salvage}}{\text{Estimated life (in units)}} \times \text{usage} = \text{depreciation}$$

This method has the advantage of relating depreciation cost directly to income.

EXAMPLE 4

Cost of a machine, $17,000; salvage, $2,000; estimated life, 8,000 hours.

$$\frac{\$17,000 - \$2,000}{8,000 \text{ h}} = \$1.875 \text{ depreciation/h}$$

Over a 5-year lifetime, the machine was in operation for 1,800, 1,200, 2,000, 1,400, and 1,600 hours for years 1 to 5, respectively. The computation of the depreciation for those years is

Year 1	1,800 h × $1.875/h =	$	3,375
Year 2	1,200 h × $1.875/h =		2,250
Year 3	2,000 h × $1.875/h =		3,750
Year 4	1,400 h × $1.875/h =		2,625
Year 5	1,600 h × $1.875/h =		3,000
Total depreciation (8,000 h) =			$15,000

SOLVED PROBLEMS

4.16 An item of machinery, bought on January 5 for $15,000, has an estimated useful life of 30,000 hours and a salvage value of $3,000. In its first year of operation the machine was used for 15,000 hours. What is the depreciation when calculated by the units-of-production method?

SOLUTION

$$\frac{\text{Cost} - \text{salvage}}{\text{Estimated life}} \times \text{usage} = \text{depreciation}$$

$$\frac{\$15,000 - \$3,000}{30,000 \text{ h}} \times 15,000 \text{ h} =$$

$$\frac{\$12,000}{30,000 \text{ h}} \times 15,000 \text{ h} =$$

$$\$0.40/\text{h} \times 15,000 \text{ h} =$$

$$\$6,000 =$$

4.17 Marion Enterprises bought a photocopier for $5,000. If it was used 3,000 hours the first year, 4,500 hours the second year, and 3,900 hours the third year, find the depreciation for the 3 years, using the units-of-production method. The trade-in value of the copier is $1,000, and its useful life is estimated to be 40,000 hours.

SOLUTION

$$\frac{\text{Cost} - \text{salvage}}{\text{Estimated life}} = \text{unit depreciation}$$

$$\frac{\$5,000 - \$1,000}{40,000} =$$

$$\frac{\$4,000}{40,000 \text{ h}} =$$

$$\$0.10/\text{h} =$$

Unit depreciation × usage = depreciation

Year 1	$0.10/h × 3,000 h =	$ 300
Year 2	$0.10/h × 4,500 h =	$ 450
Year 3	$0.10/h × 3,900 h =	$ 390
	Depreciation for 3 yr =	$1,140

4.18   Steph Pest Control bought a truck costing $11,000 that has an estimated useful life of 100,000 miles and a trade-in value of $2,000. Determine the depreciation if the truck was driven 7,000 miles the first year.

SOLUTION

$$\frac{\text{Cost} - \text{salvage}}{\text{Estimated life}} \times \text{usage} = \text{depreciation}$$

$$\frac{\$11,000 - \$2,000}{100,000 \text{ mi}} \times 7,000 \text{ mi} =$$

$$\frac{\$9,000}{100,000 \text{ mi}} \times 7,000 \text{ mi} =$$

$$\$0.09 \text{ mi} \times 7,000 \text{ mi} =$$

$$\$630 =$$

4.19   A used floor polisher was purchased by Liberty Floor Maintenance Company on March 25 for $750. Some repair work amounting to $75 was needed to put the machine into operating condition. Use the units-of-production method to determine the depreciation after 1,000 hours of use. The salvage value of the machine is $25, and its estimated useful life is 5,000 hours.

SOLUTION

$$\$750 + \$75 = \$825 \text{ cost}$$

$$\frac{\text{Cost} - \text{salvage}}{\text{Estimated life}} \times \text{usage} = \text{depreciation}$$

$$\frac{\$825 - \$25}{5,000 \text{ h}} \times 1,000 \text{ h} =$$

$$\frac{\$800}{5,000 \text{ h}} \times 1,000 \text{ h} =$$

$$\$0.16/\text{h} \times 1,000 \text{ h} =$$

$$\$160 =$$

4.20   Using the units-of-production method, find the depreciation of a machine that produced 3,600 units in its first year of operation. The cost of the machine was $17,000. It has a salvage value of $3,000 and an estimated lifetime output of 50,000 units.

SOLUTION

$$\frac{\text{Cost} - \text{salvage}}{\text{Estimated life}} \times \text{usage} = \text{depreciation}$$

$$\frac{\$17,000 - \$3,000}{50,000 \text{ units}} \times 3,600 \text{ units} =$$

$$\frac{\$14,000}{50,000 \text{ units}} \times 3,600 \text{ units} =$$

$$\$0.28/\text{unit} \times 3,600 \text{ units} =$$

$$\$1,008 =$$

4.21   If Miller & Co. bought a used truck for their lumber business for $6,000 and it cost them $1,500 in repairs before they were able to use it, what is the depreciation according to the units-of-

78   DEPRECIATION   [CHAP. 4

production method at the end of the second year in operation if the truck has a trade-in value of $1,500 and an estimated useful life of an additional 85,000 mi? In the first year, they drove the truck 12,000 mi and in the second year, 14,000 mi.

SOLUTION

$$\$6,000 + \$1,500 = \$7,500 \text{ cost}$$

$$\frac{\text{Cost} - \text{salvage}}{\text{Estimated life}} = \text{unit depreciation}$$

$$\frac{\$7,500 - \$1,500}{85,000 \text{ mi}} =$$

$$\frac{\$6,000}{85,000 \text{ mi}} =$$

$$\$0.07/\text{mi} =$$

Unit depreciation × usage = depreciation

Year 1	$0.07/mi × 12,000 mi = $ 840
Year 2	$0.07/mi × 14,000 mi = $ 980
	Depreciation for 2 yr = $1,820

4.22 Use the units-of-production method to find the depreciation for the following:

Cost	Salvage Value	Estimated Life	Usage
$25,000	$ 2,500	75,000 h	16,450 h
70,000	5,000	100,000 units	75,500 units
99,000	10,000	85,000 h	37,750 h
8,000	1,400	75,000 mi	55,600 mi
13,500	2,300	100,000 mi	66,000 mi

SOLUTION

$\left[\left(\text{Cost} - \dfrac{\text{Salvage}}{\text{Value}}\right)\right.$	÷	$\left.\begin{array}{c}\text{Estimated}\\\text{Life}\end{array}\right]$	×	Usage	=	Depreciation
[($25,000 − $2,500)	÷	75,000 h]	×	16,450 h	=	$4,935.00
[($70,000 − $5,000)	÷	100,000 units]	×	75,500 units	=	$49,075.00
[($99,000 − $10,000)	÷	85,000 h]	×	37,750 h	=	$39,526.47
[($8,000 − $1,400)	÷	75,000 mi]	×	55,600 mi	=	$4,892.80
[($13,500 − $2,300)	÷	100,000 mi]	×	66,000 mi	=	$7,392.00

4.23 Using the units-of-production method, find the depreciation of a tractor bought by Misner Farms on April 6 for $23,000. Mr. Misner paid $750 in transportation costs to have the tractor delivered. The tractor has an estimated useful life of 70,000 hours, and its salvage value is $2,750. Misner used the tractor 4,000 hours the first year and 3,950 hours the second year.

SOLUTION

$$\$23,000 + \$750 = \$23,750 \text{ cost}$$

$$\frac{\text{Cost} - \text{salvage}}{\text{Estimated life}} = \text{unit depreciation}$$

$$\frac{\$23,750 - \$2,750}{70,000 \text{ h}} =$$

$$\frac{\$21,000}{70,000 \text{ h}} =$$

$$\$0.30/\text{h} =$$

Unit depreciation $\times$ usage = depreciation

Year 1 $\$0.30/\text{h} \times 4,000 \text{ h} = \$1,200$

Year 2 $\$0.30/\text{h} \times 3,950 \text{ h} = \underline{\$1,185}$

Depreciation for 2 yr = $\$2,385$

4.24   Katz Home Builders started business on October 18. One month prior they purchased a truck for $5,000 and spent an additional $500 to get the truck in operating condition. They also bought a band saw for $500. The truck has an estimated useful life of 50,000 mi and a trade-in value of $1,500. The band saw has an estimated useful life of 5,000 hours and a trade-in value of $50. What is each item's depreciation at the end of the year if they (*a*) put 2,085 mi on the truck as of December 31 and (*b*) used the saw 300 hours?

SOLUTION

(*a*)   Truck

$$\$5,000 + \$500 = \$5,500 \text{ cost}$$

$$\frac{\text{Cost} - \text{salvage}}{\text{Estimated life}} \times \text{usage} = \text{depreciation}$$

$$\frac{\$5,500 - \$1,500}{50,000 \text{ mi}} \times 2,085 \text{ mi} =$$

$$\frac{\$4,000}{50,000 \text{ mi}} \times 2,085 \text{ mi} =$$

$$\$0.08/\text{mi} \times 2,085 \text{ mi} =$$

$$\$166.80 =$$

(*b*)   Band saw

$$\frac{\text{Cost} - \text{salvage}}{\text{Estimated life}} \times \text{usage} = \text{depreciation}$$

$$\frac{\$500 - \$50}{5,000 \text{ h}} \times 300 \text{ h} =$$

$$\frac{\$450}{5,000 \text{ h}} \times 300 \text{ h} =$$

$$\$0.09/\text{h} \times 300 \text{ h} =$$

$$\$27 =$$

4.25   Payne Electronics bought an assembler that would assemble 30 transformers per hour. If during the first year of operation 43,200 transformers were assembled, find the depreciation by using the units-of-production method. The assembler cost $150,000 and has a salvage value of $5,000. It is expected to assemble 500,000 transformers during its useful life.

SOLUTION

$$\frac{\text{Cost} - \text{salvage}}{\text{Estimated life}} \times \text{usage} = \text{depreciation}$$

$$\frac{\$150,000 - \$5,000}{500,000 \text{ units}} \times 43,200 \text{ units} =$$

$$\frac{\$145,000}{500,000 \text{ units}} \times 43,200 \text{ units} =$$

$$\$0.29/\text{unit} \times 43,200 \text{ units} =$$

$$\$12,528 =$$

4.26 An item of equipment that has a production capacity of 50 units per hour and an estimated life of 200,000 hours was purchased. The costs involved to get the equipment into operation were $257,500 price, $700 transportation charges, $300 insurance while in transit, and $1,500 installation charge. The trade-in value is $10,000. If it produced 125,000 units in 2,500 hours, what is the depreciation according to the units-of-production method?

SOLUTION

$$\$257,500 + \$700 + \$300 + \$1,500 = \$260,000 \text{ cost}$$

$$\frac{\text{Cost} - \text{salvage}}{\text{Estimated life}} \times \text{usage} = \text{depreciation}$$

$$\frac{\$260,000 - \$10,000}{200,000 \text{ h}} \times 2,500 \text{ h} =$$

$$\frac{\$250,000}{200,000 \text{ h}} \times 2,500 \text{ h} =$$

$$\$1.25/\text{h} \times 2,500 \text{ h} =$$

$$\$3,125 =$$

4.27 What is the book value of a piece of machinery with an estimated useful life of 750,000 hours and a trade-in value of $6,000, if the machine cost $81,000 and was used for 300,500 hours?

SOLUTION

$$\frac{\text{Cost} - \text{salvage}}{\text{Estimated life}} \times \text{usage} = \text{depreciation}$$

$$\frac{\$81,000 - \$6,000}{750,000 \text{ h}} \times 300,500 \text{ h} =$$

$$\frac{\$75,000}{750,000 \text{ h}} \times 300,500 \text{ h} =$$

$$\$0.10/\text{h} \times 300,500 \text{ h} =$$

$$\$30,050 =$$

$$\text{Cost} - \text{depreciation} = \text{book value}$$

$$\$81,000 - \$30,050 =$$

$$\$50,950 =$$

4.28 Find (*a*) the depreciation and (*b*) the book value at the end of the third year for an item of equipment that cost $60,000. Delivery of the equipment cost an additional $500, and its estimated useful life is 125,000 mi. The salvage value is $5,500. The equipment was used 22,000 mi the first year, 25,600 mi the second year, and 19,680 mi the third year.

SOLUTION

(a)
$$\$60{,}000 + \$500 = \$60{,}500 \text{ cost}$$

$$\frac{\text{Cost} - \text{salvage}}{\text{Estimated life}} = \text{unit depreciation}$$

$$\frac{\$60{,}500 - \$5{,}500}{125{,}000 \text{ mi}} =$$

$$\frac{\$55{,}000}{125{,}000 \text{ mi}} =$$

$$\$0.44/\text{mi} =$$

Unit depreciation $\times$ usage = depreciation

Year 1	$0.44/mi $\times$ 22,000 mi =	$ 9,680.00
Year 2	$0.44/mi $\times$ 25,600 mi =	11,264.00
Year 3	$0.44/mi $\times$ 19,680 mi =	8,659.20

Depreciation at end of 3 yr = $29,603.20

(b)
$$\text{Cost} - \text{depreciation} = \text{book value}$$
$$\$60{,}500.00 - \$29{,}603.20 =$$
$$\$30{,}896.80 =$$

4.29 Using the units-of-production method, find the depreciation of a used truck which cost $4,400. Additional costs incurred were $125.89 parts, $258.43 repairs, and $215.68 repainting. The original estimated useful life was 100,000 miles, but the truck had 57,500 miles on it when purchased. Its trade-in value is $750, and the truck was driven 15,899 miles the first year.

SOLUTION

$$\$4{,}400 + \$125.89 + \$258.43 + \$215.68 = \$5{,}000 \text{ cost}$$

$$\frac{\text{Cost} - \text{salvage}}{\text{Estimated life}} \times \text{usage} = \text{depreciation}$$

$$\frac{\$5{,}000 - \$750}{100{,}000 \text{ mi} - 57{,}500 \text{ mi}} \times 15{,}899 \text{ mi} =$$

$$\frac{\$4{,}250}{42{,}500 \text{ mi}} \times 15{,}899 \text{ mi} =$$

$$\$0.10/\text{mi} \times 15{,}899 \text{ mi} =$$

$$\$1{,}589.90 =$$

4.30 Cook Computer Systems, Inc. purchased a machine that welds components onto printed-circuit boards at a rate of 20 per hour. The machine cost $125,000 plus $2,000 in transportation costs and $3,000 in installation costs. Its estimated useful life is the welding of 100,000 components, and its salvage value is $10,000. Using the units-of-production method, determine the depreciation after 76,550 components have been welded.

SOLUTION

$$\$125{,}000 + \$2{,}000 + \$3{,}000 = \$130{,}000 \text{ cost}$$

$$\frac{\text{Cost} - \text{salvage}}{\text{Estimated life}} \times \text{usage} = \text{depreciation}$$

$$\frac{\$130{,}000 - \$10{,}000}{100{,}000 \text{ units}} \times 76{,}550 \text{ units} =$$

$$\frac{\$120{,}000}{100{,}000 \text{ units}} \times 76{,}550 \text{ units} =$$

$$\$1.20/\text{unit} \times 76{,}550 \text{ units} =$$

$$\$91{,}860 =$$

4.4 DOUBLE DECLINING BALANCE METHOD

The double declining balance method produces the highest amount of depreciation in the earlier years. *It does not recognize salvage or scrap value.* Instead, the book value of the asset remaining at the end of the depreciation period becomes the salvage or scrap value. Under this method, the straight-line rate is doubled and applied to the declining book balance each year. Many companies prefer the double declining balance method because of the greater "write-off" in the earlier years, a time when the asset contributes most to the business and when the expenditure was actually made. The procedure is to apply a *fixed rate* to the declining book value of the asset each year. As the book value declines, the depreciation becomes smaller.

EXAMPLE 5

A \$17,000 asset is to be depreciated over 5 years. The double declining balance rate is thus 40%/yr from

$$\frac{100\%}{\text{Estimated life in years}} \times 2 = \text{depreciation rate}$$

$$\frac{100\%}{5 \text{ yr}} \times 2 = 40\%/\text{yr}$$

The yearly depreciation and book value are shown in the following table.

Year	Book Value at Beginning of Year	Rate (%)	Depreciation for Year	Book Value at End of Year
1	$17,000	40	$6,800	$10,200
2	10,200	40	4,080	6,120
3	6,120	40	2,448	3,672
4	3,672	40	1,468	2,204
5	2,204	40	881	1,323

The \$1,322 book value at the end of the fifth year becomes the scrap value. If, however, a scrap value of \$2,000 had been determined, the depreciation for the fifth year would be adjusted from \$881 to \$204 (\$2,204 − \$2,000).

The date of purchase should also be considered. In the previous example, we assumed that the equipment was purchased at the beginning of the year, which is usually not a common occurrence. Therefore, a change in the computation for the first partial year of service is needed if we determine that the equipment was purchased later in the year.

EXAMPLE 6

If the equipment in Example 5 had been purchased and put to use at the end of the ninth month of the fiscal year, the pro rata portion of the first full year's depreciation would be

$$\frac{3}{12}(40\% \times \$17,000) = \$1,700$$

The method of computation for the remaining years would not be affected (although the *amounts* would change). Thus, the depreciation for the second year would be

$$40\%(\$17,000 - \$1,700) = \$6,120$$

and the book value at the end of the second year would be

$$\$9,180 = [\$17,000 - (\$1,700 + \$6,120)]$$

SOLVED PROBLEMS

4.31 On January 1, Morgan Company purchased office furniture for $1,000. The furniture has an estimated useful life of 10 years, and its salvage value is $100. Using the double declining balance method of depreciation, what is the depreciation at the end of the first year?

SOLUTION

$$\frac{100\%}{\text{Estimated life (yr)}} \times 2 = \text{depreciation rate}$$
$$100\%/10 \text{ yr} \times 2 =$$
$$20\%/\text{yr} =$$

$$\text{Cost} \times \text{depreciation rate} = \text{depreciation}$$
$$\$1,000 \times 0.20/\text{yr} =$$
$$\$200/\text{yr} =$$

Note that the salvage value is not considered when determining depreciation with this method.

4.32 Equipment was bought on January 5 for $25,000. It has an estimated useful life of 40 years and a trade-in value of $5,000. Using the double declining balance method, determine the book value at the end of the third year.

SOLUTION

$$100\%/\text{estimated life (yr)} \times 2 = \text{depreciation rate}$$
$$100\%/40 \text{ yr} \times 2 =$$
$$5\%/\text{yr} =$$

	Cost × depreciation rate = depreciation	Cost − depreciation = book value
Year 1	$25,000.00 × 0.05/yr = $1,250.00	$25,000.00 − $1,250.00 = $23,750.00
Year 2	$23,750.00 × 0.05/yr = $1,187.50	$23,750.00 − $1,187.50 = $22,562.50
Year 3	$22,562.50 × 0.05/yr = $1,128.13	$22,562.50 − $1,128.13 = $21,434.37

Note that in calculating the depreciation for years 2 and 3, we use the preceding year's book value as the cost in each case. We can state this in mathematical terms as follows:

[Cost (from prevoius yr) − depreciation (from previous yr)] × depreciation rate = depreciation

or more simply,

Book value × depreciation rate = depreciation

4.33   Using the double declining balance method of depreciation, determine the book value at the end of the first year on an item that was bought on April 8 for $60,000 and that has a salvage value of $8,000 and an estimated useful life of 50 years.

SOLUTION

$$100\%/\text{estimated life (yr)} \times 2 = \text{depreciation rate}$$
$$100\%/50 \text{ yr} \times 2 =$$
$$4\%/\text{yr} =$$

$$\text{Cost} - \text{depreciation rate} = \text{depreciation}$$
$$\$60,000 \times 0.04/\text{yr} =$$
$$\$2,400/\text{yr} =$$

End of first-year depreciation:

$$\$2,400/\text{yr} \div 12 \text{ mo/yr} = \$200/\text{mo}$$
$$\$200/\text{mo} \times 9 \text{ mo} = \$1,800$$

Book value at end of first year:

$$\text{Cost} - \text{depreciation} = \text{book value}$$
$$\$60,000 - \$1,800 =$$
$$\$58,200 =$$

4.34   Using the double declining balance method, determine the accumulated depreciation at the end of the second year for a bulldozer that cost $6,000. The bulldozer's estimated useful life is 20 years, and its trade-in value is $500. It was bought on November 27.

SOLUTION

$$100\%/\text{estimated life} \times 2 = \text{depreciation rate}$$
$$100\%/20 \text{ yr} \times 2 =$$
$$10\%/\text{yr} =$$

End of first-year depreciation:

$$\text{Cost} \times \text{depreciation rate} = \text{depreciation}$$
$$\$6,000 \times 0.10/\text{yr} =$$
$$\$600/\text{yr} =$$

$$\$600/\text{yr} \div 12 \text{ mo/yr} = \$50/\text{mo}$$
$$\$50/\text{mo} \times 1 \text{ mo} = \$50$$

Depreciation for second year:

$$(\text{Cost} - \text{depreciation})^* \times \text{depreciation rate} = \text{depreciation}$$
$$(\$6,000 - \$50) \times 0.10/\text{yr} =$$
$$\$5,950 \times 0.10/\text{yr} =$$
$$\$595/\text{yr} =$$

Accumulated depreciation at end of second year:

$$\$50 + \$595 = \$645$$

-----

*See Prob. 4.32.

4.35 Using the double declining balance method of depreciation, prepare a depreciation schedule for the first 5 years on a piece of machinery that cost $80,000, has a trade-in value of $5,000 and an estimated life of 25 years.

SOLUTION

$$100\%/\text{estimated life} \times 2 = \text{depreciation rate}$$
$$100\%/25 \text{ yr} \times 2 =$$
$$8\%/\text{yr} =$$

Year	Book Value*	Depreciation Rate	Amount of Depreciation	Accumulated Depreciation
1	$80,000.00	0.08	$6,400.00	$ 6,400.00
2	73,600.00	0.08	5,888.00	12,288.00
3	67,712.00	0.08	5,416.96	17,704.96
4	62,295.04	0.08	4,983.60	22,688.56
5	57,311.44	0.08	4,584.92	27,273.48

*Note that the book values shown are for the *beginning* of each year.

4.36 Using the double declining balance method of depreciation, prepare a depreciation schedule to the end of the third year for the March 29 purchase of 20 typewriters at a cost of $600 each by Starr Office Management, Inc. The typewriters have an estimated useful life of 5 years and a trade-in value of $100 each.

SOLUTION

$$20 \text{ typewriters} \times \$600 \text{ each} = \$12,000 \text{ total cost}$$

$$100\%/\text{estimated life} \times 2 = \text{depreciation rate}$$
$$100\%/5 \text{ yr} \times 2 =$$
$$40\%/\text{yr} =$$

End of first-year depreciation:

$$\text{Cost} \times \text{depreciation rate} = \text{depreciation}$$
$$\$12,000 \times 0.40/\text{yr} =$$
$$\$4,800/\text{yr} =$$

$$\$4,800/\text{yr} \div 12 \text{ mo/yr} = \$400/\text{mo}$$
$$\$400/\text{mo} \times 9 \text{ mo} = \$3,600$$

Year	Book Value	Depreciation Rate	Amount of Depreciation	Accumulated Depreciation
1	$12,000	0.40	$3,600	$3,600
2	8,400	0.40	3,360	6,960
3	5,040	0.40	2,016	8,976

4.37 If machinery that cost $60,000 and has a trade-in value of $5,000 was put into use on January 1, what is the book value at the end of the fifth year, if said machinery has an estimated useful life of 25 years?

SOLUTION

Year	Book Value	Depreciation Rate*	Amount of Depreciation	Accumulated Depreciation
1	$60,000.00	0.08	$4,800.00	$ 4,800.00
2	55,200.00	0.08	4,416.00	9,216.00
3	50,784.00	0.08	4,062.72	13,278.72
4	46,721.28	0.08	3,737.70	17,016.42
5	42,983.58	0.08	3,438.69	20,455.11

*100%/25 yr × 2 = 8%/yr

Book value at *end* of fifth year:

$$\text{Cost (at beginning of year 5)} - \text{depreciation} = \text{book value}$$
$$\$42,983.58 - \$3,438.69 = \$39,544.89$$

or

$$\text{Original cost} - \text{accumulated depreciation to date} = \text{book value}$$
$$\$60,000.00 - \$20,455.11 = \$39,544.89$$

4.38 Wilson Vending Company bought machines costing a total of $27,000. The machines have an estimated trade-in value of $7,000 and a life expectancy of 8 years. Using the double declining balance method, what is the accumulated depreciation at the end of the fourth year?

SOLUTION

Year	Book Value	Depreciation Rate*	Amount of Depreciation	Accumulated Depreciation
1	$27,000.00	0.25	$6,750.00	$ 6,750.00
2	20,250.00	0.25	5,062.50	11,812.50
3	15,187.50	0.25	3,796.88	15,609.38
4	11,390.62	0.25	2,847.66	18,457.04

*100%/8 yr × 2 = 25%/yr

4.39 A conveyor with an estimated useful life of 20 years and a salvage value of $700 was purchased for $7,000. Using the double declining balance method of depreciation, determine the book value at the end of the third year.

SOLUTION

Year	Book Value	Depreciation Rate*	Amount of Depreciation	Accumulated Depreciation
1	$7,000	0.10	$700	$ 700
2	6,300	0.10	630	1,330
3	5,670	0.10	567	1,897

*100%/20 yr × 2 = 10%/yr

Book value at end of third year:

$$\text{Original cost} - \text{accumulated depreciation to date} = \text{book value}$$
$$\$7,000 - \$1,897 = \$5,103$$

4.40 Using the double declining balance method of depreciation, find the book value to the nearest dollar at the end of the second year for the following:

(a)
Cost	$120,000
Trade-in value	$5,700
Estimated life	25 yr
Purchased	May 3

(b)
Cost	$3,000
Trade-in value	$0
Estimated life	8 yr
Purchased	August 16

(c)
Cost	$18,000
Trade-in value	$3,200
Estimated life	10 yr
Purchased	October 6

SOLUTION

(a)
$$100\%/\text{estimated life} \times 2 = \text{depreciation rate}$$
$$100\%/25 \text{ yr} \times 2 = 8\%/\text{yr}$$

Depreciation at end of year 1:

$$\text{Cost} \times \text{depreciation rate} = \text{depreciation}$$
$$\$120,000 \times 0.08/\text{yr} = \$9,600$$

$$\$9,600/\text{yr} \div 12 \text{ mo/yr} = \$800/\text{mo}$$
$$\$800/\text{mo} \times 8 \text{ mo} = \$6,400$$

Depreciation at end of year 2:

$$\text{(Cost} - \text{depreciation)} \times \text{depreciation rate} = \text{depreciation}$$
$$(\$120{,}000 - \$6{,}400) \times 0.08/\text{yr} =$$
$$\$113{,}600^* \times 0.08/\text{yr} =$$
$$\$9{,}088 =$$

Book value at end of year 2:

$$\text{Cost (at beginning of year 2)} - \text{depreciation} = \text{book value}$$
$$\$113{,}600^* - \$9{,}088 = \$104{,}512$$

----

*Note that, as before, the original cost less the depreciation for the first year (i.e., the book value) becomes the cost of the item at the beginning of the second year.

(b) $$100\%/\text{estimated life} \times 2 = \text{depreciation rate}$$
$$100\%/8 \text{ yr} \times 2 = 25\%/\text{yr}$$

Depreciation at end of year 1:

$$\text{Cost} \times \text{depreciation rate} = \text{depreciation}$$
$$\$3{,}000 \times 0.25/\text{yr} = \$750/\text{yr}$$
$$\$750/\text{yr} \div 12 \text{ mo/yr} = \$62.50/\text{mo}$$
$$\$62.50/\text{mo} \times 4 \text{ mo} = \$250$$

Depreciation at end of year 2:

$$\text{(Cost} - \text{depreciation)} \times \text{depreciation rate} = \text{depreciation}$$
$$(\$3{,}000 - \$250) \times 0.25/\text{yr} =$$
$$\$2{,}750 \times 0.25/\text{yr} =$$
$$\$687.50/\text{yr} =$$

Book value at end of year 2:

$$\text{Cost (at beginning of year 2)} - \text{depreciation} = \text{book value}$$
$$\$2{,}750 - \$687.50 = \$2{,}062.50$$

(c) $$100\%/\text{estimated life} \times 2 = \text{depreciation rate}$$
$$100\%/10 \text{ yr} \times 2 = 20\%/\text{yr}$$

Depreciation at end of year 1:

$$\text{Cost} \times \text{depreciation rate} = \text{depreciation}$$
$$\$18{,}000 \times 0.20/\text{yr} = \$3{,}600/\text{yr}$$
$$\$3{,}600/\text{yr} \div 12 \text{ mo/yr} = \$300/\text{mo}$$
$$\$300/\text{mo} \times 3 \text{ mo} = \$900$$

Depreciation at end of year 2:

$$\text{(Cost} - \text{depreciation)} \times \text{depreciation rate} = \text{depreciation}$$
$$(\$18{,}000 - \$900) \times 0.20/\text{yr} =$$
$$\$17{,}100 \times 0.20/\text{yr} =$$
$$\$3{,}420/\text{yr} =$$

Book value at end of year 2:

$$\text{Cost (at beginning of year 2)} - \text{depreciation} = \text{book value}$$
$$\$17{,}100 - \$3{,}420 = \$13{,}680$$

4.41 By preparing a depreciation schedule based on the double declining balance method of depreciation, determine the accumulated depreciation at the end of 5 years on 25 tables purchased at $150 each by Mohawk Restaurant. Their estimated useful life is 16 years, and they have no salvage value. The date of purchase was January 1. (Round the depreciation to the nearest dollar.)

SOLUTION

Year	Book Value	Depreciation Rate*	Amount of Depreciation	Accumulated Depreciation
1	$3,750**	0.125	$469	$ 469
2	3,281	0.125	410	879
3	2,871	0.125	359	1,238
4	2,512	0.125	314	1,552
5	2,198	0.125	275	1,827

*100%/16 yr $\times$ 2 = $12\frac{1}{2}$/yr
**25 tables $\times$ $150/table = $3,750 total cost

4.42 Using the double declining balance method, prepare a depreciation schedule for a truck costing $8,800 purchased on January 1. The truck has an estimated useful life of 5 years and a salvage value of $1,000. (Round the depreciation to the nearest dollar.)

SOLUTION

Year	Book Value	Depreciation Rate*	Amount of Depreciation	Accumulated Depreciation
1	$8,800	0.40	$3,520	$3,520
2	5,280	0.40	2,112	5,632
3	3,168	0.40	1,267	6,899
4	1,901	0.40	760	7,659
5	1,141		141	7,800

*100%/5 yr $\times$ 2 = 40%/yr

When an item has a salvage value, the depreciation for the final year of useful life is calculated as follows (see also Example 5):

$$\text{Cost (at beginning of final year)} - \text{salvage value} = \text{depreciation}$$
$$\$1,141 - \$1,000 = \$141$$

4.43 McGuire Enterprises purchased a copy machine on December 21 for $5,200. The copier has an estimated useful life of 8 years and a salvage value of $500. Using the double declining balance method of depreciation, find the book value at the end of the second year.

SOLUTION

$$100\%/\text{estimated life} \times 2 = \text{depreciation rate}$$
$$100\%/8 \text{ yr} \times 2 = 25\%/\text{yr}$$

Cost × depreciation rate = depreciation   Cost − depreciation = book value

Year 1 $5,200 × 0.25/yr = $1,300* $5,200 − $1,300 = $3,900

Year 2 $3,900 × 0.25/yr = $975 $3,900 − $975 = $2,925

*December 21 to December 31 of the year in which copier was bought is not counted.

4.44   Using the double declining balance method, prepare a depreciation schedule for an item bought on September 1 for $12,000. It has a trade-in value of $1,000 and an estimated useful life of 4 years.

SOLUTION

Year	Book Value	Depreciation Rate*	Amount of Depreciation	Accumulated Depreciation
1	$12,000	**	$2,000	$ 2,000
2	10,000	0.50	5,000	7,000
3	5,000	0.50	2,500	9,500
4	2,500		1,500	11,000

*100%/4 yr × 2 = 50%/yr
**Depreciation for year 1:

$$\text{Cost} \times \text{depreciation rate} = \text{depreciation}$$
$$\$12,000 \times 0.50/\text{yr} = \$6,000$$
$$\$6,000/\text{yr} \div 12 \text{ mo/yr} = \$500/\text{mo}$$
$$\$500/\text{mo} \times 4 \text{ mo} = \$2,000$$

Since the item has a salvage value and year 4 is the last year of this item's useful life, the depreciation for year 4 is calculated as follows (see Example 5):

$$\text{Cost (at beginning of final year)} - \text{salvage value} = \text{depreciation}$$
$$\$2,500 - \$1,000 = \$1,500$$

4.45   Using the double declining balance method, what is the accumulated depreciation at the end of 4 years for a piece of equipment bought on January 1 for $6,100, if the equipment has an estimated useful life of 10 years and a salvage value of $570? (Round the depreciation to the nearest dollar.)

SOLUTION

Year	Book Value	Depreciation Rate*	Amount of Depreciation	Accumulated Depreciation
1	$6,100	0.20	$1,220	$1,220
2	4,880	0.20	976	2,196
3	3,904	0.20	781	2,977
4	3,123	0.20	625	3,602

*100%/10 yr × 2 = 20%/yr

4.5 SUM-OF-THE-YEARS'-DIGITS METHOD

With this method, the years of the asset's lifetime are labeled 1, 2, 3, and so on, and the depreciation amounts are based on a series of fractions that have the sum of the years' digits as their common denominator. The greatest digit assigned to a year is used as the numerator for the first year, the next greatest digit for the second year, and so forth.

EXAMPLE 7

Cost of machine $17,000; salvage value, $2,000; estimated life, 5 years.
The depreciable amount is the cost less any salvage value:

$$\$17,000 - \$2,000 = \$15,000$$

To find the fraction of this amount that is to be written off each year, proceed as follows:

1. Label the years 1, 2, 3, 4, and 5.
2. Calculate the sum (S) of the years' digits by adding the digits assigned in step 1:

$$S = 1 + 2 + 3 + 4 + 5 = 15$$

3. Convert the sum to a series of fractions by placing each digit assigned in step 1 in the numerator of each respective fraction and placing the sum of the digits found in step 2 in the denominator:

$$\frac{1}{15} + \frac{2}{15} + \frac{3}{15} + \frac{4}{15} + \frac{5}{15} = 1$$

4. Take the above series of fractions *in reverse order* as the depreciation rates. Thus,

Year	Fraction	× Amount	=	Depreciation
1	5/15	× $15,000	=	$ 5,000
2	4/15	× $15,000	=	$ 4,000
3	3/15	× $15,000	=	$ 3,000
4	2/15	× $15,000	=	$ 2,000
5	1/15	× $15,000	=	$ 1,000
		Total depreciation =		$15,000

For a machine that has a short life expectancy, such as the one in the previous example, the method outlined in step 2 for finding the sum of the years' digits suffices. However, for a machine that has a long life expectancy, it is much simpler to use the following formula:

$$S = \frac{N(N+1)}{2}$$

where S is the sum of the years' digits and N is the life expectancy.

For the machine in Example 7, the calculation for the sum of the years' digits would be

$$S = \frac{5(5+1)}{2} = \frac{30}{2} = 15$$

EXAMPLE 8

The life expectancy of a piece of equipment is estimated to be 30 yr. The sum of the years' digits by the formula used in the preceding example would be

$$S = \frac{N(N+1)}{2}$$

In this case, $N = 30$ yr. Therefore

$$S = \frac{30(30+1)}{2} = \frac{930}{2} = 465$$

SOLVED PROBLEMS

4.46 Find the sum of the years' digits for the following life expectancies: (a) 5 years, (b) 10 years, (c) 8 years, (d) 20 years, and (e) 15 years.

SOLUTION

$$S = \text{sum of the years' digits}$$
$$N = \text{estimated life}$$

$$S = \frac{N(N+1)}{2}$$

(a) $\qquad\qquad\qquad\qquad S = 5(5+1)/2 = 5(3) = 15$

(b) $\qquad\qquad\qquad\qquad S = 10(10+1)/2 = 5(11) = 55$

(c) $\qquad\qquad\qquad\qquad S = 8(8+1)/2 = 4(9) = 36$

(d) $\qquad\qquad\qquad\qquad S = 20(20+1) = 10(21) = 210$

(e) $\qquad\qquad\qquad\qquad S = 15(15+1) = 15(8) = 120$

4.47 Determine the first year's depreciation fraction that would be used in the sum-of-the-years'-digits method of depreciation for the following estimated useful lives: (a) 4 years, (b) 12 years, (c) 6 years, (d) 18 years, and (e) 3 years.

SOLUTION

Since N is the estimated life, it would also be the numerator of the first year's fraction. S is the sum of the years' digits, and as such would be the denominator. Therefore, the first year's depreciation fraction may be expressed as N/S.

For each of the given cases, we need to find S first:

$$S = \frac{N(N+1)}{2}$$

First Year's Fraction

(a) $\qquad S = 4(4+1)/2 = 2(5) = 10$ $\qquad$ and $\qquad$ $N/S = 4/10$

(b) $\qquad S = 12(12+1)/2 = 6(13) = 78$ $\qquad$ and $\qquad$ $N/S = 12/78$

(c) $\qquad S = 6(6+1)/2 = 3(7) = 21$ $\qquad$ and $\qquad$ $N/S = 6/21$

(d) $\qquad S = 18(18+1)/2 = 9(19) = 171$ $\qquad$ and $\qquad$ $N/S = 18/171$

(e) $\qquad S = 3(3+1)/2 = 3(2) = 6$ $\qquad$ and $\qquad$ $N/S = 3/6$

4.48 Using the sum-of-the-years'-digits method, find the first year's depreciation for a snowplow that cost the town of Holiday $8,000 and has an estimated useful life of 15 years and a salvage value of $1,500.

SOLUTION

$$S = \frac{N(N+1)}{2} = \frac{15(15+1)}{2} = 15(8) = 120$$

First year's depreciation fraction = N/S = 15/120.*

$$\text{Cost} - \text{salvage} = \text{depreciable amount}$$
$$\$8,000 - \$1,500 = \$6,500$$

$$\text{Depreciable amount} \times \text{depreciation fraction} = \text{depreciation}$$
$$\$6,500 \times 15/120* = \$812.50$$

---

*Note that for ease of calculation, 15/120 can be reduced to 1/8 and/or written as the decimal 0.125.

4.49   If on January 1 Cliver Transport purchased two vans costing $50,000 each for their moving and storage business, what is the depreciation on both after the first year? The vans have a trade-in value of $5,000 each and an estimated life of 10 years each. (Round the depreciation to the nearest dollar.)

SOLUTION

$$S = \frac{N(N+1)}{2}$$

$$= \frac{10(10+1)}{2} = 55$$

Depreciation fraction for year 1 $= N/S = 10/55$.

$$2 \text{ vans} \times \$50,000/\text{van} = \$100,000 \text{ total cost}$$
$$2 \text{ vans} \times \$5,000/\text{van} = \$10,000 \text{ total trade-in value}$$

$$\text{Cost} - \text{salvage} = \text{depreciable amount}$$
$$\$100,000 - \$10,000 = \$90,000$$

$$\text{Depreciable amount} \times \text{depreciation fraction} = \text{depreciation}$$
$$\$90,000 \times 10/55 = \$16,364$$

4.50   ABC Lighting purchased display cases totaling $5,670. Their estimated useful life is 8 years, and their salvage value is $1,200. Using the sum-of-the-years'-digits method, determine the depreciation to the nearest cent for the first 2 years.

SOLUTION

$$S = \frac{N(N+1)}{2}$$

$$= \frac{8(8+1)}{2} = 36$$

Depreciation fraction for year 1 $= N/S = 8/36$.

Recall from Example 7 that we take the sequence of fractions in reverse order for our calculations. Hence, the numerator of year 1 fraction is the last year of useful life (i.e., the estimated life) of the item. Since we are moving backward, the numerator of the next year's fraction is the estimated life minus 1 year. This may be stated as follows:

$$\text{Depreciation fraction for year 2} = \frac{N-1}{S}$$

$$= \frac{8-1}{36} = \frac{7}{36}$$

$$\text{Cost} - \text{salvage} = \text{depreciable amount}$$
$$\$5,670 - \$1,200 = \$4,470$$

$$\text{Depreciable amount} \times \text{depreciation fraction} = \text{depreciation}$$
$$\text{Year 1} \quad \$4,470 \times 8/36 = \$993.33$$
$$\text{Year 2} \quad \$4,470 \times 7/36 = \$869.17$$

4.51   A piano was purchased by Melody Disco for $6,750. Using the sum-of-the-years'-digits method, what is the depreciation to the nearest cent for the first 3 years if the piano has a salvage value of $960 and an estimated useful life of 25 years?

SOLUTION

$$S = \frac{N(N+1)}{2} = \frac{25(25+1)}{2} = 325$$

	Year 1	**Year 2***	**Year 3****
Depreciation fraction	$\dfrac{N}{S} = \dfrac{25}{325}$	$\dfrac{N-1}{S} = \dfrac{24}{325}$	$\dfrac{N-2}{S} = \dfrac{23}{325}$

---

*See previous problem.

**Because we are moving in reverse sequential order from the total years of estimated life, we subtract yet one more year from N to find the numerator of the depreciation fraction for year 3.

$$\text{Cost} - \text{salvage} = \text{depreciable amount}$$
$$\$6{,}750 - \$960 = \$5{,}790$$

Depreciable amount $\times$ depreciation fraction = depreciation

Year 1	$\$5{,}790 \times 25/325 = \$445.38$
Year 2	$\$5{,}790 \times 24/325 = \$427.57$
Year 3	$\$5{,}790 \times 23/325 = \$409.75$

4.52 Using the sum-of-the-years'-digits method of depreciation, what is the book value (to the nearest cent) at the end of the first year on a piece of equipment that cost \$20,650? The equipment has a salvage value of \$3,650 and an estimated useful life of 50 years.

SOLUTION

$$S = \frac{N(N+1)}{2} = \frac{50(50+1)}{2} = 1{,}275$$

Depreciation fraction for year 1 = N/S = 50/1,275.

$$\text{Cost} - \text{salvage} = \text{depreciable amount}$$
$$\$20{,}650 - \$3{,}650 = \$17{,}000$$

Depreciable amount $\times$ depreciation fraction = depreciation

$$\$17{,}000.00 \times \frac{50}{1{,}275} = \$666.67$$

$$\text{Cost} - \text{depreciation} = \text{book value}$$
$$\$20{,}650.00 - \$666.67 = \$19{,}983.33$$

4.53 Using the sum-of-the-years'-digits method, determine the accumulated depreciation after 3 years on an item that cost \$125,000 and has an estimated useful life of 75 years and a salvage value of \$10,000. (Round the depreciation to the nearest dollar.)

SOLUTION

$$S = \frac{N(N+1)}{2} = \frac{75(75+1)}{2} = 2{,}850$$

	Year 1	**Year 2***	**Year 3****
Depreciation fraction:	$\dfrac{N}{S} = \dfrac{75}{2{,}850}$	$\dfrac{N-1}{S} = \dfrac{74}{2{,}850}$	$\dfrac{N-2}{S} = \dfrac{73}{2{,}850}$

---

*See Prob. 4.50.

**See Prob. 4.51.

$$\text{Cost} - \text{salvage} = \text{depreciable amount}$$
$$\$125,000 - \$10,000 = \$115,000$$

Depreciable amount $\times$ depreciable fraction = depreciation

Year 1	$\$115,000 \times 75/2,850 = \$3,026$
Year 2	$\$115,000 \times 74/2,850 = \$2,986$
Year 3	$\$115,000 \times 73/2,850 = \$2,946$

Accumulated depreciation = $8,958

4.54 Using the sum-of-the-years'-digits method, prepare a depreciation schedule for a pizza oven that was purchased for $3,000 and has an estimated useful life of 5 years and a salvage value of $900.

SOLUTION

Year	Depreciable Amount*	Depreciation Fraction	Amount of Depreciation	Accumulated Depreciation	Book Value at End of Year
1	$2,100	5/15**	$700	$ 700	$2,300
2	2,100	4/15	560	1,260	1,740
3	2,100	3/15	420	1,680	1,320
4	2,100	2/15	280	1,960	1,040
5	2,100	1/15	140	2,100	900

*Cost − salvage = depreciable amount
   $3,000 − $900 = $2,100

$$**S = \frac{N(N+1)}{2} = \frac{5(5+1)}{2} = 15; \text{ see also Example 7.}$$

4.55 Using the sum-of-the-years'-digits method, prepare a depreciation schedule for the first 5 years for machinery that cost $75,000. The machinery has a salvage value of $6,000 and an estimated useful life of 40 years. (Round depreciation to the nearest cent.)

SOLUTION

Year	Depreciable Amount*	Depreciation Fraction	Amount of Depreciation	Accumulated Depreciation	Book Value at End of Year
1	$69,000.00	40/820**	$3,365.85	$ 3,365.85	$71,634.15
2	69,000.00	39/820	3,281.71	6,647.56	68,352.44
3	69,000.00	38/820	3,197.56	9,845.12	65,154.88
4	69,000.00	37/820	3,113.41	12,958.53	62,041.47
5	69,000.00	36/820	3,029.27	15,987.80	59,012.20

* Cost − salvage = depreciable amount
    $75,000 − $6,000 = $69,000

$$**S = \frac{N(N+1)}{2} = \frac{40(40-1)}{2} = 820; \text{ see also Probs. 4.50 and 4.51.}$$

4.56 Use the sum-of-the-years'-digits method to find the depreciation (to the nearest cent) for the first year for each of the following:

(*a*)
Cost	$4,825
Salvage value	$600
Estimated life	6 yr

(*b*)
Cost	$17,164
Salvage value	$2,600
Estimated life	12 yr

(*c*)
Cost	$65,300
Salvage value	$9,000
Estimated life	25 yr

(*d*)
Cost	$9,999
Salvage value	$1,000
Estimated life	8 yr

SOLUTION

(*a*) $S = N(N + 1)/2 = 6(6 + 1)/2 = 21$; depreciation fraction $= N/S = 6/21$

$$(\text{Cost} - \text{salvage value})^* \times \text{depreciation fraction} = \text{depreciation}$$
$$(\$4,825 - \$600) \times 6/21 =$$
$$\$4,225 \times 6/21 =$$
$$\$1,207.14 =$$

(*b*) $S = N(N + 1)/2 = 12(12 + 1)/2 = 78$; depreciation fraction $= N/S = 12/78$

$$(\text{Cost} - \text{salvage value})^* \times \text{depreciation fraction} = \text{depreciation}$$
$$(\$17,164 - \$2,600) \times 12/78 =$$
$$\$14,564 \times 12/78 =$$
$$\$2,240.62 =$$

(*c*) $S = N(N + 1)/2 = 25(25 + 1)/2 = 325$; depreciation fraction $= N/S = 25/325$

$$(\text{Cost} - \text{salvage value})^* \times \text{depreciation fraction} = \text{depreciation}$$
$$(\$65,300 - \$9,000) \times 25/325 =$$
$$\$56,300 \times 25/325 =$$
$$\$4,330.77 =$$

(*d*) $S = N(N + 1)/2 = 8(8 + 1)/2 = 36$; depreciation fraction $= N/S = 8/36$

$$(\text{Cost} - \text{salvage value})^* \times \text{depreciation fraction} = \text{depreciation}$$
$$(\$9,999 - \$1,000) \times 8/36 =$$
$$\$8,999 \times 8/36 =$$
$$\$1,999.78 =$$

---

*Depreciable amount = cost − salvage value

4.57 Using the sum-of-the-years'-digits method, prepare a depreciation schedule for the first 5 years for 40 beds purchased by Hansen Motel. The beds cost $200 each. The charge to have all of them delivered was $200. Their life expectancy is 15 years with no salvage value. (Round depreciation to the nearest dollar.)

SOLUTION

Year	Depreciable Amount*	Depreciation Fraction	Amount of Depreciation	Accumulated Depreciation	Book Value at End of Year
1	$8,200	15/120**	$1,025	$1,025	$7,175
2	8,200	14/120	957	1,982	6,218
3	8,200	13/120	888	2,870	5,330
4	8,200	12/120	820	3,690	4,510
5	8,200	11/120	752	4,442	3,758

*40 beds $\times$ $200/bed = $8,000 purchase cost
$8,000 + $200 delivery charge = $8,200 total cost
Cost $-$ salvage = depreciable amount
   $8,200 $-$ $0 = $8,200
**$S = N(N + 1)/2 = 15(15 + 1)/2 = 120$

4.58 Using the sum-of-the-years'-digits method, prepare a depreciation schedule for the first 4 years for an item that cost $56,400 and has a salvage value of $4,500 and an estimated useful life of 30 years. (Round the depreciation to the nearest cent.)

SOLUTION

Year	Depreciable Amount*	Depreciation Fraction	Amount of Depreciation	Accumulated Depreciation	Book Value at End of Year
1	$51,900	30/465**	$3,348.39	$ 3,348.39	$53,051.61
2	51,900	29/465	3,236.77	6,585.16	49,814.84
3	51,900	28/465	3,125.16	9,710.32	46,689.68
4	51,900	27/465	3,013.55	12,723.87	43,676.13

* Cost $-$ salvage = depreciable amount
$56,400 $-$ $4,500 = $51,900
**$S = N(N + 1)/2 = 30(30 + 1)/2 = 465$

4.59 Use the sum-of-the-years'-digits method to determine the accumulated depreciation at the end of the second year on a backhoe purchased by Van Dyke Excavating, Inc. on April 1 for $8,500. The backhoe has an estimated useful life of 5 years and a trade-in value of $1,000. (Round the depreciation to the nearest dollar.)

SOLUTION

$$S = \frac{N(N + 1)}{2}$$

$$= \frac{5(5 + 1)}{2} = 15$$

Depreciation fraction:

        Year 1: $N/S = 5/15$

        Year 2: $(N - 1)/S = (5 - 1)/15 = 4/15$

      Cost $-$ salvage value = depreciable amount
         $8,500 $-$ $1,000 = $7,500

Year 1.

$$\text{Depreciable amount} \times \text{depreciation fraction} = \text{depreciation}$$
$$\$7,500 \times 5/15 = \$2,500 \text{ for 1st full year of useful life}$$

Portion applicable to first calendar year:

$$\$2,500 \times 9 \text{ mo}/12 \text{ mo in a year} = \$1,875*$$

Year 2. Since the first 3 months of the *second calendar* year are still part of the equipment's *first* year of *useful life*, the depreciation for these months is calculated on the basis of the first year's fraction as follows:

$$\text{Depreciation for first full year} \times \text{applicable portion of year} = \text{depreciation}$$
$$\$2,500 \times 3 \text{ mo}/12 \text{ mo in year} = \$625 \text{ for Jan. 1–Apr. 1 of 2d year}$$

Depreciation for remaining 9 months of second year:

$$\text{Depreciable amount} \times \text{depreciation fraction} = \text{depreciation}$$
$$\$7,500 \times 4/15 = \$2,000 \text{ for 2d full year of useful life}$$

Portion applicable to second calendar year:

$$\$2,000 \times 9 \text{ mo}/12 \text{ mo in a year} = \$1,500*$$

The full depreciation for the second calendar year is therefore

$$\$625 + \$1,500 = \$2,125$$

Accumulated depreciation at end of second year:

$$\$1,875 + \$2,125 = \$4,000$$

---

*Note that this calculation is the same as

$$\text{Depreciation/yr} \div 12 \text{ mo/yr} = \text{depreciation/mo}$$
$$\text{Depreciation/mo} \times \text{applicable mo} = \text{depreciation for applicable portion of yr}$$

4.60 Using the sum-of-the-years'-digits method, determine the depreciation for the second year on an item that cost $22,000, has a salvage value of $2,000, and has an estimated useful life of 10 years. It was purchased on September 24. (Round the depreciation to the nearest dollar.)

SOLUTION

$$S = \frac{N(N+1)}{2}$$

$$= \frac{10(10+1)}{2} = 55$$

Depreciation fraction:

$$\text{Year 1} \quad N/S = 10/55$$
$$\text{Year 2} \quad (N-1)/S = (10-1)/55 = 9/55$$

$$\text{Cost} - \text{salvage} = \text{depreciable amount}$$
$$\$22,000 - \$2,000 = \$20,000$$

Since the first 9 months of the second calendar year are still part of the item's first year of useful life. the depreciation for these months is calculated on the basis of the first year's fraction as follows:

$$\text{Depreciable amount} \times \text{depreciation fraction} = \text{depreciation}$$
$$\$20,000 \times 10/55 = \$3,636 \text{ for 1st full year of useful life}$$

Portion applicable to second calendar year:

$$\$3,636 \times 9 \text{ mo}/12 \text{ mo in yr} = \$2,727 \text{ for Jan. 1–Oct. 1 of 2nd calendar year}$$

The last 3 months of the second calendar year are calculated on the basis of the second year's depreciation fraction:

Depreciable amount × depreciation fraction = depreciation

$$\$20,000 \times 9/55 = \$3,273 \text{ for 2d full year of useful life}$$

Portion applicable to second calendar year:

$$\$3,273 \times 3 \text{ mo}/12 \text{ mo in year} = \$818 \text{ for Oct. 1–Dec. 31 of 2d calendar year}$$

Depreciation for 2d year:

$$\$2,727 + \$818 = \$3,545$$

4.6 SUMMARY

The four principal methods of depreciation are compared in Table 4.1. Over a 5-year lifetime, the asset was in operation for 1,800, 1,200, 2,000, 1,400, and 1,600 hours per year, respectively. The cost of the asset was $17,000, and the scrap value is $2,000.

Table 4.1 Annual Depreciation Charge

Year	Straight-Line	Sum-of-the-Years' Digits	Double Declining Balance	Units of Production
1	$ 3,000	$ 5,000	$ 6,800	$ 3,375
2	3,000	4,000	4,080	2,250
3	3,000	3,000	2,448	3,750
4	3,000	2,000	1,468	2,625
5	3,000	1,000	204	3,000
Total	$15,000	$15,000	$15,000	$15,000

SOLVED PROBLEM

4.61 A fixed asset costing $60,000 and having an estimated salvage value of $5,000 has a life expectancy of 10 years. Compare the results of the various depreciation methods by filling in the tables below. Take twice the straight-line rate as the rate in the double declining balance method.

Straight-Line Method

Year	Depreciation Expense	Accumulated Depreciation	Book Value at End of Year
1			
2			
3			
4			

Sum-of-the-Years'-Digits Method

Year	Fraction	Depreciation Expense	Accumulated Depreciation	Book Value at End of Year
1				
2				
3				
4				

Double Declining Balance Method

Year	Rate	Depreciation Expense	Accumulated Depreciation	Book Value at End of Year
1				
2				
3				
4				

SOLUTION

Straight-Line Method

Year	Depreciation Expense	Accumulated Depreciation	Book Value at End of Year
1	$5,500*	$ 5,500	$54,500**
2	5,500	11,000	49,000
3	5,500	16,500	43,500
4	5,500	22,000	38,000

*($60,000 − $5,000) ÷ 10/yr = $5,500/yr
**$60,000 − $5,500 = $54,500

Sum-of-the-Years'-Digits Method

Year	Fraction*	Depreciation Expense	Accumulated Depreciation	Book Value at End of Year
1	10/55	$10,000	$10,000	$50,000
2	9/55	9,000	19,000	41,000
3	8/55	8,000	27,000	33,000
4	7/55	7,000	34,000	26,000

$$*S = \frac{10(10 + 1)}{2} = 55$$

Double Declining Balance Method

Year	Rate*	Depreciation Expense	Accumulated Depreciation	Book Value at End of Year
1	0.20	$12,000	$12,000	$48,000
2	0.20	9,600	21,600	38,400
3	0.20	7,680	29,280	30,720
4	0.20	6,144	35,424	24,576

$*\dfrac{100\%}{10 \text{ yr}} \times 2 = 20\%$; note that this is twice the straight-line rate.

**20% × ($60,000 − $12,000) = $9,600.

Supplementary Problems

4.62   Using the straight-line method of depreciation, find the amount of depreciation per year if a fixed asset bought on January 6 for $17,000 has an estimated life of 15 years and a salvage value of $2,000.

4.63   Muller Printers bought printing equipment on July 6. The purchase price was $3,700, and the estimated useful life is 4 years. The salvage value is $700. Find the depreciation as of December 31 (same year) by using the straight-line method.

4.64   Using the straight-line method, calculate the amount of depreciation at the end of the second year on a piece of machinery purchased on October 28 for $4,650. The estimated useful life is 5 years and the trade-in value is $1,650.

4.65   A computer was purchased by Hill Enterprises on February 1. The purchase price was $2,000, and installation cost was $720. The estimated useful life is 10 years, and the salvage value is $500. What is the amount of straight-line depreciation (to the nearest cent) at the end of the third year?

4.66   If a photocopier purchased on January 3 for $13,400 has an estimated useful life of 15 years and a trade-in value of $950, what is the book value at the end of the sixth year according to the straight-line method of depreciation?

4.67   Determine the depreciation rate per year for the following estimated useful lives: 4 years, 25 years, and 32 years.

4.68   Prepare a depreciation schedule for a piece of equipment purchased on January 8 for $5,000. Transportation costs amounted to $500. The estimated useful life is 4 years, and the salvage value is $500. Use the straight-line method of depreciation.

4.69   Using the straight-line method of depreciation, determine the book value at the end of the fourth year for the following:

(a)	Cost	$12,000
	Salvage value	$1,000
	Estimated life	10 yr
(b)	Cost	$7,400
	Salvage value	$600
	Estimated life	8 yr
(c)	Cost	$35,000
	Salvage value	$4,000
	Estimated life	20 yr

4.70   An item of equipment was bought on January 1 for $30,000. It has an estimated useful life of 100,000 hours and a salvage value of $4,000. If it was used for 35,650 hours in its first year of operation, what is the depreciation according to the units-of-production method?

4.71   A used dishwasher was purchased by Faine Restaurant on April 3 for $1,500. Repair work totaling $300 was needed before putting the machine into operation. Using the units-of-production method, determine the depreciation after 5,760 hours of use if the salvage value is $50 and the estimated useful life is 57,750 hours.

4.72   Using the units-of-production method, find the depreciation on a piece of assembly-line equipment that produced 9,750 units during its first year in operation. The cost of the equipment was $40,000. It has a salvage value of $2,500 and an estimated lifetime output of 75,000 units.

4.73 K&M Painting Contractors started business on June 1. One month prior they purchased a van for $8,000 and incurred additional costs amounting to $1,000 to get the van in operating condition. They also bought a paint sprayer for $300. The van has an estimated useful life of 100,000 mi and a trade-in value of $2,000. The paint sprayer has an estimated useful life of 2,750 hours and a trade-in value of $25. What is the depreciation, based on the units-of-production method, at the end of the year if they put 5,670 mi on the van as of December 31 and used the paint sprayer 250 hours?

4.74 Roe Computers bought an assembler that assembles 50 circuit parts per hour. If during the first year of operation the machine assembled 68,430 circuits, find the depreciation by using the units-of-production method. The assembler cost $230,000, has a salvage value of $10,000, and is expected to assemble 1 million circuits during its useful life.

4.75 What is the book value of a piece of equipment that cost $70,000, was used 237,000 hours, and has an estimated useful life of 500,000 hours and a trade-in value of $5,000?

4.76 Using the units-of-production method, find the depreciation of a used truck that cost $3,700. Additional costs incurred were $335.69 parts, $312.97 repairs, and $151.34 repainting. The original estimated useful life was 150,000 mi, but the truck had 87,965 miles on it when purchased. The trade-in value is $500, and the truck was driven 9,623 mi during the year.

4.77 Office furniture was purchased by Chester Company on January 1 for $2,000. Its estimated useful life is 20 years, and it has a salvage value of $250. Using the double declining balance method of depreciation, what is the depreciation at the end of the first year?

4.78 Equipment was bought on January 10 for $30,000. It has an estimated useful life of 25 years and a trade-in value of $3,000. Determine the book value at the end of the first year by using the double declining balance method of depreciation.

4.79 Determine the accumulated depreciation at the end of the second year by using the double declining balance method of depreciation on a tractor that cost $9,000. Its estimated useful life is 10 years, and the trade-in value is $500. It was bought on October 20.

4.80 If equipment that cost $100,000 and has a trade-in value of $10,000 was put into use on January 3, what is the book value at the end of the second year if said equipment has an estimated useful life of 50 years and the double declining balance method of depreciation is used?

4.81 For the following, find the book value to the nearest dollar at the end of the first year by using the double declining balance method of depreciation:

Cost	$3,000
Trade-in value	$50
Estimated life	10 yr
Purchased	January 1
Cost	$27,000
Trade-in value	$5,000
Estimated life	25 yr
Purchased	May 1

4.82 A conveyor with an estimated useful life of 8 years and a salvage value of $400 was purchased for $5,000. Determine the book value at the end of the second year by using the double declining balance method of depreciation.

4.83 Mullen Corporation purchased a computer on December 31 for $7,000. Its estimated useful life is 20 years, and the salvage value is $1,000. Find the book value at the end of the first year by using the double declining balance method of depreciation.

4.84   According to the double declining balance method, what is the accumulated depreciation at the end of 2 years on a piece of machinery bought on January 13 for $4,000? The estimated useful life is 5 years, and the salvage value is $200. (Round the depreciation to the nearest dollar.)

4.85   Find the sum of the years for the following life expectancies: 4 years, 3 years, and 20 years.

4.86   Determine the first year's depreciation fraction in the sum-of-the-years'-digits method of depreciation for the following estimated useful lives: 15 years, 5 years, and 8 years.

4.87   Using the sum-of-the-years'-digits method, find the first year's depreciation on a tractor that cost the town of Hill $10,000 and has an estimated useful life of 20 years and a salvage value of $1,000.

4.88   Billy purchased three trucks costing $10,000 each for his painting business. The trucks have a trade-in value of $1,000 each and an estimated life of 15 years each. What is the depreciation on all three at the end of the first year if purchase was made on January 10? (Round the depreciation to the nearest dollar.)

4.89   Use the sum-of-the-years'-digits method to find the book value (to the nearest cent) at the end of the first year on a piece of machinery that cost $15,425. It has a salvage value of $2,425 and an estimated useful life of 10 years.

4.90   Using the sum-of-the-years'-digits method, determine the accumulated depreciation at the end of 2 years on an item that cost $90,000 and has an estimated useful life of 50 years and a salvage value of $5,000. (Round the depreciation to the nearest dollar.)

4.91   Use the sum-of-the-years'-digits method to find the depreciation at the end of the first year for the following:

(*a*)

Cost	$9,687
Salvage value	$500
Estimated life	8 yr

(*b*)

Cost	$2,450
Salvage value	$250
Estimated life	6 yr

Answers to Supplementary Problems

4.62 $1,000

4.63 $375

4.64 $700

4.65 $647.50

4.66 $8,420

4.67   25%, 4%, $3\frac{1}{8}$%

4.68

Year	Depreciation Rate (%)	Yearly Depreciation	Book Value (End of Year)	Accumulated Depreciation
1	25	$1,250	$4,250	$1,250
2	25	1,250	3,000	2,500
3	25	1,250	1,750	3,750
4	25	1,250	500	5,000

4.69 (a) $7,600, (b) $4,000, (c) $28,800

4.70 $9,269

4.71 $172.80

4.72 $4,875

4.73 $396.90 van, $25 paint sprayer

4.74 $15,054.60

4.75 $39,190

4.76 $620.49

4.77 $200

4.78 $27,600

4.79 $2,040

4.80 $92,160

4.81 $2,400, $25,560

4.82 $2,812.50

4.83 $6,300

4.84 $2,560

4.85 10, 6, 210

4.86 15/120, 5/15, 8/36

4.87 $857.14

4.88 $3,375

4.89 $13,061.36

4.90 $6,600

4.91 (a) $2,041.56, (b) $628.57

Interest and Discount

5.1 SIMPLE INTEREST

When an investor lends money to a borrower, the borrower must pay back the money originally borrowed, called the *principal*, and also the fee charged for the use of the money, called *interest*. From the investor's point of view, interest is income from invested capital. The sum of the principal and the interest due is called the *amount* or *accumulated value* or *maturity value*.

The amount of interest is based on three factors: the principal, the rate of interest, and the time span of the loan. At *simple interest*, the formula for computing the interest I on principal P for t years at annual rate r is given by

$$\text{Interest} = \text{principal} \times \text{rate} \times \text{time}$$
$$I = Prt$$

The maturity value S is given by

$$\text{Maturity value} = \text{principal} + \text{interest}$$
$$S = P + I$$

EXAMPLE 1

Anne Geisler requests a 2-year loan of $6,500 from Traders Bank. The bank approves the loan at an annual interest rate of 14%. (*a*) What is the simple interest on the loan? (*b*) What is the maturity value of the loan?

(*a*)
$$\text{Principal} = \$6,500$$
$$\text{Rate} = 14\% = 0.14$$
$$\text{Time} = 2 \text{ yr}$$

Substituting these values into $I = Prt$, we get

$$I = Prt$$
$$= \$6,500 \times 0.14 \times 2 = \$1,820$$

(*b*) The maturity value is defined as the sum of the principal and the interest. Hence, the maturity value of this loan is equal to

$$S = P + I = \$6,500 + \$1,820 = \$8,320$$

Although the time span of a loan may be given in days, months, or years, the rate of interest is an annual rate. Thus, when the duration of a loan is given in months or days, the time must be converted to years. When the time is given in months, then

$$t = \frac{\text{number of months}}{12}$$

EXAMPLE 2

Find the simple interest on Anne Geisler's loan of $6,500 if the loan is offered at a rate of 21% and is due in 3 months. What is the maturity value of the loan at these terms?

$$P = \$6,500 \quad r = 21\% = 0.21 \quad t = 3/12$$

$$I = Prt$$

$$= \$6,500 \times 0.21 \times \frac{3}{12} = \$341.25$$

The maturity value of the loan now equals

$$S = P + I$$
$$= \$6,500 + \$341.25 = \$6,841.25$$

SOLVED PROBLEMS

5.1   Find the simple interest on $800 loaned at an annual interest rate of 12% for 2 years.

SOLUTION

$$\text{Interest} = \text{principal} \times \text{rate} \times \text{time}$$

The principal $(P) = \$800$, the rate $(r) = 12\% = 0.12$, and time $(t) = 2$:

$$I = Prt$$
$$= \$800 \times 0.12 \times 2 = \$192$$

5.2   What is the maturity value of the loan in Prob. 5.1?

SOLUTION

The maturity value is equal to the principal plus the interest:

$$S = I + P$$
$$= \$800 + \$192 = \$992$$

5.3   (a) Find the simple interest on a $30,000 loan due in 5 years when the annual interest rate on the loan is 16%. (b) What is the maturity value of this loan?

SOLUTION

(a)

$$P = \$30,000 \quad r = 16\% = 0.16 \quad t = 5$$
$$I = Prt$$
$$= \$30,000 \times 0.16 \times 5 = \$24,000$$

(b)

$$S = P + I$$
$$= \$30,000 + \$24,000 = \$54,000$$

5.4   Find the simple interest on a $3,000 loan at 17% annual interest for 4 months.

SOLUTION

$$P = \$3,000 \quad r = 17\% = 0.17 \quad t = \frac{4}{12} = \frac{1}{3}$$

$$I = Prt$$

$$= \$3,000 \times 0.17 \times \frac{1}{3} = \$170$$

5.5   Find the simple interest on a $5,000 loan at $14\frac{1}{2}\%$ for 7 months.

SOLUTION

$$P = \$5,000 \quad r = 14\tfrac{1}{2}\% = 0.145 \quad t = \frac{7}{12}$$

$$I = Prt$$

$$= \$5,000 \times 0.145 \times \frac{7}{12} = \$422.92$$

5.2   CALCULATING DUE DATES

If the term of a loan is given in months, the due date of the loan is a corresponding day in the *maturity month*. There are two qualifying conditions:

1. If the maturity month does not have the required number of days, then the last day of the month serves as the maturity date. Thus, a 2-month loan dated December 31 is due on February 28 (or February 29 in a leap year).

2. If the due date of a loan falls on a nonbusiness day, the maturity date is the next business day, with the additional day(s) added to the period, for which interest is charged.

EXAMPLE 3

(*a*) A 15-month loan dated February 2 is due May 2 of the following year. (*b*) A loan dated May 31 and due in 4 months has a maturity date of September 30. (*c*) A 7-month loan dated December 4 is due July 5, since July 4 is a holiday.

Interest is charged for the extra day the loan is outstanding. For simplicity, we have assumed that the maturity dates in (*a*) and (*b*) fall on a business day. Should this not be the case, then the due date is postponed until the next business day and interest is charged [just as in (*c*)].

When the time is given in days, we may calculate either (1) *exact simple interest* on the basis of a 365-day year (leap year or not) or (2) *ordinary simple interest* on the basis of a 360-day year, called a *banker's year*. Of the two, ordinary interest brings greater revenue to the lender.

The formulas for calculating time (*t*) for exact and ordinary simple interest are

Exact simple interest:

$$t = \frac{\text{number of days}}{365}$$

Ordinary simple interest:

$$t = \frac{\text{number of days}}{360}$$

EXAMPLE 4

Find the exact and the ordinary simple interest on a 60-day loan of $1,950 at $13\frac{1}{2}\%$.

We know that $P = \$1,950$ and $r = 13\frac{1}{2}\% = 0.135$, but we must calculate t for each type of interest:

$$t_{\text{exact}} = \frac{60}{365} \qquad t_{\text{ordinary}} = \frac{60}{360}$$

The respective simple interests are

Exact simple interest:

$$I = Prt$$

$$= \$1,950 \times 0.135 \times \frac{60}{365} = \$43.27$$

Ordinary simple interest:

$$I = Prt$$

$$= \$1,950 \times 0.135 \times \frac{60}{360} = \$43.88$$

There are two ways to calculate the number of days between calendar dates.

1. *Exact time* is the count of the actual number of days, including all except the first day. Exact time can be easily found from Table 5.1 by subtracting the serial numbers of the given dates. (April 15, for example, has a serial number of 105 since it is the 105th day of the year.) In leap years, serial numbers of all days after February 28 are increased by 1 (so that the serial number for April 15 would be 106).

2. *Approximate time* is found by assuming that each month has 30 days.

Table 5.1   The Number of Each Day of the Year

Day of Month	Jan.	Feb.	Mar.	Apr.	May	June	July	Aug.	Sept.	Oct.	Nov.	Dec.	Day of Month
1	1	32	60	91	121	152	182	213	244	274	305	335	1
2	2	33	61	92	122	153	183	214	245	275	306	336	2
3	3	34	62	93	123	154	184	215	246	276	307	337	3
4	4	35	63	94	124	155	185	216	247	277	308	338	4
5	5	36	64	95	125	156	186	217	248	278	309	339	5
6	6	37	65	96	126	157	187	218	249	279	310	340	6
7	7	38	66	97	127	158	188	219	250	280	311	341	7
8	8	39	67	98	128	159	189	220	251	281	312	342	8
9	9	40	68	99	129	160	190	221	252	282	313	343	9
10	10	41	69	100	130	161	191	222	253	283	314	344	10
11	11	42	70	101	131	162	192	223	254	284	315	345	11
12	12	43	71	102	132	163	193	224	255	285	316	346	12
13	13	44	72	103	133	164	194	225	256	286	317	347	13
14	14	45	73	104	134	165	195	226	257	287	318	348	14
15	15	46	74	105	135	166	196	227	258	288	319	349	15
16	16	47	75	106	136	167	197	228	259	289	320	350	16
17	17	48	76	107	137	168	198	229	260	290	321	351	17
18	18	49	77	108	138	169	199	230	261	291	322	352	18
19	19	50	78	109	139	170	200	231	262	292	323	353	19
20	20	51	79	110	140	171	201	232	263	293	324	354	20
21	21	52	80	111	141	172	202	233	264	294	325	355	21
22	22	53	81	112	142	173	203	234	265	295	326	356	22
23	23	54	82	113	143	174	204	235	266	296	327	357	23
24	24	55	83	114	144	175	205	236	267	297	328	358	24
25	25	56	84	115	145	176	206	237	268	298	329	359	25
26	26	57	85	116	146	177	207	238	269	299	330	360	26
27	27	58	86	117	147	178	208	239	270	300	331	361	27
28	28	59	87	118	148	179	209	240	271	301	332	362	28
29	29		88	119	149	180	210	241	272	302	333	363	29
30	30		89	120	150	181	211	242	273	303	334	364	30
31	31		90		151		212	243		304		365	31

Note: For leap year add 1 to the tabulated number after February 28.

EXAMPLE 5

(*a*) Find the exact time from January 18 to July 9 of the same year, when the year is a leap year. From Table 5.1:

Date	Day Number
July 9	$190 + 1^* = 191$
Jan. 18	-18
Exact time	173 days

*Since the year is a leap year, 1 is added
to all days after February 28.

(*b*) Find the approximate time between January 18 and July 9. To do this, we set up a table and subtract, as shown:

Date	Month	Day	Month	Day
July 9	7	9 $\longrightarrow$	6	39*
Jan. 18	1	18	1	18
Difference			5	21

*Although July has 31 days, we assumed that all months have only
30 days to carry out the subtraction. This is because approximate
time is based on a year having 12 equal months of 30 days each.
Consequently, leap years are also not considered when dealing
with approximate time.

To restate in days the approximate time of 5 months and 21 days, we proceed as follows:

$$(5 \text{ mo} \times 30 \text{ days/mo}) + 21 \text{ days} = 150 \text{ days} + 21 \text{ days} = 171 \text{ days}$$

SOLVED PROBLEMS

5.6 Find the exact simple interest on a 90-day loan of $900 at $15\frac{1}{4}\%$.

SOLUTION

$$P = \$900 \quad r = 15\frac{1}{4}\% = 0.1525 \quad t = \frac{90}{365}$$

$$I = Prt$$

$$= \$900 \times 0.1525 \times \frac{90}{365} = \$33.84$$

5.7 Find the ordinary simple interest for the loan in Prob. 5.6.

SOLUTION

$$P = \$900 \quad r = 15\frac{1}{4}\% = 0.1525 \quad t = \frac{90}{360}$$

$$I = Prt$$

$$= \$900 \times 0.1525 \times \frac{90}{360} = \$34.31$$

5.8 Find the (*a*) exact and (*b*) ordinary simple interest on a 120-day loan of $145,000 that has an annual interest rate of $19\frac{3}{4}\%$. (*c*) Which gives the lender a greater return on the $145,000 investment and by how much?

SOLUTION

(*a*) Exact simple interest

$$P = \$145{,}000 \qquad r = 19\tfrac{3}{4}\% = 0.1975 \qquad t = \frac{120}{365}$$

$$I = Prt$$

$$= \$145{,}000 \times 0.1975 \times \frac{120}{365} = \$9{,}415.07$$

(*b*) Ordinary simple interest

$$P = \$145{,}000 \qquad r = 19\tfrac{3}{4}\% = 0.1975 \qquad t = \frac{120}{360}$$

$$I = Prt$$

$$= \$145{,}000 \times 0.1975 \times \frac{120}{360} = \$9{,}545.83$$

(*c*) Of the two, ordinary simple interest gives the lender $130.76 more interest on this investment.

5.9 Find the exact time from April 9 to December 3 of the same year.

SOLUTION

From Table 5-1:

Date	Day Number
Dec. 3	337
Apr. 9	−99
Exact time	238 days

5.10 Find the exact time from February 4 to April 21 of the same leap year.

SOLUTION

Date	Day Number
April 21	111
Add 1 for leap year	+1
	112
Feb. 4	−35
Exact time	77 days

5.11 Find the exact time from May 18 to July 5 of the following year.

SOLUTION

Date	Day Number
July 5	186
Add 365 for extending into next year	+365
	551
May 18	−138
Exact time	413 days

5.12   Find the approximate time in Prob. 5.9.

SOLUTION

Date	Month	Day	Month	Day
Dec. 3 Apr. 9	12 4	3 ⟶ 11 9	11 4	33 9
Difference			7	24

The approximate time is 7 months and 24 days, or $(7 \times 30) + 24 = 234$ days.

5.13   Find the approximate time in Prob. 5.11.

SOLUTION

Date	Month	Day	Month	Day
July 5 May 18	12 + 7 5	5 ⟶ 18 18	18 5	35 18
Difference			13	17

The approximate time is 13 months and 17 days, or $(13 \times 30) + 17 = 407$ days.

5.14   Find the maturity date of a 60-day loan dated June 15.

SOLUTION

Date	Day Number
June 15	166
Add term of loan	+60
Maturity date	226, which is Aug. 14

5.15   Find the maturity date on a 120-day loan dated August 1.

SOLUTION

Date	Day Number
August 1	213
Add term of loan	+120
	333, which is Nov. 29

5.16   Find the due date on a 3-month loan dated April 4.

SOLUTION

Three months after April 4 is July 4, which is a legal holiday. Therefore the due date is July 5 (if a business day), and interest is charged for 91 days if approximate time is used or for 92 days if exact time is used.

5.3 METHODS FOR COMPUTING SIMPLE INTEREST

There are four distinct methods for computing simple interest between two dates:

1. Exact time and ordinary interest
2. Exact time and exact interest
3. Approximate time and ordinary interest
4. Approximate time and exact interest

Method 1 is also known as the "banker's rule" and is the common method used in business in the United States and in international business transactions. Method 2 is used by the U.S. government. Method 3 is used for periodic repayment plans, such as monthly payments on real estate mortgages, installment purchases, and certain types of personal borrowing, and in computing accrued bond interest on corporate bonds. Method 4 is theoretically possible but never used.

EXAMPLE 6

A sum of $75,000 is invested from March 13 until December 20 of the same year at $15\frac{1}{2}\%$ simple interest. For each of the four methods, the interest earned is illustrated below.

$$P = \$75,000 \quad \text{and} \quad r = 15\tfrac{1}{2}\% = 0.1550$$

(a) Exact time and ordinary interest:

The calculation to find the exact time is as follows:

Date	Day Number
Dec. 20	354
Mar. 13	−72
Exact time	282 days

To find t for ordinary interest, we have to use a year based on 360 days:

$$t = \frac{282}{360}$$

We can now calculate the interest:

$$I = Prt$$
$$= \$75,000 \times 0.1550 \times \frac{282}{360} = \$9,106.25$$

(b) Exact time and exact interest:

From (a) we know the exact number of days is 282. To find t for exact interest, we have to use a 365-day year:

$$t = \frac{282}{365}$$

$$I = Prt$$
$$= \$75,000 \times 0.1550 \times \frac{282}{365} = \$8,981.51$$

(c) Approximate time and ordinary interest:

To find approximate time, we construct a table and subtract:

Date	Month	Day
Dec. 20	12	20
Mar. 13	3	13
Difference	9	7

We then convert to approximate time in days:

$$(9 \text{ mo} \times 30 \text{ days/mo}) + 7 \text{ days} = 277 \text{ days}$$

For ordinary interest we use a 360-day year to calculate t:

$$t = \frac{277}{360}$$

$$I = Prt$$

$$= \$75{,}000 \times 0.1550 \times \frac{277}{360} = \$8{,}944.79$$

(d) Approximate time and exact interest:

From (c) we know that the number of approximate days is 277. Using a 365-day year to calculate t, we get

$$t = \frac{277}{365}$$

$$I = Prt$$

$$= \$75{,}000 \times 0.1550 \times \frac{277}{365} = \$8{,}822.26$$

SOLVED PROBLEMS

5.17   A sum of \$2,000 is invested from April 9 to December 3 of the same year at 15% simple interest. Find the interest earned using the four methods.

SOLUTION

From Prob. 5.9 the exact time is 238 days, and from Prob. 5.12 the approximate time is 234 days.

$$P = \$2{,}000 \qquad r = 15\% = 0.15 \qquad t \text{ depends on the method used}$$

$$I = Prt$$

1. Exact time and ordinary interest: $I = \$2{,}000(0.15)\left(\dfrac{238}{360}\right) = \$198.33$

2. Exact time and exact interest: $I = \$2{,}000(0.15)\left(\dfrac{238}{365}\right) = \$195.62$

3. Approximate time and ordinary interest: $I = \$2{,}000(0.15)\left(\dfrac{234}{360}\right) = \$195.00$

4. Approximate time and exact interest: $I = \$2{,}000(0.15)\left(\dfrac{234}{365}\right) = \$192.33$

5.18   Using the banker's rule, find the simple interest on \$1,800 at $17\frac{1}{4}\%$ from February 4 to April 21 of the same leap year.

SOLUTION

From Prob. 5.10 the exact time is 77 days:

$$P = \$1{,}800 \qquad r = 17\tfrac{1}{4}\% = 0.1725 \qquad t = \frac{77}{360}$$

$$I = Prt$$

$$= \$1{,}800(0.1725)(77/360) = \$66.41$$

5.19 Find the maturity value (see Sec. 5.1) of a note for $1,500 at 12% ordinary simple interest for 182 days.

SOLUTION

$$P = \$1,500 \qquad r = 0.12 \qquad t = \frac{182}{360}$$

$$I = Prt$$
$$= \$1,500(0.12)(182/360) = \$91$$
$$S = P + I$$
$$= \$1,500 + \$91 = \$1,591$$

5.20 Joe borrowed $1,200 on September 10 to start college. He repaid the loan on July 20 of the following year. What amount did he pay back if the bank calculated the exact interest at 11% and used the exact time?

SOLUTION

Exact time from September 10 to July 20 of the following year:

Date	Day Number
July 20	201
Add 365 for extending	
into next year	+365
	566
Sept. 10	−253
Exact time	313 days

Interest paid:

$$P = \$1,200 \qquad r = 0.11 \qquad t = \frac{313}{365}$$

$$I = Prt$$
$$= \$1,200 \times 0.11 \times \frac{313}{365} = \$113.19$$

To determine how much Joe paid back, we calculate the maturity value of the loan.

$$S = P + I$$
$$= \$1,200 + \$113.19 = \$1,313.19$$

Joe paid the bank $1,313.19.

5.4 PROMISSORY NOTES AND BANK DISCOUNT

A *promissory note* is a written promise by a debtor, called the *maker* of the note, to pay the creditor, called the *payee* of the note, a sum of money on a specified date. Promissory notes are used when money is borrowed or goods or services are sold on credit. There are two types of promissory notes, *interest-bearing* notes and *non-interest-bearing* notes. Figure 5.1 is an example of an interest-bearing note.

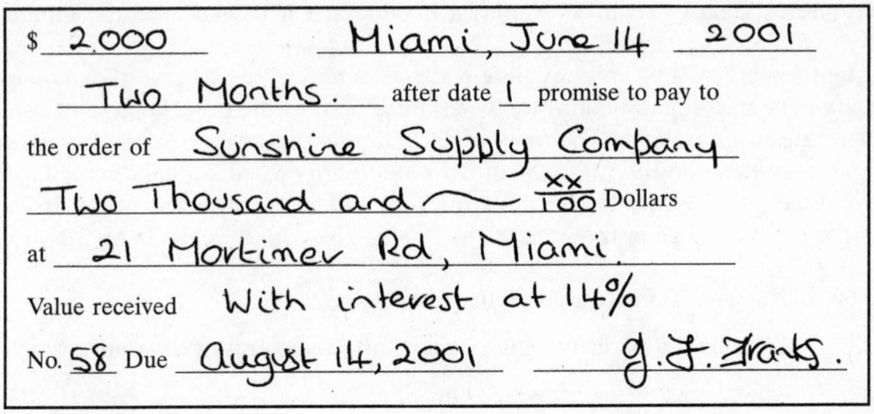

CHAP. 5] INTEREST AND DISCOUNT 115

Fig. 5.1

Looking at the promissory note in Fig. 5.1 we learn the following terms:

1. The *face value* of the note, which is the amount of money stated in the note ($2,000)
2. The *date* of the note (June 14, 2001), which is the date on which the note was made and from which the interest is computed
3. The *term* of the note (2 months)
4. The *payee* of the note (Sunshine Supply Company)
5. The *maker* of the note (I. J. Franks)
6. The *interest rate* on the note (14% ordinary simple interest)
7. The *maturity date* of the note (August 14, 2001, 2 months after June 14, 2001)

On the maturity date, August 14, 2001, the principal of $2,000 and the simple interest at 14% for 2 months must be paid. The total of principal and interest is called the *maturity value* of the note. (If the term of the note is in days, ordinary simple interest is used to calculate the maturity value.)

Figure 5.2 is an example of a non-interest-bearing note.

The interest rate is not stated on the note in Fig. 5.2. The maturity value of the note is equal to its face value and $500 must be paid on May 9, 2001 (assuming a nonleap year). Note that interest is

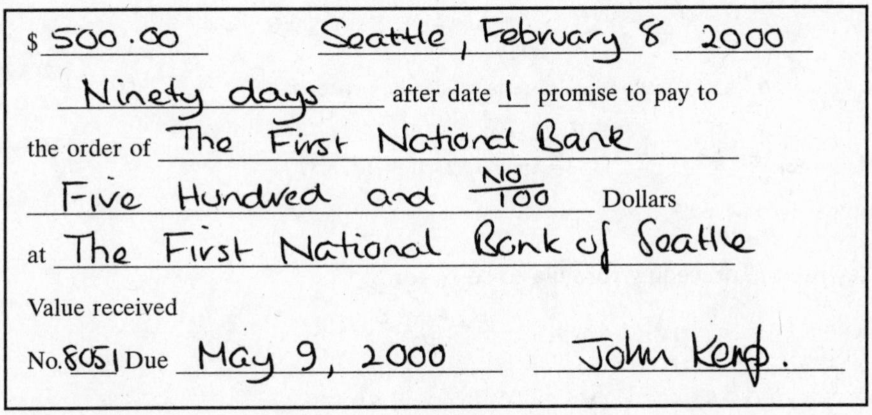

Fig. 5.2

paid on a non-interest-bearing loan. The interest is deducted in advance, at the time the money is borrowed.

An important feature of a promissory note is that it is *negotiable*. That is, it can be transferred to another payee (a person, company, bank) by the endorsement of the present payee. Cashing a note at a bank is called *discounting a note*. The bank collects interest in advance, called *bank discount (D)*, which is computed on the *maturity value (S)* of the note at a specified annual *discount rate (d)* for the *term (t)* of the discount in years. The term of the discount is the time (in years) from the date of discount until the maturity date of the note. If the time is given in days, the banker's year of 360 days is used.

Thus the bank discount (D) is computed by

$$\text{Discount} = \text{maturity value} \times \text{discount rate} \times \text{term of discount}$$

$$D = Sdt$$

The money received for the discounted note is called the *proceeds*. The proceeds (P) are obtained by deducting the bank discount (D) from the maturity value (S) of the note:

$$\text{Proceeds} = \text{maturity value} - \text{bank discount}$$

$$P = S - D$$

By combining the preceding two formulas, we can calculate proceeds directly from the discount rate and the term:

$$P = S - D = S - Sdt = S(1 - dt)$$

EXAMPLE 7

Refer to Fig. 5.2. If the First National Bank of Seattle charged 18.5% interest in advance on the 90-day, $500 loan, how much did John Kemp actually receive?

$$S = \$500 \qquad d = 18.5\% = 0.185 \qquad t = \frac{90}{360}$$

The interest collected in advance is called the bank discount (D):

$$D = Sdt$$

$$= \$500 \times 0.185 \times \frac{90}{360} = \$23.125 \cong \$23.13$$

The money received for the discounted note is called the proceeds (P):

$$P = S - D$$
$$= \$500 - \$23.13 = \$476.87$$

John Kemp received $476.87.

We can rewrite the preceding formula to solve for S:

$$P = S(1 - dt)$$

$$\frac{P}{1 - dt} = S$$

This formula is used to calculate the maturity value of a loan for specified proceeds.

EXAMPLE 8

Celeste Curtis wants to get a 180-day, non-interest-bearing note from a bank that charges $14\frac{1}{4}\%$ interest. What should be the face value of the note if Celeste needs $1,000 in cash?

We want to find the maturity value (S) of the 180-day note for specified proceeds (P) of $1,000.

$$S = \frac{P}{1 - dt}$$

$$= \frac{\$1,000}{1 - (0.1425)(180/360)} = \$1,076.72$$

The face value of the note should be $1,076.72.

SOLVED PROBLEMS

5.21   Find the maturity value of the note in Fig. 5.1.

SOLUTION

$$P = \$2,000 \qquad r = 14\% = 0.14 \qquad t = \frac{2}{12}$$

From Sec. 5.4:

$$S = P(1 + rt)$$

$$= \$2,000\left(1 + 0.14 \times \frac{2}{12}\right) = \$2,046.67$$

5.22   Sunshine Supply Company cashed the note in Fig. 5.1 on July 17 at their bank at a 12% bank discount rate. Find the bank discount and the proceeds.

SOLUTION

The term of discount is the time from July 17 to August 14, that is, 28 days.

$$S = \$2,046.67 \qquad d = 0.12 \qquad t = \frac{28}{360}$$

$$D = Sdt$$

$$= \$2,046.67 \times 0.12 \times \frac{28}{360} = \$19.10$$

$$P = S - D$$

$$= \$2,046.67 - \$19.10 = \$2,027.57$$

The bank discount charged by the bank is $19.10 and Sunshine Supply Company receives proceeds of $2,027.57.

5.23   What rate of interest did the bank in Prob. 5.22 realize on its investment if it held the note until the maturity date?

SOLUTION

The bank paid $2,027.57 for the note on July 17 and received $2,046.67 from I. J. Franks on August 14. The bank realized a profit of $2,046.67 − $2,027.57 = $19.10 on their investment of $2,027.57 over a period of 28 days. The rate of interest realized by the bank is

$$r = \frac{I}{Pt}$$

$$= \frac{\$19.10}{\$2,027.57(28/360)} = 0.1211 = 12.11\%$$

Note that the interest rate is 0.11% higher than the corresponding discount rate (d). This is because the discount rate (d) is applied to the maturity value (S), whereas the interest rate (r) is applied to the principal (proceeds) (P). Both rates result in the same amount of interest $19.10 and are said to be *equivalent rates*.

5.24 Referring to the note in Fig. 5.2, find the proceeds to John Kemp if the First National Bank of Seattle charged 15% interest in advance on the loan.

SOLUTION

$$S = \$500 \qquad d = 0.15 \qquad t = \frac{90}{360}$$

$$D = Sdt$$

$$= \$500 \times 0.15 \times \frac{90}{360} = \$18.75$$

$$P = S - D$$

$$= \$500 - \$18.75 = \$481.25$$

5.25 What is the true interest rate (at ordinary simple interest) that John Kemp paid on his loan in Prob. 5.24?

SOLUTION

The principal of the loan is $481.25, and the interest is $18.75 for 90 days:

$$P = \$481.25 \qquad I = \$18.75 \qquad t = \frac{90}{360}$$

$$r = \frac{I}{Pt}$$

$$= \frac{\$18.75}{\$481.25(90/360)} = 0.1558 = 15.58\%$$

5.26 Find the maturity date and the term of discount for each of the following:

	Date of Note	Term of Note	Date of Discount
(a)	June 12	120 days	July 15
(b)	Nov. 8	3 months	Jan. 10

SOLUTION

(*a*) Maturity date: June 12 + 120 days = Oct. 10
  Term of discount: Number of days from July 15 to Oct. 10 = 87 days

(*b*) Maturity date: Nov. 8 + 3 months = Feb. 8
  Term of discount: Number of days from Jan. 10 to Feb. 8 = 29 days

Supplementary Problems

5.27 Find the simple interest on a loan of (*a*) $500 at $8\frac{1}{4}$% for 1 year, (*b*) $2,000 at $16\frac{1}{2}$% for 30 months, and (*c*) $1,200 at 10.82% for 6 months.

5.28 Find the ordinary simple interest on a loan of (*a*) $900 at $14\frac{1}{2}$% for 120 days, (*b*) $1,400 at 13% for 90 days, and (*c*) $750 at 9.21% for 60 days.

5.29 Find the exact simple interest on each loan in Prob. 5.28.

5.30 Find the exact time from (*a*) April 21 to June 29 of the same year, (*b*) November 7 to February 28 of the following year, (*c*) March 17, 2000 to November 8, 2000, and (*d*) July 8, 2000, to January 18, 2001.

5.31 Find the approximate time for each term in Prob. 5.30.

5.32 Find the maturity date of (*a*) a 90-day loan dated August 17, (*b*) a 60-day loan dated December 8, (*c*) a 6-month loan dated May 3, and (*d*) a 182-day loan dated March 7.

5.33 Using the four methods (exact time and ordinary interest, exact time and exact interest, approximate time and ordinary interest, and approximate time and exact interest), find the simple interest on (*a*) an $800 loan at 17% from April 21 to June 29 and (*b*) a $5,000 loan at $12\frac{3}{4}$% from July 8, 2000, to January 18, 2001.

5.34 Using the banker's rule, find the simple interest on investments of (*a*) $1,500 at 9% from March 17, 2000 to November 8, 2000, (*b*) $650 at $15\frac{1}{2}$% from October 1, 2000, to January 29, 2001, (*c*) $2,000 at $10\frac{5}{8}$% from March 15, 2001, to September 3, 2001.

5.35 Using exact time and exact interest, find the simple interest on the investments in Prob. 5.34.

5.36 Find the maturity value of (*a*) a $2,500 loan for 85 days, (*b*) a $1,200 loan for 120 days, and (*c*) a $10,000 loan for 60 days, all at 14% ordinary simple interest.

5.37 Find the maturity value of the loans in Prob. 5.36 at 12% exact simple interest.

5.38 At what rate of simple interest will (*a*) $500 accumulate $10 interest in 2 months, (*b*) money double itself in 7 years, and (*c*) $2,000 grow to $2,100 in 1 year.

5.39 Find the rate of ordinary simple interest charged on the following loans:

	Principal	Maturity Value	Time (Days)
(*a*)	$800	$830.50	90
(*b*)	$1,500	$1,640.62	270

5.40   Freda invested $1,200 for 180 days and earned $65.10 interest. What rate of exact simple interest did she earn?

5.41   How many days will it take $1,000 (a) to earn $50 at 12% ordinary simple interest and (b) to accumulate to at least $1,500 at $18\frac{3}{4}$% exact simple interest?

5.42   What principal will earn (a) ordinary simple interest of $25 at 12.5% in 120 days, (b) exact simple interest of $19.50 at 9.75% in 73 days, and (c) simple interest of $21.25 at 10% in 3 months?

5.43   Find the principal and the interest on the following loans at ordinary simple interest:

	Maturity Value	Time (Days)	Rate (%)
(a)	$856.40	217	16.25
(b)	$11,748.96	730	$8\frac{5}{8}$
(c)	$1,831.25	25	25

5.44   A couple borrows $20,000. The annual interest rate is $12\frac{1}{2}$%, payable monthly, and the monthly payment is $300. How much of the first payment goes to interest and how much to principal?

5.45   Questions (a) through (e) refer to Fig. 5.3.

   (a)   Who is the maker of the note?
   (b)   What is the face value?
   (c)   What is the maturity date of the note?
   (d)   Who is the payee?
   (e)   What is the maturity value of the note?

Fig. 5.3

5.46   Find the maturity date and the maturity value of each of the following promissory notes:

	Face	Date	Term	Interest Rate
(a)	$750	Nov. 3	3 mo	$8\frac{1}{4}\%$
(b)	$2,000	June 18	120 days	$17\frac{1}{2}\%$
(c)	$5,000	Sept. 5	341 days	11.073%

5.47   Referring to Fig. 5.3, in Prob. 5.45, find the proceeds to Robert Gilbert if Jennifer Brown charged him 18% interest in advance.

5.48   Jennifer Brown cashed the note in Prob. 5.45 on December 20, at a 14% bank discount rate. Find the bank discount and the proceeds.

5.49   Find the maturity date and the term of discount for each of the following notes:

	Date of Note	Term of Note	Date of Discount
(a)	Sept. 1	60 days	Oct. 7
(b)	Feb. 4	2 mo	Mar. 1
(c)	Dec. 14, 2000	192 days	Mar. 1, 2001

5.50   Find the proceeds when each of the following notes is discounted:

	Face Value	Date	Term	Interest Rate	Date of Discount	Discount Rate
(a)	$3,000	Nov. 3	3 mo		Dec. 1	$10\frac{1}{4}\%$
(b)	$1,200	Sept. 1	60 days	$15\frac{1}{2}\%$	Oct. 7	$14\frac{3}{4}\%$
(c)	$500	Dec. 14	192 days	17%	Dec. 24	17%
(d)	$4,000	Feb. 4	2 mo		Mar. 1	$8\frac{1}{2}\%$

5.51   A bank charges 11% interest in advance on short-term loans. Find the proceeds of the loan if the borrower signs a non-interest-bearing note for (a) $1,800 due in 6 months and (b) $600 due in 90 days.

5.52   A bank charges $15\frac{1}{4}\%$ interest in advance on short-term loans. Find the face value of the non-interest-bearing note given the bank if the borrower receives (a) $800 for 4 months, (b) $1,200 for 90 days, and (c) $2,000 from June 12 to December 12.

5.53   The Travelers Trust discounted at 15% bank discount a non-interest-bearing note for $20,000 due in 180 days. On the same day the note was discounted again at 14% bank discount at a Federal Reserve bank. Find the profit made by the Travelers Trust.

5.54   On June 29, a retailer buys goods worth $3,000. To take advantage of a 5% cash discount, the retailer signs a 60-day non-interest-bearing note at his bank. The bank charges 11% interest in advance on short-term loans. What should be the face value of this note to give the retailer the exact amount needed to pay cash for the goods?

Answers to Supplementary Problems

5.27 (*a*) $41.25, (*b*) $825, (*c*) $64.92

5.28 (*a*) $43.50, (*b*) $45.50, (*c*) $11.51

5.29 (*a*) $42.90, (*b*) $44.88, (*c*) $11.35

5.30 (*a*) 69 days, (*b*) 113 days, (*c*) 236 days, (*d*) 194 days

5.31 (*a*) 68 days, (*b*) 111 days, (*c*) 231 days, (*d*) 190 days

5.32 (*a*) November 15, (*b*) February 6, (*c*) November 3, (*d*) September 5

5.33 (*a*) $26.07, $25.71, $25.69, $25.34; (*b*) $343.54, $338.84, $336.46, $331.85

5.34 (*a*) $88.50, (*b*) $33.58, (*c*) $101.53

5.35 (*a*) $87.29, (*b*) $33.12, (*c*) $100.14

5.36 (*a*) $2,582.64, (*b*) $1,256, (*c*) $10,233.33

5.37 (*a*) $2,569.86, (*b*) $1,247.34, (*c*) $10,197.26

5.38 (*a*) 12%, (*b*) 14.29%, (*c*) 5%

5.39 (*a*) $15\frac{1}{4}$%, (*b*) $12\frac{1}{2}$%

5.40 11%

5.41 (*a*) 150 days, (*b*) 974 days

5.42 (*a*) $600, (*b*) $1,000, (*c*) $850

5.43 (*a*) $P = \$780$, $I = \$76.40$; (*b*) $P = \$10,000$, $I = \$1,748.96$; (*c*) $P = \$1,800$, $I = \$31.25$

5.44 $I = \$208.33$, $P = \$91.67$

5.45 (*a*) Robert Gilbert, (*b*) $1,500, (*c*) February 3, 2001, (*d*) Jennifer Brown, (*e*) $1,500

5.46 (*a*) Feb. 3, $765.47; (*b*) Oct. 16, $2,116.67; (*c*) Aug. 12, $5,524.43

5.47 $1,455

5.48 $D = \$26.25$, $P = \$1,473.75$

5.49 (*a*) Oct. 31, $t = 24$ days; (*b*) Apr. 4, $t = 34$ days; (*c*) June 24, $t = 115$ days

5.50 (*a*) $2,945.33, (*b*) $1,218.90, (*c*) $498.46, (*d*) $3,967.89

5.51 (*a*) $1,701, (*b*) $583.50

5.52 (*a*) $842.84, (*b*) $1,247.56, (*c*) $2,168.07

5.53 $100

5.54 $2,903.23

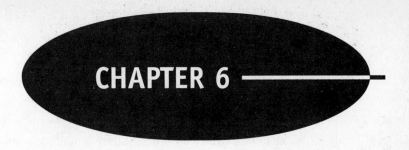

CHAPTER 6

Annuities and Their Applications

6.1 ANNUITIES

An *annuity* is a sequence of payments made at regular intervals. Payments may be made *to you* by an insurance company or a retirement fund, for example, or *by you* to an account which you may use later to make a purchase or pay for your children's education.

The time between payments is called the *payment interval* or *conversion period*, and the time over which the money is to be paid is called the *term* of the annuity.

When the term of the annuity is fixed, the annuity is said to be *certain*; otherwise it is called a *contingent annuity*. A 30-year mortgage is an example of a *certain annuity* because there are precisely 360 monthly payments made during the duration of the loan. An example of a *contingent annuity* is a monthly retirement payment paid during the life of a retiree. The number of payments to be made is unknown and is estimated by actuaries using mortality tables. In this book we consider only *certain* annuities.

Interest is paid at regular intervals called *payment intervals*. When the payment period coincides with the conversion period, the annuity is said to be *simple*; otherwise it is called a *general annuity*. We shall consider only *simple* annuities in this book.

When payments are made at the end of each payment interval the annuity is called an *ordinary annuity*. An *annuity due* is an annuity whose payments are made at the beginning of the payment interval. Unless otherwise stated, all annuities in this chapter are assumed to be ordinary annuities.

In dealing with annuity formulas we shall use the following symbols:

R: The periodic payment of the annuity.

n: The number of payments made.

i: The interest rate per payment interval.

S: The *accumulated value* of the annuity; the amount of money you will have at the end of the annuity's term.

A: The *present value* of the annuity, or *discounted value*; the amount of money which must be set aside today to allow a specified payment for a predetermined period of time. The present value is the amount of money the annuity is worth *today*.

Remember that i = annual interest rate (expressed as a decimal) divided by the number of payments per year, so for a monthly annuity at 6% annual interest, $i = 0.06/12 = 0.005$.

> The accumulated value of an ordinary annuity is computed by the formula[1]
>
> $$S = R \times \text{accumulation factor}$$

The accumulation factor is computed by a rather complex mathematical formula. Table 6.1 shows accumulation factors for a variety of periods and interest rates.

EXAMPLE 1

To determine the accumulation factor for an ordinary annuity of four payments whose periodic interest rate is 2%, we go to Table 6.1 and look in the row corresponding to $n = 4$ and the column corresponding to $i = 0.02$. The accumulation factor is 4.12161.

EXAMPLE 2

Compute the accumulated value of an *ordinary* annuity of $500 which is compounded quarterly for one year at an annual rate of 8%.

In this example $R = 500$, $n = 4$, and $i = 0.08/4 = 0.02$. From Example 1 the accumulation factor is 4.12161: $S = R \times \text{accumulation factor} = \$500 \times 4.12161 = \$2,060.80$.

EXAMPLE 3

To understand how money accumulates in an ordinary annuity, we can compute the value of the annuity after each payment. Since each payment of $500 is made at the *end* of the quarter, interest is compounded at most three times. The following table illustrates the growth of the money.

Payment Period	Payment (R)	Number of Times Compounded (k)	Value at End of Year $R(1 + i)^k$
1	500.00	3	$500(1.02)^3 = 530.60$
2	500.00	2	$500(1.02)^2 = 520.20$
3	500.00	1	$500(1.02)\ \ = 510.00$
4	500.00	0	500.00
Total			$2,060.80

Next we consider an *annuity due*, where each payment is made at the beginning of the payment interval.

---

[1] Some books use the notation $S_{\overline{n}|i}$ to denote the accumulation factor $[(1 + i)^n - 1]/i$. Thus $S = R \times S_{\overline{n}|i}$. However, we shall not use this notation in this book.

Table 6.1   Accumulation Factors for Simple Annuities

	Periodic Interest Rate (i)							
n	0.005	0.0075	0.01	0.0125	0.02	0.025	0.03	0.04
1	1.00000	1.00000	1.00000	1.00000	1.00000	1.00000	1.00000	1.00000
2	2.00500	2.00750	2.01000	2.01250	2.02000	2.02500	2.03000	2.04000
3	3.01503	3.02256	3.03010	3.03766	3.06040	3.07562	3.09090	3.12160
4	4.03010	4.04523	4.06040	4.07563	4.12161	4.15252	4.18363	4.24646
5	5.05025	5.07556	5.10101	5.12657	5.20404	5.25633	5.30914	5.41632
6	6.07550	6.11363	6.15202	6.19065	6.30812	6.38774	6.46841	6.63298
7	7.10588	7.15948	7.21354	7.26804	7.43428	7.54743	7.66246	7.89829
8	8.14141	8.21318	8.28567	8.35889	8.58297	8.73612	8.89234	9.21423
9	9.18212	9.27478	9.36853	9.46337	9.75463	9.95452	10.15911	10.58280
10	10.22803	10.34434	10.46221	10.58167	10.94972	11.20338	11.46388	12.00611
11	11.27917	11.42192	11.56683	11.71394	12.16872	12.48347	12.80780	13.48635
12	12.33556	12.50759	12.68250	12.86036	13.41209	13.79555	14.19203	15.02581
13	13.39724	13.60139	13.80933	14.02112	14.68033	15.14044	15.61779	16.62684
14	14.46423	14.70340	14.94742	15.19638	15.97394	16.51895	17.08632	18.29191
15	15.53655	15.81368	16.09690	16.38633	17.29342	17.93193	18.59891	20.02359
16	16.61423	16.93228	17.25786	17.59116	18.63929	19.38022	20.15688	21.82453
17	17.69730	18.05927	18.43044	18.81105	20.01207	20.86473	21.76159	23.69751
18	18.78579	19.19472	19.61475	20.04619	21.41231	22.38635	23.41444	25.64541
19	19.87972	20.33868	20.81090	21.29677	22.84056	23.94601	25.11687	27.67123
20	20.97912	21.49122	22.01900	22.56298	24.29737	25.54466	26.87037	29.77808
21	22.08401	22.65240	23.23919	23.84502	25.78332	27.18327	28.67649	31.96920
22	23.19443	23.82230	24.47159	25.14308	27.29898	28.86286	30.53678	34.24797
23	24.31040	25.00096	25.71630	26.45737	28.84496	30.58443	32.45288	36.61789
24	25.43196	26.18847	26.97346	27.78808	30.42186	32.34904	34.42647	39.08260
25	26.55912	27.38488	28.24320	29.13544	32.03030	34.15776	36.45926	41.64591
26	27.69191	28.59027	29.52563	30.49963	33.67091	36.01171	38.55304	44.31174
27	28.83037	29.80470	30.82089	31.88087	35.34432	37.91200	40.70963	47.08421
28	29.97452	31.02823	32.12910	33.27938	37.05121	39.85980	42.93092	49.96758
29	31.12439	32.26094	33.45039	34.69538	38.79223	41.85630	45.21885	52.96629
30	32.28002	33.50290	34.78489	36.12907	40.56808	43.90270	47.57542	56.08494
31	33.44142	34.75417	36.13274	37.58068	42.37944	46.00027	50.00268	59.32834
32	34.60862	36.01483	37.49407	39.05044	44.22703	48.15028	52.50276	62.70147
33	35.78167	37.28494	38.86901	40.53857	46.11157	50.35403	55.07784	66.20953
34	36.96058	38.56458	40.25770	42.04530	48.03380	52.61289	57.73018	69.85791
35	38.14538	39.85381	41.66028	43.57087	49.99448	54.92821	60.46208	73.65222
36	39.33610	41.15272	43.07688	45.11551	51.99437	57.30141	63.27594	77.59831
37	40.53279	42.46136	44.50765	46.67945	54.03425	59.73395	66.17422	81.70225
38	41.73545	43.77982	45.95272	48.26294	56.11494	62.22730	69.15945	85.97034
39	42.94413	45.10817	47.41225	49.86623	58.23724	64.78298	72.23423	90.40915
40	44.15885	46.44648	48.88637	51.48956	60.40198	67.40255	75.40126	95.02552
60	69.77003	75.42414	81.66967	88.57451	114.05154	135.99159	163.05344	237.99069
80	98.06771	109.07253	121.67152	136.11880	193.77196	248.38271	321.36302	551.24498
120	163.87935	193.51428	230.03869	275.21706	488.25815	734.32599	1,123.69957	2,741.56402

EXAMPLE 4

Compute the accumulated value of an *annuity due* of $500 which is compounded quarterly for one year at an annual rate of 8%.

As in Example 3, $R = 500$, $n = 4$, and $i = 0.08/4 = 0.02$. However, since each $500 payment is made at the beginning of the payment interval rather than the end, the value of each payment is multiplied by a factor of $1 + i$. The total value of the annuity at the end of its term is also increased by a factor of $1 + i$. Therefore

$$S = R \times \text{accumulation factor} \times (1 + i) = \$500 \times 4.12161 \times 1.02 = 2,102.02$$

The growth of the money is illustrated below. Note that the end-of-year value of each $500 payment is 1.02 times what it was in Example 3:

Payment Period	Payment (R)	Number of Times Compounded (k)	Value at End of Year $R(1 + i)^k$
1	500.00	4	$500(1.02)^4 = 541.22$
2	500.00	3	$500(1.02)^3 = 530.60$
3	500.00	2	$500(1.02)^2 = 520.20$
4	500.00	1	$500(1.02) = 510.00$
Total			$2,102.02

> The accumulated value of an annuity due is computed by the formula
> $$S = R \times \text{accumulation factor} \times (1 + i)$$

EXAMPLE 5

Compute the accumulated value of an annuity of $100 invested at the end of each month for one year at an annual rate of 6%.

Since the payment interval is one month, the annual rate of 0.06 must be divided by 12 to give $i = 0.005$. $R = \$100$ and $n = 12$. The accumulation factor is 12.33556 from Table 6.1.

$$S = R \times \text{accumulation factor} = \$100 \times 12.33556 = \$1,233.56$$

EXAMPLE 6

Suppose that Ryan deposits $1,000 every 3 months in a savings account which pays 8% annual interest compounded quarterly. How much will Ryan have in the bank at the end of 5 years?

$$R = \$1,000, n = 5 \times 4 = 20 \text{ payments, and } i = 0.08/4 = 0.02$$

Assuming that Ryan deposits his money at the *beginning* of each 3-month period,

$$S = R \times \text{accumulation factor} \times (1 + i) = \$1,000 \times 24.29737 \times 1.02 = \$24,783.32$$

The next example illustrates how much money to put aside each period in order to accumulate a specified amount.

EXAMPLE 7

How much must Sylvia save each month if she would like to accumulate $5,000 in 3 years? Assume interest is paid at the rate of 6% compounded monthly and that Sylvia makes her deposit at the end of each month.

In this problem we wish to compute R. $S = \$5,000$, $n = 12 \times 3 = 36$, $i = 0.06/12 = 0.005$. The accumulation factor from Table 6.1 is 39.33610. Since $S = R \times$ accumulation factor,

$$\$5,000 = R \times 39.33610$$

We divide both sides of the equation by 39.3361 and obtain $R = \$127.11$. Sylvia must save \$127.11 each month.

If the deposits are made at the beginning of each payment interval, the calculation is just a bit different.

EXAMPLE 8

How much must Sylvia save each month (see Example 7) if deposits are made at the *beginning* of each month?

This is an annuity due. As in the previous example, the accumulation factor is 39.33610, so

$$\$5,000 = R \times 39.33610 \times 1.005$$
$$\$5,000 = R \times 39.53278$$

Dividing \$5,000 by 39.53278, we obtain $R = \$126.48$. Note that Sylvia's deposits are a bit less if she makes them at the beginning of the month. (Does this make sense to you?)

The *present value* of the annuity, or *discounted value*, is the amount of money which must be set aside to allow a specified payment for a specified period of time. The present value indicates, for example, how much money should be invested in order to provide a fixed monthly stipend for retirement for the next 20 years.

The present value of an ordinary annuity is computed by the formula

$$A = R \times \text{discount factor}$$

Table 6.2 shows discount factors for a variety of periods and interest rates.

EXAMPLE 9

Bill would like to invest some money so that he can receive a monthly retirement supplement. How much money must he invest at 9% compounded monthly in order to receive \$500 at the end of each month for the next 5 years?

In this example $R = \$500$, $n = 5 \times 12 = 60$, and $i = 0.09/12 = 0.0075$. The discount factor from Table 6.2 is 48.17337.

$$A = R \times \text{discount factor} = \$500 \times 48.17337 = \$24,086.69$$

The present value of an annuity due is computed by the formula

$$A = R \times \text{discount factor} \times (1 + i)$$

EXAMPLE 10

How much would Bill (see Example 9) have to invest if payments are to be made at the *beginning* of the month?

$$A = R \times \text{discount factor} \times (1 + i) = \$500 \times 48.17337 \times 1.0075 = \$24,267.34$$

Note that this amount is larger than in Example 9. (Does this seem reasonable?)

Table 6.2   Discount Factors for Simple Annuities

n	\multicolumn{8}{c}{Periodic Interest Rate (i)}							
	0.005	0.0075	0.01	0.0125	0.02	0.025	0.03	0.04
1	0.99502	0.99256	0.99010	0.98765	0.98039	0.97561	0.97087	0.96154
2	1.98510	1.97772	1.97040	1.96312	1.94156	1.92742	1.91347	1.88609
3	2.97025	2.95556	2.94099	2.92653	2.88388	2.85602	2.82861	2.77509
4	3.95050	3.92611	3.90197	3.87806	3.80773	3.76197	3.71710	3.62990
5	4.92587	4.88944	4.85343	4.81784	4.71346	4.64583	4.57971	4.45182
6	5.89638	5.84560	5.79548	5.74601	5.60143	5.50813	5.41719	5.24214
7	6.86207	6.79464	6.72819	6.66273	6.47199	6.34939	6.23028	6.00205
8	7.82296	7.73661	7.65168	7.56812	7.32548	7.17014	7.01969	6.73274
9	8.77906	8.67158	8.56602	8.46234	8.16224	7.97087	7.78611	7.43533
10	9.73041	9.59958	9.47130	9.34553	8.98259	8.75206	8.53020	8.11090
11	10.67703	10.52067	10.36763	10.21780	9.78685	9.51421	9.25262	8.76048
12	11.61893	11.43491	11.25508	11.07931	10.57534	10.25776	9.95400	9.38507
13	12.55615	12.34235	12.13374	11.93018	11.34837	10.98318	10.63496	9.98565
14	13.48871	13.24302	13.00370	12.77055	12.10625	11.69091	11.29607	10.56312
15	14.41662	14.13699	13.86505	13.60055	12.84926	12.38138	11.93794	11.11839
16	15.33993	15.02431	14.71787	14.42029	13.57771	13.05500	12.56110	11.65230
17	16.25863	15.90502	15.56225	15.22992	14.29187	13.71220	13.16612	12.16567
18	17.17277	16.77918	16.39827	16.02955	14.99203	14.35336	13.75351	12.65930
19	18.08236	17.64683	17.22601	16.81931	15.67846	14.97889	14.32380	13.13394
20	18.98742	18.50802	18.04555	17.59932	16.35143	15.58916	14.87747	13.59033
21	19.88798	19.36280	18.85698	18.36969	17.01121	16.18455	15.41502	14.02916
22	20.78406	20.21121	19.66038	19.13056	17.65805	16.76541	15.93692	14.45112
23	21.67568	21.05331	20.45582	19.88204	18.29220	17.33211	16.44361	14.85684
24	22.56287	21.88915	21.24339	20.62423	18.91393	17.88499	16.93554	15.24696
25	23.44564	22.71876	22.02316	21.35727	19.52346	18.42438	17.41315	15.62208
26	24.32402	23.54219	22.79520	22.08125	20.12104	18.95061	17.87684	15.98277
27	25.19803	24.35949	23.55961	22.79630	20.70690	19.46401	18.32703	16.32959
28	26.06769	25.17071	24.31644	23.50252	21.28127	19.96489	18.76411	16.66306
29	26.93302	25.97589	25.06579	24.20002	21.84438	20.45355	19.18845	16.98371
30	27.79405	26.77508	25.80771	24.88891	22.39646	20.93029	19.60044	17.29203
31	28.65080	27.56832	26.54229	25.56929	22.93770	21.39541	20.00043	17.58849
32	29.50328	28.35565	27.26959	26.24127	23.46833	21.84918	20.38877	17.87355
33	30.35153	29.13712	27.98969	26.90496	23.98856	22.29188	20.76579	18.14765
34	31.19555	29.91278	28.70267	27.56046	24.49859	22.72379	21.13184	18.41120
35	32.03537	30.68266	29.40858	28.20786	24.99862	23.14516	21.48722	18.66461
36	32.87102	31.44681	30.10751	28.84727	25.48884	23.55625	21.83225	18.90828
37	33.70250	32.20527	30.79951	29.47878	25.96945	23.95732	22.16724	19.14258
38	34.52985	32.95808	31.48466	30.10250	26.44064	24.34860	22.49246	19.36786
39	35.35309	33.70529	32.16303	30.71852	26.90259	24.73034	22.80822	19.58448
40	36.17223	34.44694	32.83469	31.32693	27.35548	25.10278	23.11477	19.79277
60	51.72556	48.17337	44.95504	42.03459	34.76089	30.90866	27.67556	22.62349
80	65.80231	59.99444	54.88821	50.38666	39.74451	34.45182	30.20076	23.91539
120	90.07345	78.94169	69.70052	61.98285	45.35539	37.93369	32.37302	24.77409
180	118.50351	98.59341	83.32166	71.44964	48.58440	39.53036	33.17034	24.97852
240	139.58077	111.14495	90.81942	75.94228	49.56855	39.89326	33.30567	24.99796
360	166.79161	124.28187	97.21833	79.08614	49.95992	39.99449	33.33254	24.99998

EXAMPLE 11

Gene's grandmother left him $10,000 when she died. So that he would not squander the money, she stipulated in her will that the money be invested in a bank account paying 8% interest compounded quarterly and paid out in equal installments every 3 months for a period of 10 years. How much will Gene receive each quarter?

In this problem $A = $10,000$, $n = 10 \times 4 = 40$, and $i = 0.08/4 = 0.02$. The discount factor from Table 6.2 is 27.35548.

$$A = R \times \text{discount factor}$$
$$\$10,000 = R \times 27.35548$$

Dividing $10,000 by 27.35548, we obtain $R = 365.56 per month.

SOLVED PROBLEMS

6.1   Find the accumulated value of an annuity of $750 invested at the end of each quarter for 5 years at an annual rate of 8% compounded quarterly.

SOLUTION

$R = 750, $n = 5 \times 4 = 20$, $i = 0.08/4 = 0.02$. The accumulation factor (from Table 6.1) is 24.29737:

$$S = R \times \text{accumulation factor} = \$750 \times 24.29737 = \$18,223.03$$

6.2   Find the accumulated value of an annuity of $50 invested at the end of each month for 2 years at an annual rate of 9% compounded monthly.

SOLUTION

$R = 50, $n = 12 \times 2 = 24$ payments, and $i = 0.09/12 = 0.0075$. The accumulation factor (from Table 6.1) is 26.18847.

$$A = R \times \text{accumulation factor} = \$50 \times 26.18847 = \$1,309.42.$$

The value of the annuity is $1,309.42.

6.3   XYZ Savings Bank pays interest at the rate of 4% annually compounded quarterly. How much money will Roger have in the bank at the end of 5 years if he deposits $250 at the end of each quarter?

SOLUTION

$R = 250. There are 20 quarters in a 5-year period, so $n = 20$, and $i = 0.04/4 = 0.01$. The accumulation factor is 22.01900 (from Table 6.1):

$$S = R \times \text{accumulation factor} = \$250 \times 22.01900 = \$5,504.75$$

Roger will have saved $5,504.75.

6.4   How much money will Roger (see Example 6.3) have in the bank at the end of 5 years if he deposits $250 at the beginning of each quarter?

SOLUTION

As before, $R = 250, $n = 20$, and $i = 0.01$:

$$S = R \times \text{accumulation factor} \times (1 + i) = \$250 \times 22.01900 \times 1.01 = \$5,559.80$$

6.5 How much interest is earned in 10 years if $100 is deposited at the end of each month in an account that pays 15% compounded monthly?

SOLUTION

$R = \$100$, $n = 10 \times 12 = 120$, $i = 0.15/12 = 0.0125$. The accumulation factor (Table 6.1) is 275.21706:

$$S = R \times \text{accumulation factor} = \$100 \times 275.21706 = \$27,521.71$$

Since the total amount deposited is $100 \times 120 = \$12,000$, the interest earned is $27,521.71 - \$12,000.00 = \$15,521.71$.

6.6 Barney makes a New Year's resolution to put $100 into the bank at the *beginning* of each month, beginning January 2000. If the bank pays 6% interest compounded monthly on the last day of each month, how much will Barney have one year later?

SOLUTION

$R = \$100$, $n = 12$, $i = 0.06/12 = 0.005$. The accumulation factor (Table 6.1) is 12.33556. Since this is an annuity due, it follows that

$$S = R \times \text{accumulation factor} \times (1 + i) = \$100 \times 12.33556 \times 1.005 = \$1,239.72$$

6.7 Find the present value of an annuity of $350 at the end of each month for 5 years at 9% compounded monthly.

SOLUTION

$R = \$350$, $n = 12 \times 5 = 60$, $i = 0.09/12 = 0.0075$. The discount factor obtained from Table 6.2 is 48.17337:

$$A = R \times \text{discount factor} = \$350 \times 48.17337 = \$16,860.68$$

6.8 A refrigerator can be purchased for $150 down and $50 a month for 18 months. What is the equivalent price if the refrigerator is purchased for cash? Assume that the interest rate on credit is 15% compounded monthly.

SOLUTION

$R = \$50$, $n = 18$, $i = 0.15/12 = 0.0125$. The present value of an annuity of $50 per month for 18 months is computed using a discount factor of 16.02955, obtained from Table 6.2:

$$A = R \times \text{discount factor} = \$50 \times 16.02955 = \$801.48$$

The equivalent cash price for the refrigerator is $150.00 + \$801.48 = \$951.48$.

6.9 Mr. Smith would like to receive $4,000 each quarter for 10 years after he retires. How much money (to the nearest dollar) does he have to save in a money market fund which pays at the rate of 8% compounded quarterly?

SOLUTION

$R = \$4,000$, $n = 10 \times 4 = 40$, and $i = 0.08/4 = 0.02$. The discount factor (Table 6.2) is 27.35548:

$$A = R \times \text{discount factor} = \$4,000 \times 27.35548 = \$109,422$$

6.10 Bob Turner has saved a total of $170,000 for retirement. He has put the money in a mutual fund which pays 9% annual interest compounded monthly. How much should he withdraw each month in order to have enough money to last for 15 years?

SOLUTION

$A = \$170,000$, $n = 12 \times 15 = 180$, and $i = 0.09/12 = 0.0075$. The discount factor (Table 6.2) is 98.59341:

$$A = R \times \text{discount factor}$$
$$\$170,000 = R \times 98.59341$$

Dividing \$170,000 by 98.59341, we get \$1,724.25. This is the amount Bob should withdraw each month.

6.11 When Sarah James' husband died, she became the beneficiary of a \$100,000 life insurance policy. Instead of taking the money in a lump sum, she elects to receive a monthly stipend over a period of 20 years. If the insurance company pays interest at the rate of 6% compounded monthly, what will her monthly income be?

SOLUTION

$A = \$100,000$, $n = 20 \times 12 = 240$, $i = 0.06/12 = 0.005$. The discount factor is 139.58077:

$$A = R \times \text{discount factor}$$
$$\$100,000 = R \times 139.58077$$

Dividing by 139.58077, we obtain $R = \$716.43$ as her monthly income.

6.12 At age 30, Mr. Bixby begins to save for his retirement by depositing \$200 every 3 months into a savings account that pays 5% interest compounded quarterly. At age 60 he decides to retire, using his savings account as the basis of an annuity. How much will he get every quarter if he wants to get equal payments for the next 20 years? Assume the interest rate to be fixed at 5% over the full 50-year period.

SOLUTION

First we must compute how much Mr. Bixby will have saved up in 30 years: $R = \$200$, $n = 30 \times 4 = 120$, and $i = 0.05/4 = 0.0125$. The accumulation factor from Table 6.1 is 275.21706.

$$S = R \times \text{accumulation factor} = \$200 \times 275.21706 = \$55,043.41$$

Now we compute the quarterly payment. $A = \$55,043.41$, $n = 20 \times 4 = 80$, $i = 0.0125$. The discount factor from Table 6.2 is 50.38666.

$$A = R \times \text{accumulation factor}$$
$$55,043.41 = R \times 50.38666$$
$$R = \$1,092.42$$

Mr. Bixby will receive \$1,092.42 every 3 months for the next 20 years.

6.13 A sofa sells for \$600. As an incentive, a furniture store offers to accept \$50 per month for one year with no finance charge. If the actual rate of interest charged by the bank is 12% compounded monthly, what is the actual cost of the sofa?

SOLUTION

The present value of the annuity is the actual cost of the sofa. (The difference between this number and the \$600 paid goes to the bank as interest.) $R = \$50$, $n = 12$, and $i = 0.12/12 = 0.01$. The discount factor (Table 6.2) is 11.25508:

$$A = R \times \text{discount factor} = \$50 \times 11.25508 = \$562.75$$

6.14   Tom Evans purchases a life insurance policy which has an annual premium of $1,500 due at the beginning of the year. If he elects to pay his premium in quarterly installments, how much should he pay at the beginning of each quarter if the interest rate is 10% compounded quarterly?

SOLUTION

The present value of the premium, A, is $1500, $n = 4$, and $i = 0.10/4 = 0.025$. The discount factor is 3.76197 (from Table 6.2):

$$A = R \times \text{discount factor} \times (1 + i)$$
$$1,500 = R \times 3.76197 \times 1.025$$
$$1,500 = R \times 3.85602$$
$$R = 389.00$$

Tom should pay $389 at the beginning of each 3-month period.

6.15   The monthly rent for a one-bedroom apartment in Manhattan is $1,500, payable at the beginning of the month. If the current interest rate is 9%, what would be a fair amount to charge someone if they wish to pay their yearly rental in advance?

SOLUTION

$A = 1,500$, $n = 12$, $i = 0.09/12 = 0.0075$. The discount factor from Table 6.2 is 11.43491:

$$A = R \times \text{discount factor} \times (1 + i)$$
$$A = \$1,500 \times 11.43491 \times 1.0075$$
$$A = \$17,281 \text{ (to the nearest dollar)}$$

6.2   SINKING FUNDS

Often a specific amount of money, needed at some future date, is accumulated by a series of equal periodic payments. Such a fund, known as a *sinking fund*, is frequently used to pay off debts or to replace worn-out or antiquated equipment.

The total amount of money in the fund is simply the accumulated value S of an annuity. Thus the periodic payment R can be computed from our previous formula,

$$S = R \times \text{accumulation factor}$$

by algebraically solving for R:

$$\boxed{R = \frac{S}{\text{accumulation factor}}}$$

EXAMPLE 12

The owners of a tool and die company want to accumulate $50,000 to replace worn-out equipment 8 years from now. How much should they contribute each month into a sinking fund which pays 8% compounded quarterly?

The number of payments, $n = 8 \times 4 = 32$, $i = 0.08/4 = 0.02$, and $S = \$50,000$:

$$R = \frac{S}{\text{accumulation factor}} = \frac{\$50,000}{44.22703} = \$1,130.53$$

Thus, the monthly payment should be $1,130.53.

A *sinking fund schedule* can be constructed if we wish to observe how the fund accumulates.

EXAMPLE 13

Construct a sinking fund schedule which describes the accumulation of a sinking fund in which $10,000 is to be accumulated in 3 years if payments are made quarterly into an account which pays 5% compounded quarterly.

First we compute the quarterly payment:

$$n = 4 \times 3 = 12; \qquad i = \frac{0.05}{4} = 0.0125$$

$$R = \frac{S}{\text{accumulation factor}} = \frac{\$10,000}{12.86036} = \$777.58$$

For each period, the amount accumulated is increased by the quarterly payment, $766.80, and the interest on the amount at the beginning of that period.

Period	Initial Amount	Interest at 1.25%	+	Quarterly Payment (R)	=	Increase in Fund	Final Amount
1	0	0	+	777.58	=	777.58	777.58
2	777.58	9.72	+	777.58	=	787.30	1,564.88
3	1,564.88	19.56	+	777.58	=	797.14	2,362.02
4	2,362.02	29.53	+	777.58	=	807.11	3,169.13
5	3,169.13	39.61	+	777.58	=	817.19	3,986.32
6	3,986.32	49.83	+	777.58	=	827.41	4,813.73
7	4,813.73	60.17	+	777.58	=	837.75	5,651.48
8	5,651.48	70.64	+	777.58	=	848.22	6,499.70
9	6,499.70	81.25	+	777.58	=	858.83	7,358.53
10	7,358.53	91.98	+	777.58	=	869.56	8,228.09
11	8,228.09	102.85	+	777.58	=	880.43	9,108.52
12	9,108.52	113.86	+	777.58	=	891.44	9,999.96

All calculations were rounded to the nearest penny. The final amount is slightly different than the amount predicted mathematically due to rounding. This is typical of most calculations of this type.

The amount of money accumulated in a sinking fund after n payments is just the accumulated value of the annuity at that time:

$$S = R \times \text{accumulation factor}$$

EXAMPLE 14

Determine how much money is in the sinking fund of the last example at the end of 6 periods.

$$S = R \times \text{accumulation factor} = \$777.58 \times 6.19065 = \$4,813.73$$

This agrees with line 6 of the table above.

EXAMPLE 15

Jodi and Frank estimate that they will need $100,000 to send their son to college in 15 years. Assume that interest rates will remain at 8% compounded quarterly.

(a) How much should they save every 3 months?
The amount they have to put aside each period is computed by the formula

$$R = \frac{S}{\text{accumulation factor}}$$

where $S = \$100,000$, $n = 4 \times 15 = 60$, and $i = 0.08/4 = 0.02$. The accumulation factor obtained from Table 6.1 is 114.05154:

$$R = \frac{S}{\text{accumulation factor}} = \frac{\$100,000}{114.05154} = \$876.80$$

(b) How much will they have accumulated after $7\frac{1}{2}$ years?
After $7\frac{1}{2}$ years they will have made 30 payments. The accumulation factor is now 40.56808:

$$S = R \times \text{accumulation factor} = 876.80 \times 40.56808 = \$35,570.09$$

They will have saved $35,570.09 after $7\frac{1}{2}$ years. Note that this is somewhat less than half the final amount. (Does this seem reasonable?)

Sinking funds are used to discharge debts. The debtor borrows money and pays off the debt by making equal periodic payments into a sinking fund that will accumulate the amount borrowed by the end of the loan's term. At the end of the term of the loan, the borrower transfers the amount from the sinking fund to the lender.

The sum of the interest payment and the sinking fund deposit is called the *periodic expense* of the debt.

> Periodic expense = interest on the loan + deposit into sinking fund

The *book value* of the debt at any time is the original principal minus the amount in the sinking fund.

> Book value = original amount borrowed − amount in the sinking fund

EXAMPLE 16

A businessman borrows $15,000 at 18% payable monthly and makes monthly deposits into a sinking fund so that his debt may be paid off at the end of one year. The sinking fund earns 9% compounded monthly.

(a) What is the monthly expense of the debt?
The monthly interest on the loan is computed by multiplying the amount borrowed by the monthly interest rate, $0.18/12 = 0.015$:

$$\text{Monthly interest} = R \times i = 15,000 \times 0.015 = \$225.00$$

Next we compute the amount which must be deposited into the sinking fund in order to accumulate $15,000 in one year:

$$i = \frac{0.09}{12} = 0.0075$$

$$R = \frac{S}{\text{accumulation factor}} = \frac{\$15,000}{12.50759} = \$1,199.27$$

Monthly expense = interest on the loan + deposit into sinking fund
$$= \$225.00 + \$1,199.27 = \$1,424.27$$

(b) What is the book value of the debt at the end of 6 months?
The amount in the sinking fund at the end of 6 months is

$$S = R \times \text{accumulation factor} = \$1,199.27 \times 6.11363 = \$7,331.89$$

Book value = original amount borrowed − amount in the sinking fund
$$= \$15,000.00 - \$7,331.89 = \$7,668.11$$

SOLVED PROBLEMS

6.16 Barbara wants to save up enough money to put a $24,000 down payment on a house in 2 years. How much money should she deposit each month into an account which pays 6% interest compounded monthly in order to save enough money for the down payment?

SOLUTION

In this problem $S = \$24,000$, $n = 12 \times 2 = 24$, and $i = 0.06/12 = 0.005$. The accumulation factor (from Table 6.1) is 25.43196:

$$R = \frac{S}{\text{accumulation factor}} = \frac{\$24,000}{25.43196} = \$943.69$$

Barbara should deposit $943.69 at the end of each month.

6.17 Trevor owns a machine shop. One of his machines is rather old and will have to be replaced in 3 years. Trevor predicts that a new machine will cost $80,000. How much should he put aside into a sinking fund which pays an annual rate of 6% compounded semiannually in order to accumulate enough money to replace the machine?

SOLUTION

$S = \$80,000$, $n = 3 \times 2 = 6$, and $i = 0.06/2 = 0.03$. The accumulation factor is 6.46841:

$$R = \frac{S}{\text{accumulation factor}} = \frac{\$80,000}{6.46841} = \$12,367.80$$

Trevor should put $12,367.80 into the bank at the end of each semiannual period.

6.18 A condominium association wants to establish a sinking fund to accumulate $250,000 in 3 years to repair the roofs. The fund earns 9% interest compounded monthly. If there are 200 units in the condominium, how much should each unit owner be assessed each month as a fair contribution into the fund? Assume that all units are of equal size and hence have equal assessments.

SOLUTION

The total monthly assessment is computed from the formula $R = S/\text{accumulation factor}$ where $S = \$250,000$, $n = 12 \times 3 = 36$, and $i = 0.09/12 = 0.0075$. The accumulation factor (from Table 6.1) is 41.15272. Hence

$$R = \frac{S}{\text{accumulation factor}} = \frac{\$250,000}{41.15272} = \$6,074.93$$

Since the assessment is to be divided equally among the 200 unit owners, each should pay $6,074.93/200 = $30.37 each month.

6.19 How much interest does the sinking fund in Prob. 6.18 earn?

SOLUTION

Since the total payments are $6,074.93 per month × 36 months = $218,697.48, the interest earned is $250,000 − $218,697.48 = $31,302.52.

6.20 A city issues $1,000,000 worth of bonds to raise capital to improve its sewage treatment system. What semiannual deposits must be made into a sinking fund earning interest at 8% compounded semiannually in order to redeem the bonds at the end of 15 years?

SOLUTION

The accumulated value S must be \$1,000,000 after 15 years, $n = 15 \times 2 = 30$, and $i = 0.08/2 = 0.04$. The accumulation factor (Table 6.1) is 56.08494:

$$R = \frac{S}{\text{accumulation factor}} = \frac{\$1,000,000}{56.08494} = \$17,830.10$$

The city must deposit \$17,830.10 every 6 months.

6.21 Construct a sinking fund schedule for the *first 2 years* of problem 6.20.

SOLUTION

Period	Initial Amount	Interest	+	Monthly Payment (R)	=	Increase in Fund	Final Amount
1	0	0	+	17,830.10	=	17,830.10	17,830.10
2	17,830.10	713.20	+	17,830.10	=	18,543.30	36,373.40
3	36,373.40	1,454.94	+	17,830.10	=	19,285.04	55,658.44
4	55,658.44	2,226.34	+	17,830.10	=	20,056.44	75,714.88

6.22 Construct a sinking fund schedule for the *last 2 years* of problem 6.20.

SOLUTION

First we must determine the final amount after the 13th year (26th deposit).

$$S = R \times \text{accumulation factor} = 17,830.10 \times 44.31174 = \$790,082.76$$

Now we can complete the sinking fund schedule.

Period	Initial Amount	Interest	+	Monthly Payment (R)	=	Increase in Fund	Final Amount
27	790,082.76	31,603.31	+	17,830.10	=	49,433.41	839,516.17
28	839,516.17	33,580.65	+	17,830.10	=	51,410.75	890,926.92
29	890,926.92	35,637.08	+	17,830.10	=	53,467.18	944,394.10
30	944,394.10	37,775.76	+	17,830.10	=	55,605.86	999,999.96

The final amount is 4 cents short because of rounding.

6.23 A debt of \$50,000, whose quarterly interest rate is 4%, must be repaid in 5 years. To discharge the debt, quarterly deposits are made into a sinking fund which earns interest at the rate of 10% compounded quarterly. What is the quarterly expense of the debt?

SOLUTION

The quarterly interest on the debt is

$$R \times i = \$50,000 \times 0.04 = \$2,000.00$$

The quarterly deposit into the sinking fund is

$$R = \frac{S}{\text{accumulation factor}} = \frac{\$50,000}{25.54466} = 1,957.36 \quad \left(n = 20, i = \frac{0.10}{4} = 0.025\right)$$

Quarterly expense = interest on the loan + deposit into sinking fund
$$= \$2,000.00 + \$1,957.36 = \$3,957.36$$

6.24 What is the book value of the debt in problem 6.23 at the end of 3 years?

SOLUTION

After 3 years ($n = 12$) the amount of money in the sinking fund is

$$S = R \times \text{accumulation factor} = \$1,957.36 \times 13.79555 = \$27,002.86$$

Book value = original amount borrowed − amount in the sinking fund
$$= \$50,000 - \$27,002.86 = \$22,997.14$$

6.3 AMORTIZATION

A loan is *amortized* if both the principal and interest are paid off with a single periodic payment whose amount is *fixed* for the life of the loan. The most common example of an amortized loan is a home mortgage which is typically paid off in monthly installments lasting from 15 to 30 years.

The amount of interest is computed monthly based on the *principal balance* and is taken from the monthly payment. The part of the monthly payment not used to pay interest is used to reduce the principal balance. Thus the following month, less interest is paid and the principal balance is reduced further.

To compute the monthly payment, we can think of an amortized loan as a simple annuity whose present value A is the amount of money borrowed. The payment R can be computed from the formula discussed previously.

$$A = R \times \text{discount factor}$$

by solving for R:

$$\boxed{R = \frac{A}{\text{discount factor}}}$$

EXAMPLE 17

Compute the monthly payment on a $10,000 loan at a 6% annual interest rate which is amortized over 15 years.

$$A = \$10,000, i = \frac{0.06}{12} = 0.005, n = 15 \times 12 = 180$$

$$R = \frac{A}{\text{discount factor}} = \frac{\$10,000}{118.50351} = \$84.39$$

Thus the monthly payment should be $84.39.

Instead of calculating the monthly payments using the discount factor, as shown above, tables can be used to compute monthly payments. Table 6.3 is an abbreviated table of monthly loan payments.

Table 6.3   Monthly Payments per $1,000 Financed

Annual Interest Rate

Yrs	6.0%	6.5%	7.0%	7.5%	8.0%	8.5%	9.0%	9.5%	10.0%	10.5%	11.0%	11.5%	12.0%	12.5%	13.0%	13.5%
1	86.06643	86.29642	86.52675	86.75742	86.98843	87.21978	87.45148	87.68351	87.91589	88.14860	88.38166	88.61505	88.84879	89.08286	89.31728	89.55203
2	44.32061	44.54625	44.77258	44.99959	45.22729	45.45568	45.68474	45.91449	46.14493	46.37604	46.60784	46.84032	47.07347	47.30731	47.54182	47.77701
3	30.42194	30.64900	30.87710	31.10622	31.33637	31.56754	31.79973	32.03295	32.26719	32.50244	32.73872	32.97601	33.21431	33.45363	33.69395	33.93529
4	23.48503	23.71495	23.94624	24.17890	24.41292	24.64830	24.88504	25.12314	25.36258	25.60338	25.84552	26.08901	26.33384	26.58000	26.82750	27.07632
5	19.33280	19.56615	19.80120	20.03795	20.27639	20.51653	20.75836	21.00186	21.24704	21.49390	21.74242	21.99261	22.24445	22.49794	22.75307	23.00985
6	16.57289	16.80993	17.04901	17.29011	17.53324	17.77839	18.02554	18.27469	18.52584	18.77897	19.03408	19.29116	19.55019	19.81118	20.07411	20.33896
7	14.60855	14.84944	15.09268	15.33828	15.58621	15.83649	16.08908	16.34398	16.60118	16.86067	17.12244	17.38646	17.65273	17.92124	18.19196	18.46489
8	13.14143	13.38623	13.63372	13.88387	14.13668	14.39213	14.65020	14.91089	15.17416	15.44002	15.70843	15.97937	16.25284	16.52881	16.80726	17.08816
9	12.00575	12.25451	12.50628	12.76102	13.01872	13.27935	13.54291	13.80936	14.07869	14.35086	14.62586	14.90366	15.18423	15.46755	15.75359	16.04231
10	11.10205	11.35480	11.61085	11.87018	12.13276	12.39857	12.66758	12.93976	13.21507	13.49350	13.77500	14.05954	14.34710	14.63762	14.93107	15.22743
11	10.36703	10.62377	10.88410	11.14801	11.41545	11.68639	11.96080	12.23865	12.51988	12.80446	13.09235	13.38350	13.67788	13.97543	14.27611	14.57987
12	9.75850	10.01921	10.28381	10.55226	10.82453	11.10056	11.38031	11.66373	11.95078	12.24141	12.53555	12.83317	13.13419	13.43857	13.74625	14.05717
13	9.24723	9.51190	9.78074	10.05370	10.33074	10.61179	10.89681	11.18572	11.47848	11.77502	12.07527	12.37918	12.68666	12.99766	13.31210	13.62992
14	8.81236	9.08096	9.35401	9.63143	9.91318	10.19919	10.48938	10.78368	11.08203	11.38434	11.69054	12.00055	12.31430	12.63168	12.95264	13.27707
15	8.43857	8.71107	8.98828	9.27012	9.55652	9.84740	10.14267	10.44225	10.74605	11.05399	11.36597	11.68190	12.00168	12.32522	12.65242	12.98319
16	8.11438	8.39075	8.67208	8.95828	9.24925	9.54491	9.84516	10.14990	10.45902	10.77242	11.09000	11.41165	11.73725	12.06670	12.39988	12.73668
17	7.83101	8.11121	8.39661	8.68709	8.98257	9.28292	9.58804	9.89781	10.21210	10.53081	10.85381	11.18096	11.51216	11.84726	12.18615	12.52869
18	7.58162	7.86561	8.15502	8.44973	8.74963	9.05458	9.36445	9.67912	9.99844	10.32228	10.65050	10.98295	11.31950	11.66001	12.00433	12.35231
19	7.36083	7.64856	7.94192	8.24079	8.54501	8.85446	9.16897	9.48840	9.81259	10.14139	10.47464	10.81218	11.15386	11.49951	11.84898	12.20211
20	7.16431	7.45573	7.75299	8.05593	8.36440	8.67823	8.99726	9.32131	9.65022	9.98380	10.32188	10.66430	11.01086	11.36141	11.71576	12.07375
21	6.98857	7.28363	7.58472	7.89166	8.20428	8.52239	8.84581	9.17434	9.50780	9.84599	10.18871	10.53578	10.88700	11.24218	11.60114	11.96370
22	6.83074	7.12939	7.43424	7.74510	8.06178	8.38406	8.71174	9.04461	9.38246	9.72507	10.07223	10.42374	10.77938	11.13896	11.50226	11.86911
23	6.68847	6.99065	7.29919	7.61389	7.93453	8.26087	8.59268	8.92974	9.27182	9.61867	9.97008	10.32581	10.68565	11.04937	11.41676	11.78761
24	6.55978	6.86543	7.17760	7.49605	7.82054	8.15082	8.48664	8.82775	9.17389	9.52481	9.88027	10.24002	10.60382	10.97145	11.34267	11.71727
25	6.44301	6.75207	7.06779	7.38991	7.71816	8.05227	8.39196	8.73697	9.08701	9.44182	9.80113	10.16469	10.53224	10.90354	11.27835	11.65645
26	6.33677	6.64918	6.96838	7.29407	7.62598	7.96380	8.30723	8.65599	9.00977	9.36829	9.73127	10.09844	10.46953	10.84427	11.22244	11.60378
27	6.23985	6.55555	6.87815	7.20734	7.54280	7.88421	8.23125	8.58361	8.94098	9.30304	9.66950	10.04008	10.41449	10.79247	11.17376	11.55812
28	6.15124	6.47016	6.79609	7.12868	7.46759	7.81247	8.16300	8.51882	8.87960	9.24504	9.61480	9.98859	10.36613	10.74713	11.13133	11.51849
29	6.07005	6.39213	6.72130	7.05720	7.39946	7.74771	8.10158	8.46072	8.82477	9.19341	9.56629	9.94312	10.32359	10.70741	11.09432	11.48406
30	5.99551	6.32068	6.65302	6.99215	7.33765	7.68914	8.04623	8.40854	8.77572	9.14739	9.52323	9.90292	10.28613	10.67258	11.06200	11.45412

EXAMPLE 18

To compute tł  using Table 6.3, we obtain 8.43857 corresponding to 15   payment per $1,000 borrowed, we must multiply by 10 for a   nt.

EXAMPLE 19

Suppose we wi   n, at a rate of 8.5%, to be paid back monthly over a per   onthly payment per $1,000 borrowed: $20.51653. Since ou   5.

EXAMPLE 20

An amortization schedule shows the allocation of the monthly payment toward interest and principal. Consider a $100,000 15 year loan at 6% annual interest. The monthly payment is $843.86. Each month (1) interest is computed by multiplying the previous months balance by 0.5% (0.005), (2) interest is deducted from the monthly payment, and (3) the remainder of the monthly payment is used to reduce the principal balance.

Note how the interest, which is always 0.5% of the previous principal balance, decreases from month to month while the reduction to principal increases. The sum of these two numbers is always equal to the monthly payment of $843.86.

Payment Number	Payment Amount	Interest	Reduction to Principal	Principal Balance
				100,000.00
1	843.86	500.00	343.86	99,656.14
2	843.86	498.28	345.58	99,310.56
3	843.86	496.55	347.31	98,963.25
4	843.86	494.82	349.04	98,614.21
5	843.86	493.07	350.79	98,263.42
6	843.86	491.32	352.34	97,910.88
.	.	.	.	.
.	.	.	.	.
.	.	.	.	.
178	843.86	12.53	831.33	1,674.16
179	843.86	8.37	835.49	838.67
180	843.86	4.19	839.67	−1.00

The monthly payment is mathematically computed so that the balance at the end of the loan period is $0.00. In actuality, the amount is never $0.00 due to rounding of the interest. To account for this, the last payment is usually slightly different from the others.

EXAMPLE 21

Richard and Maddy want to buy a house that costs $240,000. They can afford to put a 20% down payment toward the cost of the house but must obtain a mortgage for the rest. We would like to determine how much they must pay each month if they elect a 30-year term and the prevailing interest rate is $7\frac{1}{2}$%.

Since the down payment is 20% of the purchase price of the house, $48,000, they must finance $192,000. Table 6.3 gives a monthly payment of 6.99213 dollars per $1,000 borrowed. Their monthly payment is $192 \times 6.99215 = \$1,342.49$ per month.

EXAMPLE 22

We would like to compute how much Richard and Maddy (Example 21) pay in finance charges for the life of the loan.

First we compute how much they paid over the 30-year life of the loan:

$$30 \times 12 = 360 \text{ payments}$$
$$360 \times \$1,342.49 = \$483,296.40$$

Now we subtract the amount borrowed:

$$\$483,296.40 - \$192,000.00 = \$291,296.40$$

The total finance charge is \$291,296.40.

SOLVED PROBLEMS

6.25   Find the monthly payment on an auto loan of \$20,000 to be amortized over a 5-year period at a rate of 9%.

SOLUTION

There are 60 monthly payments and the monthly interest rate $i = 0.09/12 = 0.0075$. The discount factor from Table 6.2 is 48.17337:

$$R = \frac{A}{\text{discount factor}} = \frac{\$20,000}{48.17337} = \$415.17$$

6.26   Calculate the monthly payment in Prob. 6.25 using Table 6.3.

SOLUTION

From Table 6.3 the rate per \$1,000 financed corresponding to 5 years and 9% is 20.7582. Since our auto loan is for \$20,000 (20 × \$1,000), we multiply 20 × 20.75836 = 415.1672. The monthly payment is \$415.17.

6.27   Bill Murphy financed a \$2,500 necklace for his wife Jane. If he will be making 36 monthly payments of \$82.44, what rate of financing did he receive?

SOLUTION

Since $2,500/1,000 = 2.5$, there are 2.5 thousands in \$2,500. His monthly payment per \$1,000 is $82.44/2.5 = 32.976$. Referring to Table 6.3 across the row labeled 3 years (36 months), we see that 32.976 corresponds closest to 11.5%. This is his annual rate of interest.

6.28   Anthony wants to buy a boat which costs \$17,000. He has saved \$5,000, which he will use as a deposit, and he will finance the rest of it by taking out a loan to be paid back in equal monthly installments, amortized over 5 years at an annual interest rate of 12%. What will his payment be?

SOLUTION A

$R = \$17,000 - \$5,000 = \$12,000$, $i = 0.12/12 = 0.01$, and there are 60 monthly payments. The discount factor from Table 6.2 is 44.95504:

$$R = \frac{A}{\text{discount factor}} = \frac{\$12,000}{44.95504} = \$266.93$$

His monthly payment will be \$266.93.

SOLUTION B

From Table 6.3, the monthly payment per $1,000 on a 5-year loan at 12% annual interest is $22.24445. Multiplying, $12 \times \$22.24445 = \$266.93$.

6.29   Construct an amortization schedule for a 3-year loan of $5,000 at 5% interest, which is to be repaid in quarterly installments over 3 years.

SOLUTION

First we compute the amount to be paid each quarter. The discount factor (Table 6.2, $n = 3 \times 4 = 12$, $r = 0.05/4 = 0.0125$) is 11.07931:

$$R = \frac{A}{\text{discount factor}} = \frac{\$5,000}{11.07931} = \$451.29$$

Payment Number	Payment Amount	Interest	Reduction to Principal	Principal Balance
				$5,000.00
1	$451.29	$62.50	$388.79	$4,611.21
2	$451.29	$57.64	$393.65	$4,217.56
3	$451.29	$52.72	$398.57	$3,818.99
4	$451.29	$47.74	$403.55	$3,415.44
5	$451.29	$42.69	$408.60	$3,006.84
6	$451.29	$37.59	$413.70	$2,593.14
7	$451.29	$32.41	$418.88	$2,174.26
8	$451.29	$27.18	$424.11	$1,750.15
9	$451.29	$21.88	$429.41	$1,320.74
10	$451.29	$16.51	$434.78	$ 885.96
11	$451.29	$11.07	$440.22	$ 445.74
12	$451.29	$5.57	$445.72	$ 0.02

6.4 CAPITAL BUDGETING

Often we have to make a decision between two different investment alternatives. The determination as to which is the best alternative is made by comparing their present values.

To determine accurately how much a fixed amount of money will be worth at a later date, we must understand how *compound interest* works. If a fixed amount of money, say, $1,000, earns simple interest at an annual rate of 8%, the interest earned in one year is $0.08 \times \$1,000 = \$80$. The original money is worth $1,080 after one year. However, if the interest is calculated at 2% every quarter (1/4 of 8% = 2%), the amount of money at the end of the year will be somewhat greater. This is easily explained with the help of the following table:

Amount before Interest Is Compounded (A)	Interest Earned $(0.02 \times A)$	Amount after Interest Is Compounded
$1,000.00	$20.00	$1,020.00
$1,020.00	$20.40	$1,040.40
$1,040.40	$20.81	$1,061.21
$1,061.21	$21.22	$1,082.43

Our $1,000 has grown to $1,082.43 after one year.

To compute the amount of money we will have after interest is compounded, we can multiply $A \times (1 + i)$ where i = annual interest rate/4. If interest is compounded more often, say, monthly or daily, then i = annual interest rate/n, where $n = 12$ for monthly compounding and $n = 360$ for daily compounding. (Most banks use 360 days in a year.)

In our example, we compounded 4 times, so the final amount can be calculated by successive multiplication:

$$\text{Final amount} = A \times (1 + i) \times (1 + i) \times (1 + i) \times (1 + i)$$

or

$$\text{Final amount} = A \times (1 + i)^4$$

At the end of n compoundings , the final amount would be

$$S = A \times (1 + i)^n$$

EXAMPLE 23

To compute how much $1,000 would be worth after 1 year if interest is compounded quarterly at 8%, use $A = \$1,000$, $i = 0.08/4 = 0.02$, and $n = 4$:

$$S = A \times (1 + i)^4 = \$1,000 \times (1.02)^4 = \$1,000 \times 1.08243 = \$1,082.43$$

The amount computed, $1,082.43, is called the *future value* of the money. The *present value* of the money is the amount of money we started with. To compute how much money is needed now so that we will have an amount S in the future, we rewrite the equation, solving for A:

$$A = \frac{S}{(1 + i)^n}$$

EXAMPLE 24

Let us compute how much money is needed today so that we will have $2,500 after 2 years if interest is 8% compounded quarterly.

Since interest is compounded quarterly, there will be eight compoundings in 2 years. Using $S = \$2,500$, $n = 8$, and $i = 0.08/4$, we compute A:

$$A = \frac{S}{(1 + i)^8} = \frac{\$2,500}{(1.02)^8} = \frac{\$2,500}{1.171659} = \$2,133.73$$

EXAMPLE 25

We wish to determine which of the following two alternatives is the better choice:

- Alternative A yields a return of $2,700 at the end of 2 years plus $11,500 at the end of 6 years.

- Alternative B gives a return of $500 at the end of each quarter for 6 years.

Assume that the bank interest rate on money borrowed is 12% compounded quarterly.

Alternative A consists of two components. We compute the present value of each.

Component 1: $S_1 = \$2,700$, $n_1 = 8$, $i = 0.12/4 = 0.03$.

$$A_1 = \frac{S_1}{(1 + i)^{n_1}} = \frac{2,700}{(1.03)^8} = \$2,131.40$$

Component 2: $S_2 = \$11,500$, $n_2 = 24$, $i = 0.12/4 = 0.03$.

$$A_2 = \frac{S_2}{(1+i)^{n_2}} = \frac{11,500}{(1.03)^{24}} = \$5,657.24$$

$A = A_1 + A_2 = \$2,131.40 + \$5,657.24 = \$7,788.64$.

Alternative B is an annuity. $R = \$500$, $n = 6 \times 4 = 24$, and $i = 0.12/4 = 0.03$. Its present value is

$$A = R \times \text{discount factor} = \$500 \times 16.93554 = \$8,467.77.$$

Since alternative B has the higher present value, it is the preferable choice.

SOLVED PROBLEMS

6.30 Frank wants to buy a car. The dealer tells him that he can pay $500 a month for 36 months, or he can pay $15,000 cash for the car. Assuming that the prevailing interest rate is 9% monthly, which is a better deal for Frank?

SOLUTION

First compute the present value of the annuity. This will tell us how much $500 a month for 36 months is worth today: $R = \$500$, $n = 36$, $i = 0.09/12 = 0.0075$. The discount factor from Table 6.2 is 31.44681:

$$A = R \times \text{discount factor} = \$500 \times 31.44681 = \$15,723.41$$

Since the present value of the cost annuity is greater than $15,000, Frank would be better off paying $15,000 cash right away.

6.31 A company must decide whether to buy new equipment for $400,000 and enter into a service contract at $1,200 per month for 5 years (option 1) or lease the equipment for $9,000 each month over a 5-year period and then purchase it at the end of 5 years for $50,000 (option 2). If the company can earn 12% compounded monthly on its money, should the company buy or lease the equipment?

SOLUTION

If we purchase the equipment, we must compute the present value of the service contract. In this problem $n = 60$, and $i = 0.12/12 = 0.01$. The discount factor is 44.95504 (Table 6.2).

Present value of service contract:

$$A = R \times \text{discount factor} = \$1,200 \times 44.95504 = \$53,946.05$$

Including the cost of purchasing the equipment, the total present value of option 1 is then

$$\$400,000 + \$53,946.05 = \$453,946.05.$$

Present value of leasing:

$$A = R \times \text{discount factor} = \$9,000 \times 44.95504 = \$404,595.36$$

Present value of the purchase of the equipment after 5 years:

$$A = \frac{S}{(1+i)^n} = \frac{\$50,000}{(1.01)^{60}} = \$27,522.48$$

The total present value of option 2 is $404,595.36 + $27,522.48 = $432,117.84. Since this amount is lower than the $453,946.05 in option 1, the company should lease its equipment.

6.32 Which would you prefer to receive: (*a*) $15,000 at the end of 3 years plus $30,000 at the end of 5 years, or (*b*) $2,250 at the end of each quarter for the next 5 years?
Assume that money is worth 10% annually and is compounded quarterly.

SOLUTION

The present value of $15,000 3 years from now is

$$A = \frac{S}{(1+i)^n} = \frac{\$15{,}000}{(1.025)^{12}} = \frac{\$15{,}000}{1.34489} = \$11{,}153.33 \qquad \left(n = 4 \times 3 = 12;\ i = \frac{0.10}{4} = 0.025 \right)$$

The present value of $30,000 5 years from now is

$$A = \frac{S}{(1+i)^n} = \frac{\$30{,}000}{(1.025)^{20}} = \frac{\$30{,}000}{1.63862} = \$18{,}308.09 \qquad \left(n = 4 \times 5 = 20;\ i = \frac{0.10}{4} = 0.025 \right)$$

The total present value under option (a) is $29,461.42.

Under option (b) the present value of $2,250 per quarter for 5 years is

$$A = R \times \text{discount factor} = \$2{,}250 \times 15.58916 = \$35{,}075.61$$

Option (b) is preferable, since the present value of the money is larger.

Supplementary Problems

6.33   Compute the accumulated value of an ordinary annuity of $100 per month for 5 years assuming that the interest rate is 9% compounded monthly.

6.34   Compute the accumulated value of an annuity due of $100 per month for 5 years assuming that the interest rate is 9% compounded monthly.

6.35   Compute the accumulated value of an ordinary annuity of $500 per quarter for 5 years assuming that the interest rate is 10% compounded quarterly.

6.36   Compute the accumulated value of an annuity due of $500 per quarter for 5 years assuming that the interest rate is 10% compounded quarterly.

6.37   Compute the accumulated value of an ordinary annuity of $1,200 every six months for 3 years assuming that the interest rate is 6% compounded semiannually.

6.38   Compute the accumulated value of an annuity due of $1,200 every 6 months for 3 years assuming that the interest rate is 6% compounded semiannually.

6.39   Compute the present value of an ordinary annuity of $150 a month for 3 years. Interest is paid at 15% compounded monthly.

6.40   Compute the present value of an annuity due of $150 a month for 3 years. Interest is paid at 15% compounded monthly.

6.41   You have just won the million-dollar lottery! You will get $100,000 at the end of each year for the next 10 years. Assuming 4% interest compounded annually at the end of each year, how much did you really win?

6.42   Bunny gets paid at the end of each month. If she deposits $50 from each paycheck into an account that pays 12% compounded monthly, how much will she have saved at the end of a year?

6.43   How much interest is accumulated at the end of 2 years if $90 per month is deposited into a savings account paying 9% compounded monthly?

6.44   How much money must Sidney save each quarter to accumulate $500 at the end of 2 years? Assume that the interest rate is 5% compounded quarterly and that Sidney makes his deposit at the *end* of each quarter.

6.45   Repeat Prob. 6.44 assuming that Sidney makes his deposit at the *beginning* of each quarter.

6.46   Pan American bank pays 6% compounded monthly on its passbook savings account. How much would you have to deposit each month in order to save $500 at the end of one year?

6.47   How much money should you put in a savings account paying 6% interest compounded monthly in order to have enough money to receive a monthly stipend of $500 per month for 10 years?

6.48   Mrs. Spector is updating her will. She wants to leave her granddaughter $1,000 a year for 10 years after her death. How much money will her executors need to invest at 4% compounded annually to accomplish this?

6.49   Mr. Bailey was sued by Mr. Smith and was ordered by the court to pay $5,000 in damages. Since Mr. Bailey didn't have the money, he agreed to pay $1,000 now and the rest in equal monthly installments over a period of one year. If interest is compounded monthly at 6% per annum, how much must Mr. Bailey pay Mr. Smith each month?

6.50   Scott and Ronnie need to save $30,000 to put a down payment on a house in 3 years. If interest at a local bank is compounded quarterly at 5% per year, how much must they save each quarter if they make their deposit (*a*) at the end of the quarter or (*b*) at the beginning of the quarter?

6.51   A washing machine sells for $450. If Mae puts $150 down, how much should she pay each month for the next 12 months if she finances the appliance? Assume that the finance charges are 15% per year compounded monthly.

6.52   Use Table 6.3 to compute the monthly payment on a 12-year loan of $17,000 at an annual interest rate of 6.5%.

6.53   Use Table 6.3 to compute the savings in interest between a 7.5% loan of $100,000 and an 8% loan of the same amount. Both have 20-year terms and are payable monthly.

6.54   A 30-year mortgage of $50,000 has a monthly payment due of $420.43. Use Table 6.3 to compute the annual interest rate.

6.55   A store advertises a refrigerator for $100 down and $100 a month for 8 months. If the interest rate is 15% compounded monthly, what is the actual value of the refrigerator?

6.56   A company wants to accumulate $200,000 in 5 years in order to purchase new equipment. How much must they deposit each month into an account which pays an interest rate of 9% per year compounded monthly?

6.57   Suppose that the interest rate in Prob. 6.56 drops to 6% after the second year. How much must the company now save each month in order to accomplish their goal?

6.58   If the annual premium on a life insurance policy is $1,200, and the interest rate is 10%, what would be a fair quarterly premium?

6.59   How much must you save each month for the next 10 years to withdraw $50 per month for the following 20 years? Assume that the interest rate stays constant at 6% compounded monthly for the entire 30-year period.

6.60 The monthly rent on a condominium is $600, payable at the beginning of the month. If the current interest rate is 6%, what would be a fair amount to charge someone who wishes to pay the yearly rent in advance?

6.61 Dr. Payne is a dentist. He estimates that his x-ray machine will have to be replaced in 5 years at a cost of $75,000. What should be his quarterly contribution into a sinking fund which pays 12% compounded quarterly so that he will have enough money to purchase a new machine?

6.62 Construct a sinking fund schedule which describes the accumulation of a sinking fund in which $20,000 is to be accumulated in 3 years if payments are made semiannually into an account which pays 8% compounded every 6 months.

6.63 The Ace plumbing supply company anticipates that they will need a new truck in 5 years which will cost $40,000. They contribute monthly into a sinking fund which pays interest at the rate of 9% compounded monthly. After 2 years, however, an emergency arises so they withdraw the entire balance from the fund. How much did they withdraw?

6.64 A tennis club has 300 members. They want to build a new clubhouse at a cost of $750,000 so they establish a sinking fund which will accumulate this amount of money in 2 years. The fund earns 12% interest compounded every two months. If all members are to pay equally, how much will their bimonthly assessment be?

6.65 A sinking fund of equal monthly payments is established to accumulate $100,000 in 5 years. If the annual interest rate is 15%, how much interest will the fund accumulate in that period of time?

6.66 The voters of the town of Brookville pass a $20,000,000 bond issue to be redeemed in 10 years. What semiannual deposits (to the nearest dollar) must the town officials make into a sinking fund paying 8% compounded semiannually in order to have enough money to redeem the bonds on time?

6.67 To have enough capital to buy new networking equipment, the Compact Computer Corporation takes out a $500,000 loan whose 12% interest is payable monthly. To pay off the debt in 5 years, monthly payments are made into a sinking fund which pays 9% interest compounded monthly. What is the monthly expense of the debt?

6.68 What is the book value of the debt, to the nearest dollar, in Prob. 6.67 at the end of 2 years?

6.69 In order to buy a new fire engine, the city of Pinewood takes out a $1,200,000 loan, whose 16% interest is payable quarterly. To pay back the debt in 4 years, quarterly payments are made to a sinking fund which pays 12% interest compounded quarterly. What is the quarterly expense of the debt (to the nearest dollar)?

6.70 What is the book value of the debt after $2\frac{1}{2}$ years (to the nearest dollar)?

6.71 What are the monthly payments on a $250,000 mortgage at 9% annual interest amortized over 20 years?

6.72 A new Cadillac costs $35,000. The interest rate on a dealer-financed auto loan, payable monthly, is 15%. If Mr. Taylor wants to pay $1,000 a month for 3 years, how much of a down payment will he have to give the dealer?

6.73 What is the total interest on the auto loan in Prob. 6.72?

6.74 What is the cost (i.e., interest) of a 30-year, $100,000 mortgage, payable monthly, whose interest rate is $7\frac{1}{2}$%?

6.75 A home computer was purchased for $100 down and $50 a month for 24 months. If the interest rate is 15%, what is the actual price of the computer?

6.76 What is the total finance charge for the computer purchase of Prob. 6.75?

6.77 Redwood Savings Bank charges an annual interest rate of 9% for a 30-year mortgage with monthly payments. Greenwood Federal charges only 8.5% for the same loan. How much would you save each month on a $100,000 mortgage if you took your business to Greenwood?

6.78 Suppose that you took your monthly savings from Prob. 6.77 and deposited it in a savings account paying 6% interest compounded monthly. How much money would be in the account after 10 years?

6.79 A new car can be purchased for $20,000 or can be leased for 36 months at $500 per month and then purchased at the end of the lease for $5,000. If the interest rate for the lease is 12% annually, and the interest rate on savings is 9% compounded monthly, which is the better alternative? Assume that you will definitely purchase the car one way or the other.

6.80 A growing company needs to increase its warehouse space. They anticipate that they will need a total of 150,000 ft^2 in 1 year, but they need only 75,000 ft^2 right away. If the cost of construction is $10/ft^2 now but will be $11/ft^2 in a year, which of the following alternatives is best? Assume that the interest rate is 12% simple interest and will not fluctuate during the year.

    (*a*) Build a 150,000-ft^2 warehouse immediately.

    (*b*) Build a 75,000-ft^2 warehouse now and add another 75,000 ft^2 next year.

6.81 Assuming interest rates remain constant at 12% compounded quarterly, which of the following alternatives is preferable?

    (*a*) An investment today of $20,000 with expected returns of $2,500 a quarter for the next 10 years.

    (*b*) An investment today of $25,000 with expected returns of $2,625 a year for the next 10 years.

Answers to Supplementary Problems

6.33 $7,542.41

6.34 $7,598.98

6.35 $12,772.33

6.36 $13,091.64

6.37 $7,762.09

6.38 $7,994.95

6.39 $4,327.09

6.40 $4,381.18

6.41 $811,090

6.42 $634.13

6.43 $2,356.96

6.44 $59.82

6.45 $59.08

6.46 $40.53

6.47 $45,036.73

6.48 $8,110.90

6.49 $344.27

6.50 (*a*) $2,332.75, (*b*) $2,303.95

6.51 $27.08

6.52 $170.33

6.53 $30.85/mo

6.54 9.5%

6.55 $856.81

6.56 $2,651.67

6.57 $3,172.50

6.58 $318.98

6.59 $42.59

6.60 $7,006.21

6.61 $2,791.18

6.62

Period	Initial Amount	Interest	+	Monthly Payment (R)	=	Increase in Fund	Final Amount
1	0	0	+	3,015.24	=	3,015.24	3,015.24
2	3,015.24	120.61	+	3,015.24	=	3,135.85	6,151.09
3	6,151.09	246.04	+	3,015.24	=	3,261.28	9,412.37
4	9,412.37	376.49	+	3,015.24	=	3,391.73	12,804.10
5	12,804.10	512.16		3,015.24	=	3,527.40	16,331.50
6	16,331.50	653.26		3,015.24	=	3,668.50	20,000.00

6.63 $13,888.53

6.64 $186.40

6.65 $32,260.60

6.66　$671,635

6.67　$11,629.18

6.68　$326,392

6.69　$107,533

6.70　$517,521

6.71　$2,249.32

6.72　$6,152.73

6.73　$7,152.73

6.74　$151,717.40

6.75　$1,131.21

6.76　$168.79

6.77　$35.71

6.78　$5,852.13

6.79　Leasing the car and purchasing it at the end of the lease

6.80　Alternative (*b*)

6.81　Alternative (*a*)

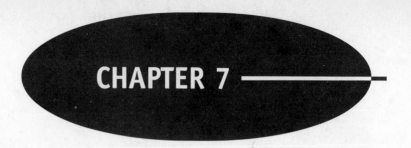

CHAPTER 7

Stocks and Bonds

7.1 STOCKS AND DIVIDENDS

One way to invest money is to buy *stock* or *shares* in a corporation. A *shareholder* is a part owner of the corporation and receives part of the corporation's profits in the form of *dividends*. The price of the share, called *par value*, is set by the company when the stock is first sold to the public. When the stock is resold on the *stock market*, its price is determined by what the buyer is willing to pay and the seller is willing to accept. This value, called the *market value*, is published in the financial section of most major newspapers. Typical stock quotations are shown in Table 7.1.

Table 7.1   Stock Quotations

High	Low	Stock	Dividend in Dollars	Sales 100s	High	Low	Close	Net Change
$27\frac{7}{8}$	20	A	1.50	1,221	$24\frac{1}{2}$	$23\frac{5}{8}$	$24\frac{1}{2}$	$+\frac{7}{8}$
$16\frac{1}{4}$	8	B	.60	48	$9\frac{3}{4}$	$9\frac{5}{8}$	$9\frac{5}{8}$	$-\frac{1}{8}$
$119\frac{1}{4}$	$97\frac{1}{8}$	C	2	54	$110\frac{3}{8}$	$108\frac{1}{2}$	$108\frac{5}{8}$	$-\frac{3}{8}$
83	$62\frac{1}{4}$	D	pf 5.50	9	$64\frac{1}{4}$	$64\frac{1}{4}$	$64\frac{1}{4}$	$+\frac{1}{4}$
$22\frac{1}{8}$	$15\frac{1}{8}$	E	pf .78	1	$20\frac{3}{4}$	$20\frac{3}{4}$	$20\frac{3}{4}$	$-\frac{1}{4}$

High price for past 12 months

Name of company

Number of shares sold that day in 100s

Low price for that day

Difference between closing prices of that day and the prior trading day

Low price for past 12 months

Dividend for year

High price for that day

Price for last trade of that day

EXAMPLE 1

Referring to Table 7.1, find (*a*) the total dividend paid for the past year to an investor owning 300 shares of stock A, and (*b*) the price of 100 shares of stock B purchased at the high price for that day.

(*a*)   Dividend per share of stock A: $1.50

Total dividend: $300 \times \$1.50 = \$450$

(*b*)   High price of a share of stock B: $\$9\frac{3}{4} = \$9.75$

Price of 100 shares at the high price: $100 \times \$9.75 = \$975$

The two kinds of stock sold are *common* and *preferred*. The dividend on preferred stock is fixed when the stock is issued. Stock D in Table 7.1 is a preferred stock (see the abbreviation "pf") paying a dividend of 5.50% of the par value (usually $100). Dividends to preferred stockholders are paid before dividends are paid to common stockholders. Most preferred stock is *cumulative*. When a company declares dividends in any given year, the holders of cumulative preferred stock will receive all dividends not declared in previous years plus the current year's dividend. On *noncumulative* preferred stock, declared dividends are paid only for the current year.

EXAMPLE 2

The ABC Corporation has issued 2,000 shares of $100 par value common stock and 500 shares of 8%, $100 par value preferred stock. If the company declared $12,000 in dividends for the year, what will be the dividend per share of common stock?

Dividend per share of preferred stock: $8\% \times \$100 = \$8$

Total dividend on preferred stock: $500 \times \$8 = \$4,000$

Total dividend on common stock: $\$12,000 - \$4,000 = \$8,000$

Dividend per share of common stock: $\dfrac{\$8,000}{2,000} = \$4$

EXAMPLE 3

Paul White owns 120 shares of a cumulative $7\frac{1}{4}\%$, $100 par value preferred stock. He has not received dividends for the previous 2 years. How much dividend will he receive this year if the company declares dividends?

Yearly dividend for each share: $7\frac{1}{4}\% \times \$100 = \$7.25$

Yearly dividend on 120 shares: $120 \times \$7.25 = \$870$

Total dividend for 3 years: $3 \times \$870 = \$2,610$

Shares are usually traded in groups of 100 shares, called *round lots*. An *odd lot* refers to fewer than 100 shares. An *odd-lot differential fee* of $\$\frac{1}{8}$ for each share traded is added to the price of stock being purchased and subtracted from the price being sold to arrive at the statement price, known as the *execution price*. A commission, based on the dollar value of the stocks traded, is paid to a stockbroker, who acts as an agent performing transactions between buyer and seller. Commission rates depend on the brokerage firm.

EXAMPLE 4

An investor bought 60 shares of stock selling at $35\frac{1}{8}$. What was the broker's commission if the commission rate was 1.4%?

Execution price per share: $\$35\frac{1}{8} + \$\frac{1}{8}$ (odd lot) $= \$35.25$

Cost of shares: $60 \times \$35.25 = \$2,115$

Commission: $1.4\% \times \$2,115 = \$29.61$

EXAMPLE 5

Mrs. Smith sold 130 shares of stock selling at $12\frac{1}{4}$. Find the broker's commission if the commission rate was 1.6%.

Round lot (100 shares)

Execution price per share:	$12.25
Gross proceeds from stock:	$100 \times 12.25 = \$1,225$

Odd lot $(130 - 100 = 30)$

Execution price per share:	$\$12\frac{1}{4} - \$\frac{1}{8}$ (odd lot) = \$12.125
Gross proceeds from stock:	$30 \times \$12.125 = \$363.75$
Total gross proceeds:	$\$1,225 + \$363.75 = \$1,588.75$
Total commission:	$1.6\% \times \$1,588.75 = \$25.42$

Several criteria may be used to evaluate investments in stocks. The *annual yield*, often expressed as a percent, is the ratio of the annual dividend per share to the price per share:

$$\text{Annual yield} = \frac{\text{annual dividend per share}}{\text{price per share}}$$

The *capital gain* is the net proceeds less the total cost:

$$\text{Capital gain} = \text{net proceeds} - \text{total cost}$$

The *total gain* is the sum of total dividends plus the capital gain:

$$\text{Total gain} = \text{total dividends} + \text{capital gain}$$

Investors usually base their decisions of whether to buy or sell stock on the *estimated total gain* for a specified period of time. This estimate ignores commission, SEC charges, and transfer taxes.

EXAMPLE 6

Find the rate of annual yield on a common stock if the semiannual dividend is $1.35 and the price per share is $18.

Annual dividend: $2 \times \$1.35 = \$2.70$

$$\text{Annual yield} = \frac{\text{annual dividend}}{\text{price per share}}$$

$$= \frac{\$2.70}{\$18} = 0.15 = 15\%$$

EXAMPLE 7

An investor bought a common stock at $22 per share. Her quarterly dividend was 45¢ a share. She sold the stock after 2 years at $37.50 per share. What is (*a*) the total gain per share and (*b*) the percent of total gain relative to cost?

(*a*)   Total dividends per share: 8 quarters $\times \$0.45/\text{quarter} = \$3.60$

$$\text{Capital gain per share} = \text{net proceeds} - \text{total cost}$$
$$= \$37.50 - \$22 = \$15.50$$

$$\text{Total gain per share} = \text{total dividends} + \text{capital gain}$$
$$= \$3.60 + \$15.50 = \$19.10$$

(b)

$$\text{Total gain percent} = \frac{\text{total gain}}{\text{total cost}} \times 100$$

$$= \frac{\$19.10}{\$22} \times 100 = 86.82\%$$

SOLVED PROBLEMS

7.1 Find the cost of 85 shares of stock B in Table 7.1 at the closing price of the day.

SOLUTION

Execution price per share: $9\frac{5}{8} + \$\frac{1}{8}$ (odd lot) = \$9.75
Cost of shares: $85 \times \$9.75 = \$828.75$

7.2 Find the gross proceeds from the sale of 215 shares of stock A in Table 7.1 at the low price of the day.

SOLUTION

Round lot (groups of 100 shares)
    Execution price per share: \$23.625
    Gross proceeds from stock: $200 \times \$23.625 = \$4,725$
Odd lot $(215 - 200 = 15)$
    Execution price per share: $\$23\frac{5}{8} - \$\frac{1}{8} = \$23.50$
    Gross proceeds from stock: $15 \times \$23.50 = \$352.50$
    Total gross proceeds from sale: $\$4,725 + \$352.50 = \$5,077.50$

7.3 Find the broker's commission on the purchase of 20 shares of stock C in Table 7.1 at the high price of the day, if the commission rate is 2.2%.

SOLUTION

Execution price per share: $\$110\frac{3}{8} + \$\frac{1}{8}$ (odd lot) = \$110.50
Cost of shares: $20 \times \$110.50 = \$2,210$
Commission: $2.2\% \times \$2,210 = \$48.62$

7.4 Find the broker's commission in Prob. 7.3 assuming that the transaction was a sale.

SOLUTION

Execution price per share: $\$110\frac{3}{8} - \$\frac{1}{8} = \$110.25$
Proceeds from shares: $20 \times \$110.25 = \$2,205$
Commission: $2.2\% \times \$2,205 = \$48.51$

7.5 The Sherlock Corporation declares a dividend of \$42,540 to its 5,000 shares of 5.5%, \$100 par value preferred stock and its 8,000 shares of common stock. What is the dividend per share of (a) preferred stock and (b) common stock?

SOLUTION

(a)   Dividend per share of preferred stock: 5.5% × $100 = $5.50

(b)   Since dividends are paid first to preferred stock, the amount available to common stock is calculated as follows:

Dividend to common stock = total dividend − dividend to preferred stock

Total dividend to preferred stock: 5,000 × $5.50 = $27,500

Total dividend to common stock: $42,540 − $27,500 = $15,040

Dividend per share of common stock: $\dfrac{\$15,040}{8,000} = \$1.88$

7.6   The Ruben Corporation declares dividends as follows from 1998 to 2001:

1998	$11,000
1999	$37,000
2000	$8,000
2001	$45,000

Its outstanding stock consists of 3,000 shares of 7%, $100 par value cumulative preferred stock and 5,000 shares of common stock. No dividends are in arrears as of the end of 1997. What amount of dividends is paid to each class of stock each year and what are the total dividends for each class for the 4 years?

SOLUTION

The normal preferred dividend is

$$7\% \times \$100 \times 3,000 \text{ shares} = \$21,000$$

Dividends

Year	Total	Preferred Stock	Arrears	Common Stock
1998	$ 11,000	$11,000	$10,000*	$ 0
1999	37,000	$21,000 + $10,000 = 31,000**	0	6,000†
2000	8,000	8,000	13,000‡	0
2001	45,000	$21,000 + $13,000 = 34,000**	0	11,000§
Total	$101,000	$84,000		$17,000

*Since the normal preferred dividend is $21,000, the amount in arrears at the end of 1998 is
$21,000 − $11,000 (the declared dividend). Note that this means that none of the 1998 dividend
is available to common stock.

**The normal preferred dividend is added to the amount in arrears to determine the dividend
available to cumulative preferred stock.

†The amount of the 1999 dividend available to common stock is the total 1999 dividend less the
amount applied to preferred stock:

$37,000 − $31,000 = $6,000

‡$21,000 − $8,000 = $13,000 in arrears

§$45,000 − $34,000 = $11,000

7.7   Solve Prob. 7.6 assuming that the preferred stock is noncumulative.

SOLUTION

Dividends

Year	Total	Preferred Stock	Common Stock
1998	$ 11,000	$11,000	$ 0*
1999	37,000	21,000**	16,000†
2000	8,000	8,000	0*
2001	45,000	21,000**	24,000†
Total	$101,000	$61,000	$40,000

*The normal preferred dividend is still $21,000, so none of the 1998 dividend is available to common stock.
**Since the stock is noncumulative, only the normal preferred dividend amount is available to preferred stock.
†Total dividend − dividend to preferred stock = dividend to common stock.

7.8   Bundy Products, Inc. declares a dividend of $45,000 to its 2,000 shares of 8%, $100 par value preferred stock and its 6,000 shares of common stock. After each common share has received $2.50, preferred shareholders participate with the common shareholders in the distribution of the remaining dividend, in the ratio of shares in each class. Find the total dividend and the dividend per share for each class of stock.

SOLUTION

Normal preferred dividend: $8\% \times \$100 \times 2{,}000 \text{ shares} = \$16{,}000$
Stated common dividend: $\$2.50 \times 6{,}000 \text{ shares} = 15{,}000$
Remainder to be distributed by ratio:
Total shareholders: $2{,}000 + 6{,}000 = 8{,}000$
Amount available: $\$45{,}000 - (\$16{,}000 + \$15{,}000) = \$14{,}000$

To preferred shareholders: $\dfrac{2{,}000}{8{,}000} \times \$14{,}000 = 3{,}500$

To common shareholders: $\dfrac{6{,}000}{8{,}000} \times \$14{,}000 = 10{,}500$

Class of Stock	Total Dividend	Dividend per Share
Preferred	$16,000 + $3,500 = $19,500	$\dfrac{\$19{,}500}{2{,}000} = \$9.75$
Common	$15,000 + $10,500 = $25,500	$\dfrac{\$25{,}500}{6{,}000} = \$4.25$

7.9   Solve Prob. 7.8 assuming that the preferred stock is not participating in the distribution of the remaining dividends.

SOLUTION

Class of Stock	Total Dividend	Dividend per Share
Preferred	$16,000	8% × $100 = $8.00
Common	$45,000 − $16,000 = $29,000	$\dfrac{\$29,000}{6,000} = \$4.83$

7.10   Determine the rate of annual yield for stock A in Table 7.1, if bought at the low price of the day.

SOLUTION

Annual dividend is $1.50 per share:

$$\text{Annual yield} = \text{annual dividend per share/price per share}$$

$$= \frac{\$1.50}{\$23.625} \cong 0.0635 = 6.35\%$$

7.11   Three years ago Jeff purchased 100 shares of stock D at $47\frac{1}{8}$ and sold it at the day's closing price, shown in Table 7.1. Assuming that dividends have been constant for the 3-year period, what is (*a*) the total gain and (*b*) the annual rate of gain based on cost?

SOLUTION

(*a*)   Gain from dividends per share: 3 yr × $5.50 = $16.50

$$\text{Capital gain per share} = \text{net proceeds} - \text{total cost}$$
$$= \$64\tfrac{1}{4} - \$47\tfrac{1}{8} = \$17\tfrac{1}{8} = \$17.125$$

$$\text{Total gain per share} = \text{total dividends} + \text{capital gain}$$
$$= \$16.50 + \$17.125 = \$33.625$$

Total gain on 100 shares: 100 × $33.625 = $3,362.50

(*b*)   Annual gain on 100 shares: $3,362.50 ÷ 3 yr = $1,120.83
Cost of shares: 100 × $47.125 = $4,712.50
Annual rate of gain $1,120.83/$4,712.50 ≅ 0.2378 = 23.78%

7.12   Two years ago, an investor bought 200 shares of stock E at $31\frac{1}{4}$ and sold it at the day's closing price, shown in Table 7.1. Calculate (*a*) the investor's total loss and (*b*) the annual rate of loss based on cost.

SOLUTION

(*a*)   Gain from dividends per share: 2 yr × $0.78 = $1.56

$$\text{Capital loss per share} = \text{total cost} - \text{net proceeds}$$
$$= \$31\tfrac{1}{4} - \$20\tfrac{3}{4} = \$10\tfrac{2}{4} = \$10.50$$

$$\text{Total loss per share} = \text{capital loss} - \text{total dividends}$$
$$= \$10.50 - \$1.56 = \$8.94$$

	Total loss on 200 shares:	$200 \times \$8.94 = \$1,788$
(b)	Annual loss on 200 shares:	$\$1,788 \div 2 \text{ yr} = \$894$
	Cost of 200 shares:	$200 \times \$31.25 = \$6,250$
	Annual rate of loss:	$\$894/\$6,250 \cong 0.1430 = 14.30\%$

7.2 BONDS

A *bond* is a long-term contract between a borrower (usually a corporation or the government) and a lender (bondholder). The bondholder is a creditor and is paid interest on the *face value* or *par value* of the bond at a specified rate of interest, called *bond rate*. The interest is usually payable semiannually on the dates specified on the bond certificate. On the *redemption date* (or *maturity date*) the bondholder receives the par value of the bond.

Table 7.2 Bond Quotations

Bond				Current Yield	Vol.	High	Low	Close	Net Change
A	$9\frac{3}{8}$	s	06	9.3	16	$102\frac{3}{8}$	$100\frac{1}{8}$	$100\frac{1}{8}$	$+\frac{1}{8}$
B	$7\frac{1}{8}$	s	03	8.0	57	89	$88\frac{1}{2}$	89	$+\frac{5}{8}$
C	$12\frac{1}{2}$	s	09	11.0	14	$110\frac{1}{8}$	110	110	$-\frac{1}{8}$
D	$4\frac{3}{4}$	s	00	6.3	51	$74\frac{7}{8}$	$74\frac{5}{8}$	$74\frac{3}{4}$	$+\frac{7}{8}$
E	8.7	s	04	8.4	265	103	$102\frac{3}{4}$	103	$+\frac{1}{8}$

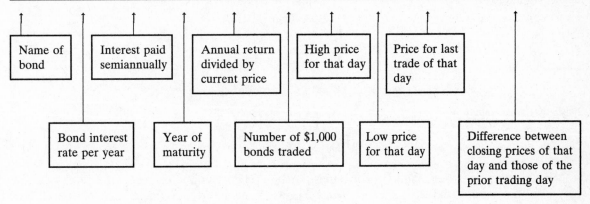

Name of bond

Interest paid semiannually

Annual return divided by current price

High price for that day

Price for last trade of that day

Bond interest rate per year

Year of maturity

Number of $1,000 bonds traded

Low price for that day

Difference between closing prices of that day and those of the prior trading day

Bonds may be bought and sold in bond exchanges. Current market prices, called *market quotations*, of $100 par value bonds are published daily in the financial pages of major newspapers. Typical bond quotations are shown in Table 7.2.

EXAMPLE 8

Find the market price of one $1,000 bond A in Table 7.2 at that day's closing price.

Day's closing price quotation:	$\$100\frac{1}{8} = \$100.125$
Market price of a $1,000 bond:	$10 \times \$100.125 = \$1001.25$

EXAMPLE 9

Find the market price of four $1,000 bonds D in Table 7.2 at the previous day's closing price.

Previous day's closing price quotation: $74\frac{3}{4} - \$\frac{7}{8} = \$73\frac{7}{8} = \$73.875$

Market price of four $1,000 bonds: $4 \times 10 \times \$73.875 = \$2,955$

EXAMPLE 10

Find the market price of a $5,000 bond C in Table 7.2 at that day's low price.

Day's low price quotation: $110 = \$110$

Market price of a $5,000 bond: $5 \times 10 \times \$110 = \$5,500$

EXAMPLE 11

How much bond interest will be paid semiannually to an investor who owns six $1,000 bonds E in Table 7.2?

Semiannual interest on $1,000 bond E: $\dfrac{8.7\%}{2} \times \$1,000 = \$43.50$

Semiannual interest on six $1,000 bonds E: $6 \times \$43.50 = \$261$

The market prices of bonds change to reflect changes in the economy and in the current interest rates. A bond priced below its face value is selling at a *discount*, and a bond priced above its face value is selling at a *premium*.

EXAMPLE 12

Find the premium on a $1,000 bond A in Table 7.2 at the day's high price.

Day's high price quotation: $102\frac{3}{8} = \$102.375$

Market price of a $1,000 bond: $10 \times \$102.375 = \$1,023.75$

Premium: $\$1,023.75 - \$1,000 = \$23.75$

EXAMPLE 13

Find the discount on a $2,000 bond B in Table 7.2 at the day's low price.

Day's low price quotation: $88\frac{1}{2} = \$88.50$

Market price of a $2,000 bond: $20 \times \$88.50 = \$1,770$

Discount: $\$2,000 - \$1,770 = \$230$

Bonds pay interest semiannually. For bonds purchased between interest dates, the purchaser pays the seller the interest earned (accrued) from the last bond interest payment date to the date of purchase. This so-called *accrued bond interest* is computed by the simple interest formula

$$I = P \times r \times t$$

where I = accrued bond interest
        P = face value of bonds purchased
        r = annual bond rate
        t = time from last interest payment date to date of purchase

Approximate time (each month = 30 days) and a 360-day year is used to determine time t.

Total purchase price of a bond purchased between bond interest dates is then the sum of the market price and the accrued bond interest. Any commission to the broker should also be added to the purchase price. Since these commissions are relatively small, they are ignored in this book.

EXAMPLE 14

A $5,000, 8% bond paying interest on February 1 and August 1 is sold on April 8. Find the accrued bond interest.

Time from:

Feb. 1 to Apr. 1 $= 2 \times 30 =$ 60 days	
Apr. 1 to Apr. 8	7 days
Feb. 1 to Apr. 8	67 days

Accrued bond interest:

$$I = Prt$$
$$= \$5,000 \times 0.08 \times \frac{67}{360} = \$74.44$$

EXAMPLE 15

On March 26, an investor bought eight $1,000 bonds D at the day's closing price, shown in Table 7.2. Calculate the total purchase price if the interest dates are June 1 and December 1.

Day's closing price quotations: $74\frac{3}{4} = \$74.75$

Market price of eight $1,000 bonds: $8 \times 10 \times \$74.75 = \$5,980$

Time from:

Dec. 1 to Mar. 1 $= 3 \times 30 =$ 90 days	
Mar. 1 to Mar. 26	25 days
Dec. 1 to Mar. 26	115 days

Accrued bond interest:

$$I = Prt$$
$$= \$8,000 \times 0.0475 \times \frac{115}{360} = \$121.39$$
$$\text{Total purchase price} = \text{market price} + \text{accrued interest}$$
$$= \$5,980 + 121.39 = \$6,101.39$$

To measure the rate of return on an investment in bonds, we may calculate either the rate of *current yield* or the rate of *yield to maturity*. The formula for the rate of current yield is

$$\text{Rate of current yield} = \frac{\text{annual interest}}{\text{market price}}$$

The estimate for the rate of yield to maturity is based on the average annual interest divided by the average investment:

$$\text{Average annual interest} = \frac{\text{total interest} + \text{par value} - \text{purchase price}}{\text{number of years to maturity}}$$
$$\text{Average investment} = \frac{\text{purchase price} + \text{par value}}{2}$$
$$\text{Rate of yield to maturity} = \frac{\text{average annual interest}}{\text{average investment}}$$

EXAMPLE 16

A $1,000, 8% bond is quoted at 110 five years before maturity. Find the rate of current yield.

Annual interest: $8\% \times \$1,000 = \$80$
Market price: $10 \times \$110 = \$1,100$

$$\text{Rate of current yield} = \frac{\text{annual interest}}{\text{market price}}$$

$$= \frac{\$80}{\$1,100} \cong 0.0727 = 7.27\%$$

EXAMPLE 17

Estimate the rate of yield to maturity for the bond in Example 16.

$$\text{Average annual interest} = \frac{\text{total interest} + \text{par value} - \text{purchase price}}{\text{number of years to maturity}}$$

$$= \frac{(5 \text{ yr} \times \$80/\text{yr}) + \$1,000 - \$1,100}{5} = \$60$$

$$\text{Average investment} = \frac{\text{purchase price} + \text{par value}}{2}$$

$$= \frac{\$1,100 + \$1,000}{2} = \$1,050$$

$$\text{Rate of yield to maturity} = \frac{\text{average annual interest}}{\text{average investment}}$$

$$= \frac{\$60}{\$1,050} \cong 0.0571 = 5.71\%$$

SOLVED PROBLEMS

7.13 Find the market price of each $5,000 bond in Table 7.2 at the day's low price.

SOLUTION

Market price of a $5,000 bond:

$$A = 50 \times 100\tfrac{1}{8} = \$5,006.25$$
$$B = 50 \times 88\tfrac{1}{2} \ = \$4,425$$
$$C = 50 \times 110 \ = \$5,500$$
$$D = 50 \times 74\tfrac{5}{8} \ = \$3,731.25$$
$$E = 50 \times 102\tfrac{3}{4} = \$5,137.50$$

7.14 Find the semiannual bond interest payment on each $10,000 bond in Table 7.2.

SOLUTION

Bond interest payment on $10,000 bond:

$$A = \frac{0.09375}{2} \times \$10,000 = \$468.75$$

$$B = \frac{0.07125}{2} \times \$10,000 = \$356.25$$

$$C = \frac{0.125}{2} \times \$10,000 \ = \$625$$

$$D = \frac{0.0475}{2} \times \$10,000 = \$237.50$$

$$E = \frac{0.087}{2} \times \$10,000 \ = \$435$$

7.15   Find the premium or discount on each \$2,000 bond in Table 7.2 at the day's closing price.

SOLUTION

Market price of bond A:	$20 \times 100\frac{1}{8} = \$2,002.50$
Premium on bond A:	$\$2,002.50 - \$2,000 = \$2.50$
Market price of bond B:	$20 \times 89 = \$1,780$
Discount on bond B:	$\$2,000 - \$1,780 = \$220$
Market price of bond C:	$20 \times 110 = \$2,200$
Premium on bond C:	$\$2,200 - \$2,000 = \$200$
Market price of bond D:	$20 \times 74\frac{3}{4} = \$1,495$
Discount on bond D:	$\$2,000 - \$1,475 = \$505$
Market price of bond E:	$20 \times 103 = \$2,060$
Premium on bond E:	$\$2,060 - \$2,000 = \$60$

7.16   Jessica Guiso bought three \$1,000, $11\frac{1}{2}\%$ bonds on August 9 at market quotation $109\frac{1}{8}$. If the interest dates are March 1 and September 1, find the accrued bond interest and the total purchase price.

SOLUTION

Time from:		
	Mar. 1 to Aug. 1 $= 5 \times 30 = 150$ days	
	Aug. 1 to Aug. 9	8 days
	Mar. 1 to Aug. 9	158 days

Accrued bond interest:

$$I = Prt$$

$$= \$3,000 \times 0.115 \times \frac{158}{360} = \$151.42$$

Market price of three \$1,000 bonds: $3 \times 10 \times \$109\frac{1}{8} = \$3,273.75$

$$\text{Total purchase price} = \text{market price} + \text{accrued interest}$$
$$= \$3,273.75 + \$151.42 = \$3,425.17$$

7.17   Find the total purchase price in Prob. 7.16 assuming that the market quotation was $87\frac{7}{8}$.

SOLUTION

Accrued bond interest is the same: \$151.42.

Market price: $3 \times 10 \times 87\frac{7}{8} = \$2,636.25$

$$\text{Total purchase price} = \text{market price} + \text{accrued interest}$$
$$= \$2,636.25 + \$151.42 = \$2,787.67$$

7.18 Andrew owns two $1,000, $9\frac{1}{4}$% bonds paying interest on May 15 and November 15. What will be his proceeds from sale of the bonds on July 20 at market quotation $92\frac{1}{4}$?

SOLUTION

Market price: $2 \times 10 \times 92\frac{1}{4} = \$1,845$

Time from:

May 15 to July 15 = 2×30 =	60 days
July 15 to July 20	5 days
May 15 to July 20	65 days

Accrued bond interest:

$$I = Prt$$

$$= \$2,000 \times 0.0925 \times \frac{65}{360} = \$33.40$$

$$\text{Proceeds} = \text{market price} - \text{accrued interest}$$
$$= \$1,845 + \$33.40 = \$1,878.40$$

7.19 How much would Andrew receive in Prob. 7.18 at market quotation $103\frac{1}{8}$?

SOLUTION

Accrued bond interest is the same: $33.40.

Market price: $2 \times 10 \times 103\frac{1}{8} = \$2,062.50$

$$\text{Proceeds} = \text{market price} + \text{accrued interest}$$
$$= \$2,062.50 + \$33.40 = \$2,095.90$$

7.20 Find the rate of current yield in Prob. 7.16.

SOLUTION

Annual interest on a $1,000 bond: $11\frac{1}{2}\% \times 1,000 = \$115$
Market price of a $1,000 bond: $10 \times 109\frac{1}{8} = \$1,091.25$

$$\text{Rate of current yield} = \frac{\text{annual interest}}{\text{market price}}$$

$$= \frac{\$115}{\$1,091.25} \cong 0.1054 = 10.54\%$$

7.21 In Prob. 7.16, at what price would Jessica have to buy a $1,000 bond for the rate of current yield to be 12%?

SOLUTION

We rewrite the formula for current yield to solve for the market price:

$$\text{Current yield} = \frac{\text{annual interest}}{\text{market price}}$$

$$\text{Market price} = \frac{\text{annual interest}}{\text{current yield}}$$

The annual interest rate in Prob. 7.16 is 11.5%. The annual interest on a $1,000 bond is therefore

$$0.115 \times \$1,000 = \$115$$

By substituting the known values into the formula for market price, we get

$$\text{Market price} = \frac{\text{annual interest}}{\text{current yield}}$$

$$= \frac{\$115}{0.12} \cong \$958.33$$

For the current yield to be 12%, the price of a $1,000 bond in Prob. 7.16 would have to be $958.33.

7.22   What market price would give the buyer of a $1,000 bond B in Table 7.2 a 10.5% rate of current yield?

SOLUTION

Annual interest: $7\frac{1}{8}\% \times \$1,000 = \$71.25$

$$\text{Market price} = \frac{\text{annual interest}}{\text{current yield}}$$

$$= \frac{\$71.25}{0.105} \cong \$678.57$$

7.23   Twelve years before maturity, a $5,000, 9% bond is quoted at $93\frac{1}{2}$. Find the rate of current yield.

SOLUTION

Annual interest: $9\% \times \$5,000 = \$450$

Market price: $5 \times 10 \times 93\frac{1}{2} = \$4,675$

$$\text{Rate of current yield} = \frac{\text{annual interest}}{\text{market price}}$$

$$= \frac{\$450}{\$4,675} \cong 0.0963 = 9.63\%$$

7.24   Estimate the rate of yield to maturity for the bond in Prob. 7.23.

SOLUTION

$$\text{Average interest} = \frac{\text{total interest} + \text{par value} - \text{purchase price}}{\text{number of years to maturity}}$$

$$= \frac{(12 \text{ yr} \times \$450/\text{yr}) + \$5,000 - \$4,675}{12} \cong \$477.08$$

$$\text{Average investment} = \frac{\text{purchase price} + \text{par value}}{2}$$

$$= \frac{\$4,675 + \$5,000}{2} = \$4,837.50$$

$$\text{Rate of yield to maturity} = \frac{\text{average annual interest}}{\text{average investment}}$$

$$= \frac{\$477.08}{\$4,837.50} \cong 0.0986 = 9.86\%$$

7.25 Estimate the rate of yield to maturity for a $2,000, 12% bond quoted at 107 eight and a half years before maturity.

SOLUTION

Annual interest: $12\% \times \$2,000 = \$240$

Market price: $2 \times 10 \times 107 = \$2,140$

$$\text{Average interest} = \frac{\text{total interest} + \text{par value} - \text{purchase price}}{\text{number of years to maturity}}$$

$$= \frac{(8.5 \text{ yr} \times \$240/\text{yr}) + \$2,000 - \$2,140}{8.5} \cong \$223.53$$

$$\text{Average investment} = \frac{\text{purchase price} + \text{par value}}{2}$$

$$= \frac{\$2,140 + \$2,000}{2} = \$2,070$$

$$\text{Rate of yield to maturity} = \frac{\text{average annual interest}}{\text{average investment}}$$

$$= \frac{\$223.53}{\$2,070} \cong 0.1080 = 10.80\%$$

7.26 Dan Thomas owns some $9\frac{1}{4}\%$ bonds from TTR, Inc. that are due in 5 years, 3 months. He is considering selling these and buying some Satco 11% bonds due in 17 years. If he can sell his TTR at $92\frac{1}{4}$ and buy Satco at $102\frac{7}{8}$, which bonds would give him a better rate of current yield?

SOLUTION

TTR $1,000 bond:

Annual interest: $9\frac{1}{4}\% \times \$1,000 = \$92.50$

Market price: $10 \times 92\frac{1}{4} = \$922.50$

$$\text{Rate of current yield} = \frac{\text{annual interest}}{\text{market price}}$$

$$= \frac{\$92.50}{\$922.50} \cong 0.1003 = 10.03\%$$

Satco $1,000 bond:

Annual interest: $11\% \times \$1,000 = \$110$

Market price $10 \times 102\frac{7}{8} = \$1,028.75$

$$\text{Rate of current yield} = \frac{\text{annual interest}}{\text{market price}}$$

$$= \frac{\$110}{\$1,028.75} \cong 0.1069 = 10.69\%$$

The Satco bond gives a better rate of current yield.

7.27 In Prob. 7.26, which bond would give Dan Thomas a better rate of yield to maturity?

SOLUTION

TTR $1,000 bond:

$$\text{Average interest} = \frac{\text{total interest} + \text{par value} - \text{purchase price}}{\text{number of years to maturity}}$$

$$= \frac{(5.25 \text{ yr} \times \$92.50/\text{yr}) + \$1,000 - \$922.50}{5.25} = \$107.26$$

$$\text{Average investment} = \frac{\text{purchase price} + \text{par value}}{2}$$

$$= \frac{\$922.50 + \$1,000}{2} = \$961.25$$

$$\text{Rate of yield to maturity} = \frac{\text{average interest}}{\text{average investment}}$$

$$= \frac{\$107.26}{\$961.25} \cong 0.1116 = 11.16\%$$

Satco $1,000 bond:

$$\text{Average interest} = \frac{\text{total interest} + \text{par value} - \text{purchase price}}{\text{number of years to maturity}}$$

$$= \frac{(17 \text{ yr} \times \$110/\text{yr}) + \$1,000 - \$1,028.75}{17} = \$108.31$$

$$\text{Average investment} = \frac{\text{purchase price} + \text{par value}}{2}$$

$$= \frac{\$1,028.75 + \$1,000}{2} \cong \$1,014.38$$

$$\text{Rate of yield to maturity} = \frac{\text{average interest}}{\text{average investment}}$$

$$= \frac{\$108.31}{\$1,014.38} \cong 0.1068 = 10.68\%$$

The TTR bond gives a better rate of yield to maturity.

Supplementary Problems

7.28 Refer to Table 7.1 and find the total dividends on (a) 120 shares of stock A, (b) 200 shares of stock B, (c) 50 shares of stock C, (d) 90 shares of stock D, and (e) 250 shares of stock E.

7.29 Find the total purchase cost of the shares in Prob. 7.28 at the closing price of the day.

7.30 Find the total purchase cost of the shares in Prob. 7.28 at the previous day's closing price.

7.31 Find the gross proceeds from the sale of the shares in Prob. 7.28 at the high price of that day.

7.32 Find the gross proceeds from the sale of the shares in Prob. 7.28 at the closing price of that day.

7.33 Fairway Electronics issued 20,000 shares of $7\frac{1}{2}\%$, $100 par value preferred stock. Calculate the total amount of dividends to be paid at the end of the year on (a) 1,500 shares, (b) 200 shares, and (c) 380 shares.

7.34 For each of the following, calculate the amount of dividends payable on $100 par value cumulative preferred stock.

	Number of Shares	Dividend Rate (%)	Time Since Last Payment (Years)
(a)	50	5	3
(b)	3,000	7	2
(c)	80	8	4
(d)	150	$6\frac{1}{4}$	1

7.35 Natco, Inc. has outstanding 4,000 shares of $6\frac{1}{2}\%$, $100 par value cumulative preferred stock and 10,000 shares of common stock. The company declares dividends as follows from 1998 to 2001.

1998	$20,000
1999	$45,000
2000	$25,000
2001	$87,000

No dividends are in arrears as of the end of 1997. What amount of dividends is paid each year to (a) preferred and (b) common stock?

7.36 Assuming that the preferred stock is noncumulative, find the total dividends for the common stock in Prob. 7.35 for the 4 years.

7.37 Gemini, Inc. has outstanding 7,000 shares of 8%, $100 par value cumulative preferred stock and 20,000 shares of common stock. Dividends on the preferred stock are currently $45,000 in arrears. If a dividend of $184,000 is declared in the current year, find the dividend per share for (a) preferred stock and (b) common stock.

7.38 Delita Corporation declares a dividend of $72,750 to its 5,000 shares of $8\frac{1}{2}\%$, $50 par value non-cumulative participating preferred stock, and its 15,000 shares of common stock. After each common share has received a dividend of $1.10, the preferred stock participates with the common stock in the distribution of remaining dividend in the ratio of shares in each class. Calculate the dividend per share for (a) preferred and (b) common stock.

7.39 Calculate the dividend per share for each class of stock in Prob. 7.38 assuming that the dividend declared is (a) $76,150, (b) $48,350.

7.40 Assuming that the preferred stock is cumulative participating preferred stock and $7,000 dividends are in arrears, calculate the dividend per share for (a) preferred and (b) common stock in Prob. 7.38.

7.41 Assuming that the preferred stock is cumulative nonparticipating preferred stock and $11,900 dividends are in arrears, calculate the dividend par value for (a) preferred and (b) common stock in Prob. 7.38.

7.42 Calculate the broker's commission at the commission rate of 1.8% on the purchase of (a) 80 shares at $17\frac{7}{8}$, (b) 100 shares at $21\frac{1}{4}$, (c) 280 shares at $31\frac{1}{8}$.

7.43 What is the broker's commission in Prob. 7.42 if the transactions were sales?

7.44 Find the total cost, including 2.1% commission, of a purchase of 320 shares of stock E in Table 7.1 at the day's closing price.

7.45   Find the net proceeds, after a commission of 1.7% has been paid, on the sale of 190 shares of stock B in Table 7.1 at the day's low price.

7.46   Find the total cost for each of the following purchases:

	Number of Shares	Price	Commission Rate (%)
(a)	220	$43\frac{1}{8}$	1.4
(b)	25	$108\frac{7}{8}$	1.8
(c)	320	$7\frac{1}{4}$	2.0

7.47   Find the net proceeds if the transactions in Prob. 7.46 were sales.

7.48   What is the investor's annual yield on common stocks with

(a)   Cost per share of $17.25 and quarterly dividend of $0.55

(b)   Cost per share of $45 and semiannual dividend of $2.12

(c)   Cost per share of $105.75 and annual dividend of $6.80

7.49   Determine the rate of annual yield for each stock in Table 7.1, if bought at the closing price of that day.

7.50   Determine the rate of annual yield for each stock in Table 7.1, if bought at the closing price of the previous day.

7.51   Arlene purchased 200 shares of stock A in Table 7.1 four years ago at $12\frac{1}{8}$ and sold it at the day's high price. If dividends have been constant for the 4-year period, what is (a) her total gain and (b) the annual rate of gain based on cost.

7.52   Assuming that Arlene bought the stock in Prob. 7.51 at $33\frac{3}{4}$, what is (a) her total loss and (b) the annual rate of loss based on cost?

7.53   Find the market price of each $2,000 bond in Table 7.2 at that day's high price.

7.54   At what market price would the $1,000 bonds in Table 7.2 give an 11% rate of current yield?

7.55   At what market price would the $1,000 bonds in Table 7.2 give a $7\frac{1}{2}$% rate of current yield?

7.56   Find the total semiannual interest payable to the owner of two $1,000 bonds A and three $1,000 bonds E in Table 7.2.

7.57   Find the total semiannual interest payable to the investor who owns one $2,000 bond of each type listed in Table 7.2.

7.58   Calculate the premium for the following bonds:

	Face Value	Market Quotation
(a)	$1,000	$107\frac{1}{8}$
(b)	5,000	$101\frac{7}{8}$
(c)	500	$117\frac{1}{2}$

7.59   Calculate the discount for the following bonds:

	Face Value	Market Quotation
(a)	$ 2,000	$73\frac{3}{4}$
(b)	10,000	91
(c)	100,000	$87\frac{1}{4}$

7.60   Find the accrued bond interest on each of the following bond transactions:

	Par Value	Bond Interest Rate	Interest Dates	Date of Sale	Market Quotation	Number of Bonds
(a)	$1,000	$9\frac{1}{4}\%$	June 15, Dec. 15	Oct. 26	$92\frac{1}{2}$	2
(b)	500	8%	Mar. 1, Sept. 1	Feb. 4	87	10
(c)	5,000	$10\frac{1}{2}\%$	Feb. 15, Aug. 15	Apr. 21	101	1
(d)	2,000	12%	June 1, Dec. 1	May 12	$105\frac{7}{8}$	4

7.61   Find the total proceeds of the bond transactions in Prob. 7.60.

7.62   Find the rate of current yield for the bonds in Prob. 7.60.

7.63   Referring to Table 7.2, find the accrued bond interest on each of the following bond transactions:

	Bond	Par Value	Number of Bonds	Last Interest Date	Date of Sale
(a)	A	$1,000	3	Oct. 1	Jan. 5
(b)	B	1,000	2	Sept. 15	Dec. 20
(c)	C	500	6	Apr. 1	June 11
(d)	D	2,000	5	Nov. 15	Mar. 26
(e)	E	5,000	2	May 1	Aug. 29

7.64   Find the total purchase price of the bonds in Prob. 7.63 if purchased at that day's closing price.

7.65   Calculate the rate of current yield for the following bonds:

	Par Value	Bond Interest Rate	Market Quotation	Time to Maturity
(a)	$1,000	$11\frac{3}{4}\%$	$102\frac{3}{8}$	5 yr
(b)	500	$7\frac{1}{2}\%$	86	10 yr
(c)	2,000	12.9%	$112\frac{1}{4}$	8 yr, 6 mo
(d)	5,000	$8\frac{1}{4}\%$	$92\frac{1}{2}$	3 yr, 3 mo

7.66   Estimate the rate of yield to maturity for the bonds in Prob. 7.65.

Answers to Supplementary Problems

7.28 (a) $180, (b) $120, (c) $100, (d) $495, (e) $195

7.29 (a) $2,942.50, (b) $1,925, (c) $5,437.50, (d) $5,793.75, (e) $5,193.75

7.30 (a) $2,837.50, (b) $1,950, (c) $5,456.25, (d) $5,771.25, (e) $5,256.25

7.31 (a) $2,937.50, (b) $1,950, (c) $5,512.50, (d) $5,771.25, (e) $5,181.25

7.32 (a) $2,937.50, (b) $1,925, (c) $5,425, (d) $5,771.25, (e) $5,181.25

7.33 (a) $11,250, (b) $1,500, (c) $2,850

7.34 (a) $750, (b) $42,000, (c) $2,560, (d) $937.50

7.35 (a) 1998: $20,000, 1999: $32,000, 2000: $25,000, 2001: $27,000; (b) 1998: 0, 1999: $13,000, 2000: 0, 2001: $60,000

7.36 $80,000

7.37 (a) $14.43, (b) $4.15

7.38 (a) $6, (b) $2.85

7.39 (a) Preferred: $6.17, common: $3.02; (b) preferred: $4.78, common: $1.63

7.40 (a) $7.05, (b) $2.50

7.41 (a) $6.63, (b) $2.64

7.42 (a) $25.92, (b) $38.25, (c) $157.05

7.43 (a) $25.56, (b) $38.25, (c) $156.69

7.44 $6,781.99

7.45 $1,786.60

7.46 (a) $9,622.86, (b) $2,774.05, (c) $2,368.95

7.47 (a) $9,352.21, (b) $2,669.81, (c) $2,271.15

7.48 (a) 12.75%, (b) 9.42%, (c) 6.43%

7.49 A, 6.12%; B, 6.23%; C, 1.84%; D, 8.56%; E, 3.76%

7.50 A, 6.35%; B, 6.15%; C, 1.83%; D, 8.59%; E, 3.71%

7.51 (a) $3,675, (b) 37.89%

7.52 (a) $650, (b) 2.41%

7.53 A, $2,047.50; B, $1,780; C, $2,202.50; D, $1,497.50; E, $2,060

7.54   A, $852.27; B, $647.73; C, $1,136.36; D, $431.82; E, $790.91

7.55   A, $1,250; B, $950; C, $1,666.67; D, $633.33; E, $1,160

7.56 $244.25

7.57 $424.50

7.58   (a) $71.25, (b) $93.75, (c) $87.50

7.59   (a) $525, (b) $900, (c) $12,750

7.60   (a) $67.32, (b) $170, (c) $96.25, (d) $429.33

7.61   (a) $1,917.32, (b) $4,520, (c) $5,146.25, (d) $8,899.33

7.62   (a) 10%, (b) 9.20%, (c) 10.40%, (d) 11.33%

7.63   (a) $73.44, (b) $37.60, (c) $72.92, (d) $172.85, (e) $285.17

7.64   (a) $3,077.19, (b) $1,817.60, (c) $3,372.92, (d) $7,647.85, (e) $10,585.17

7.65   (a) 11.48%, (b) 8.72%, (c) 11.49%, (d) 8.92%

7.66   (a) 11.14%, (b) 9.57%, (c) 10.80%, (d) 10.97%

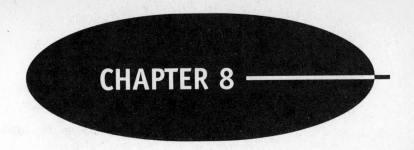

CHAPTER 8

Buying

8.1 TRADE DISCOUNTS

When merchandise is offered for sale, a *list price* or *catalog price* is determined for the item being sold. Often a *manufacturer's suggested retail price* is printed on the item's packaging or in advertisements. These, however, are only suggested prices and are often reduced significantly when the merchandise is actually sold.

Trade discounts are commonly used in trade industries. A plumber or electrician, for example, is usually able to purchase supplies at a much lower price than the consumer. Discounts are frequently given for large quantities of an item purchased or as incentives to sell older merchandise.

The advantage of using discounts is that the manufacturer can print one catalog or price sheet for merchandise being sold to different classes of buyers. Prices to wholesalers, retailers, and consumers, for example, can be changed by simply adjusting the *discount rate*.

Discount rates are expressed as decimals or percentages. The dollar amount of the discount is computed by a simple formula. To compute the net price for the item, subtract the discount from the list price of the item.

$$\boxed{\text{Amount of discount} = \text{discount rate} \times \text{list price}}$$

EXAMPLE 1

Compute the discount and net price for a $250 television set offered at a 16% discount rate.

$$\begin{aligned} \text{Amount of discount} &= \text{discount rate} \times \text{list price} \\ &= 16\% \times \$250 \\ &= 0.16 \times \$250 \\ &= \$40 \end{aligned}$$

The discount is $40. The net price for the television is $250 − $40 = $210.

EXAMPLE 2

A manufacturer of plumbing fixtures labels a sink with a list price of $300. His wholesaler gets a 50% discount, a plumber gets a 40% discount, and a consumer gets a 15% discount. How much will each pay for the sink?

$$\text{Wholesaler's discount} = 50\% \times \$300 = 0.50 \times \$300 = \$150$$
$$\text{Wholesaler's price} = \$300 - \$150 = \$150$$

$$\text{Plumber's discount} = 40\% \times \$300 = 0.40 \times \$300 = \$120$$
$$\text{Plumber's price} = \$300 - \$120 = \$180$$

$$\text{Consumer's discount} = 15\% \times \$300 = 0.15 \times \$300 = \$45$$
$$\text{Consumer's price} = \$300 - \$45 = \$255$$

The *complement* of a discount rate is the discount rate subtracted from 100%. Thus the complement of a 35% discount would be $100\% - 35\% = 65\%$. While a discount rate can be viewed as a percentage "off" the price of an item, the complement of a discount rate is viewed as the percentage of the list price actually paid for the item. The net price for the item can be more conveniently computed by the formula

$$\boxed{\text{Net price} = (100\% - \text{discount rate}) \times \text{list price}}$$

EXAMPLE 3

Use complements to compute the prices paid for the sink of Example 2.

$$\text{Amount paid by wholesaler} = (100\% - 50\%) \times \$300 = 0.50 \times \$300 = \$150$$
$$\text{Amount paid by plumber} = (100\% - 40\%) \times \$300 = 0.60 \times \$300 = \$180$$
$$\text{Amount paid by consumer} = (100\% - 15\%) \times \$300 = 0.85 \times \$300 = \$255$$

Since amount of discount = discount rate × list price, it follows that

$$\boxed{\begin{aligned}\text{Discount rate} &= \frac{\text{amount of discount}}{\text{list price}} \\ \text{List price} &= \frac{\text{amount of discount}}{\text{discount rate}}\end{aligned}}$$

Similarly, since net price = (100% − discount rate) × list price, it follows that

$$\boxed{\text{List price} = \frac{\text{net price}}{100\% - \text{discount rate}}}$$

EXAMPLE 4

Compute the discount rate for a $450 lamp which is sold for $315. The actual discount is $450 - \$315 = \$135$:

$$\text{Discount rate} = \frac{\text{amount of discount}}{\text{list price}} = \frac{\$135}{\$450} = 0.30$$

Expressed as a percentage, the discount rate is 30%.

EXAMPLE 5

Compute the list price of a telephone assuming that a 25% discount was worth $20:

$$\text{List price} = \frac{\text{amount of discount}}{\text{discount rate}} = \frac{\$20}{25\%} = \frac{\$20}{0.25} = \$80$$

EXAMPLE 6

Compute the list price of a fax machine whose net price is $195 if it sold at a 35% discount:

$$\text{List price} = \frac{\text{net price}}{100\% - \text{discount rate}} = \frac{\$195}{100\% - 35\%} = \frac{\$195}{0.65} = \$300$$

SOLVED PROBLEMS

8.1   Compute the discount on an office desk which lists for $240 if a discount of 10% is offered.

SOLUTION

Discount = 10% of $240 = 0.10 × $240 = $24.

8.2   Compute the net price for a painting whose list price is $172 and is offered on sale for 20% off.

SOLUTION

Solution 1:

$$\text{Discount} = 20\% \times \$172 = 0.20 \times \$172 = \$34.40$$
$$\text{Net price} = \$172.00 - \$34.40 = \$137.60$$

Solution 2 (using complements):

$$100\% - 20\% = 80\%$$
$$\text{Net price} = 80\% \times \$172 = 0.80 \times \$172 = \$137.60$$

8.3   A VCR with a list price of $340 went on sale for "25% off." An extended warranty, which was not on sale, sold for $17. How much did George pay (before tax) when he bought both the VCR and extended warranty?

SOLUTION

$$\text{Price of VCR} = (100\% - 75\%) \times \$340 = 0.75 \times \$340 = \$255.$$
$$\text{Price of extended warranty} = \$17 \text{ (no discount is given on the warranty).}$$
$$\text{Total price for both} = \$255 + \$17 = \$272.$$

8.4   A lamp which normally sells for $180 was purchased by a consumer for $120. How much of a discount did the consumer receive?

SOLUTION

The actual discount received was $180 − $120 = $60:

$$\text{Discount rate} = \frac{\text{amount of discount}}{\text{list price}} = \frac{60}{180} = \frac{1}{3} = 33\tfrac{1}{3}\%$$

8.5   Jane spent $150 on a printer on sale for 15% off list price. What was the list price of the printer?

SOLUTION

$$\text{List price} = \frac{\text{net price}}{100\% - \text{discount rate}}$$

Thus

$$\text{List price} = \frac{150}{0.85} = \$176.47$$

8.6 Which actually costs less: a $300 coil of 10-gage wire which is offered with a trade discount of 40% or a $450 coil of 12-gage wire which is offered with a trade discount of 65%?

SOLUTION

Net price of 10-gage wire = $(100\% - 40\%) \times \$300$

$\qquad\qquad\qquad\qquad = 60\% \times \$300 = 0.60 \times \$300 = \$180$

Net price of 12-gage wire = $(100\% - 65\%) \times \$450$

$\qquad\qquad\qquad\qquad = 35\% \times \$450 = 0.35 \times \$450 = \$157.50$

The 12-gage wire is cheaper.

8.2   CHAIN DISCOUNTS

As an extra incentive to purchase a product, some companies and retail stores offer *chain discounts*. To the uninformed consumer such discounts give the illusion of being larger than they really are.

EXAMPLE 7

A stereo unit has a list price of $1,000. It goes on sale at a discount of 30% and then goes on clearance for an additional 20% off. What is the final price of the stereo?

$$\text{First discount} = 30\% \times \$1,000 = 0.30 \times \$1,000 = \$300$$
$$\text{Price after first discount} = \$1,000 - \$300 = \$700$$

$$\text{Second discount} = 20\% \times \$700 = 0.20 \times \$700 = \$140$$
$$\text{Price after second discount} = \$700 - \$140 = \$560$$

The actual selling price is $560.

At first glance, it might appear that the combined discount should be $30\% + 20\% = 50\%$. If that were true, however, the price of the $1,000 stereo would be $500. The discount in example 7 was somewhat less than 50%.

It is a bit more convenient to use complements to compute chain discounts. Since

$\qquad$ Price after 1st discount = $(100\% - \text{1st discount rate}) \times \text{list price}$

and

$\qquad$ Price after 2d discount = $(100\% - \text{2d discount rate}) \times \text{price after 1st discount}$

it follows that

Price after 2d discount = $(100\% - \text{2d discount rate}) \times (100\% - \text{1st discount rate}) \times \text{list price}$

The order in which the discounts are taken is unimportant; the final selling price is the same if you reverse the order of the discounts.

EXAMPLE 8

Consider the stereo in Example 7. Compute the final selling price using complements:

Method 1:

$\qquad$ Price after 1st discount = $(100\% - 30\%) \times \$1000 = 0.70 \times \$1000 = \$700$

$\qquad$ Price after 2d discount = $(100\% - 20\%) \times \$700 = 0.80 \times \$700 = \$560$ (final price)

Method 2:

$$\text{Final price} = (100\% - \text{1st discount rate}) \times (100\% - \text{2d discount rate}) \times \text{list price}$$
$$= (100\% - 30\%) \times (100\% - 20\%) \times \$1,000$$
$$= 70\% \times 80\% \times \$1,000$$
$$= 0.70 \times 0.80 \times \$1,000$$
$$= \$560$$

Method 2 is a much more direct way of solving the problem of chain discounts. It extends in a natural way to three or more successive discounts.

EXAMPLE 9

An evening gown lists for $1,500. It is offered at a discount store for 30% off list price. Since it does not sell, the store offers a second discount of 40% off the discounted price. It still does not sell. In desperation, the store offers 50% off the lowest sale price. What is the final price of the gown?

$$\text{Final price} = (100\% - \text{1st discount rate}) \times (100\% - \text{2d discount rate}) \times (100\% - \text{3d discount rate}) \times \text{list price}$$
$$= (100\% - 30\%) \times (100\% - 40\%) \times (100\% - 50\%) \times \$1,500$$
$$= 70\% \times 60\% \times 50\% \times \$1,500$$
$$= 0.70 \times 0.60 \times 0.50 \times \$1,500$$
$$= \$315$$

To make intelligent comparisons, it is useful to compute the single discount which is equivalent to a chain of successive discounts. Such a number is known as the *single equivalent discount*.

EXAMPLE 10

A $400 barbecue is put on sale at 30% off. At the end of the summer, it is put on clearance for 50% off the sale price. What is the *single* discount equivalent to the chain discounts of 30% and 50% off?

$$\text{Final price} = (100\% - \text{1st discount rate}) \times (100\% - \text{2d discount rate}) \times \$40$$
$$= (100\% - 30\%) \times (100\% - 50\%) \times \$400$$
$$= 0.70 \times 0.50 \times \$400$$
$$= 0.35 \times \$400$$
$$= \$140$$

The final price of the barbecue is $140, which is $260 off the original price of $400. Even though the actual discount taken was broken up into two successive discounts, the problem can be viewed as one discount of $260. As such, the

$$\text{Discount rate} = \frac{\text{amount of discount}}{\text{list price}} = \frac{260}{400} = 0.65 = 65\%$$

In other words, the chain discounts of 30% and 50% are equivalent to the single 65% discount.

To compute the single equivalent discount, follow these steps:

(*a*) Compute the complements of each individual discount.

(*b*) Multiply the complements and express as a percent.

(*c*) Subtract from 100%.

EXAMPLE 11

Use these steps to compute the single equivalent discount in Example 10:

(*a*)   The discounts are 30 and 50%. Their complements are 70 and 50%, respectively.

(*b*) $70\% \times 50\% = 0.70 \times 0.50 = 0.35 = 35\%$

(*c*) $100\% - 35\% = 65\%$

The single equivalent discount is 65%.

SOLVED PROBLEMS

8.7   What is the selling price of a cashmere coat which lists for $400, goes on sale for 40% off, and then goes on clearance for an additional 20% off the sale price?

SOLUTION A

$$1\text{st discount} = 40\% \times \$400 = 0.40 \times \$400 = \$160$$
$$\text{Price after 1st discount} = \$400 - \$160 = \$240$$

$$2\text{d discount} = 20\% \times \$240 = \$48$$
$$\text{Price after 2d discount} = \$240 - \$48 = \$192$$

SOLUTION B

$$\text{Price after 1st discount} = (100\% - 40\%) \times \$400 = 0.60 \times \$400 = \$240$$
$$\text{Price after 2d discount} = (100\% - 20\%) \times \$240 = 0.80 \times \$240 = \$192$$

SOLUTION C

$$\text{Final price} = (100\% - 40\%) \times (100\% - 20\%) \times \$400$$
$$= 0.60 \times 0.80 \times \$400$$
$$= 0.48 \times \$400$$
$$= \$192$$

8.8   The list price of a dining-room set is $3,500 with discounts of 20% and 30%. What is the final selling price?

SOLUTION

$$\text{Final selling price} = (100\% - 20\%) \times (100\% - 30\%) \times \$3,500$$
$$= 80\% \times 70\% \times \$3,500$$
$$= 0.80 \times 0.70 \times \$3,500$$
$$= 0.56 \times \$3,500$$
$$= \$1,960$$

8.9   Compute the sale price of a kitchen stove whose list price is $1,400 if it is given successive discounts of 25% and 40%. Verify that the price is the same regardless of the order in which the discounts are taken.

SOLUTION

25% discount followed by 40% discount:

$$\text{Price after 25\% discount} = (100\% - 25\%) \times \$1,400 = 0.75 \times \$1,400 = \$1,050$$
$$\text{Price after 40\% discount} = (100\% - 40\%) \times \$1,050 = 0.60 \times \$1,050 = \$630$$

40% discount followed by 25% discount:

$$\text{Price after 40\% discount} = (100\% - 40\%) \times \$1,400 = 0.60 \times \$1,400 = \$840$$
$$\text{Price after 25\% discount} = (100\% - 25\%) \times \$840 = 0.75 \times \$840 = \$630$$

Either way the price after both discounts is $630.

8.10 Determine the single discount equivalent to a chain discount of 25% and 40%. Then compute the price of the stove in problem 8.9.

SOLUTION

The complements of the two discounts are 75% and 60%, respectively:

$$75\% \times 60\% = 0.75 \times 0.60 = 0.45 = 45\%$$
$$100\% - 45\% = 55\%$$

The single equivalent discount is 55%.

$$\text{Price of stove} = (100\% - 55\%) \times \$1,400 = 45\% \times 1,400 = 0.45 \times 1,400 = \$630$$

8.11 Which is the best deal?

(*a*) A 10% discount followed by a 60% discount

(*b*) A 20% discount followed by a 50% discount

(*c*) A 30% discount followed by a 40% discount

SOLUTION

We compute the equivalent single discount for each case:

(*a*) $(100\% - 10\%) \times (100\% - 60\%) = 0.90 \times 0.40 = 0.36 = 36\%$:

$$\text{Single equivalent discount} = 100\% - 36\% = 64\%$$

(*b*) $(100\% - 20\%) \times (100\% - 50\%) = 0.80 \times 0.50 = 0.40 = 40\%$:

$$\text{Single equivalent discount} = 100\% - 40\% = 60\%$$

(*c*) $(100\% - 30\%) \times (100\% - 40\%) = 0.70 \times 0.60 = 0.42 = 42\%$:

$$\text{Single equivalent discount} = 100\% - 42\% = 58\%$$

Clearly (*a*) gives the largest discount.

8.12 Compute the single equivalent discount of three successive 20% discounts.

SOLUTION

$$
\begin{aligned}
(100\% - 20\%) \times (100\% - 20\%) \times (100\% - 20\%) &= 80\% \times 80\% \times 80\% \\
&= 0.80 \times 0.80 \times 0.80 \\
&= 0.512 \\
&= 51.2\% \\
100\% - 51.2\% &= 48.8\%.
\end{aligned}
$$

8.3 CASH DISCOUNTS

Cash discounts are discounts applied to bills which are paid within a specified period of time. They are given by large companies as an inducement to pay bills quickly.

Cash discounts are often listed under the heading *terms* on a bill or invoice. For example, 2/10, net 30 (sometimes written 2/10, n/30) means that the customer is entitled to receive a 2% discount if the bill is paid within 10 days; otherwise the customer has 30 days to pay the bill at the invoice price. After that there may be a late charge or interest may be imposed on the past due balance.

Delivery charges and other special fees are seldom included in a cash discount.

EXAMPLE 12

An invoice of $520 dated April 1 has terms 2/10, net 30. What is the discount if the bill is paid on or before April 11? How much should the customer pay?

$$\text{Discount} = 2\% \text{ of } \$520 = 0.02 \times 520 = \$10.40$$

The customer should pay $520.00 − $10.40 = $509.60. If the bill is paid between April 12 and May 1, the full $520 must be paid.

Sometimes a company will offer several different payment options. These must be clearly stated on the bill.

EXAMPLE 13

Budget Press received a $720 bill from its paper supplier, dated August 1, with terms 3/10, 2/20, 1/30, net/60. How much should Budget Press pay their supplier?

(*a*)   If the bill is paid on before August 11, the discount is 3% × $720 = $21.60. Budget Press should pay $720.00 − $21.60 = $698.40.

(*b*)   If the bill is paid between August 12 and 21, the discount is 2% × $720 = $14.40. They should pay $720.00 − $14.40 = $705.60.

(*c*)   If the bill is paid between August 22 and 31, the discount is 1% × $720 = $7.20. In this case $720 − $7.20 = $712.80 must be paid.

(*d*)   If the bill is paid between September 1 and 30, the full $720 is due.

Discount periods do not always start on the invoice date. There are additional ways of stating the time a bill is due:

End of month (EOM) or prox.	2/10 EOM means that the 10-day discount period begins on the first day of the month following the invoice. Thus if a bill is received Jan. 28, the customer has until Feb. 10 to receive a 2% discount.
Receipt of goods (ROG)	2/10 ROG means that the discount period begins when the merchandise is received by the buyer. Typically, invoices are mailed the same day the goods are shipped, but usually arrive sooner. The buyer has 10 days after receiving the merchandise to pay the discounted price.
X (extra)	2/10–90X means that the buyer has an extra 90 days (100 in total) to pay for the merchandise at 2% discount. This is used as an extra incentive for customers to buy out-of-season merchandise. Because they can delay payment, they are likely to order sooner.

EXAMPLE 14

An invoice for $5,000 in merchandise is dated July 27 and has credit terms 3/10, 1/20, net 30 EOM. How much money should be paid if payment is received on (a) August 1? (b) August 15? (c) August 25?

(a) Since the invoice is labeled EOM, the buyer has until August 10 to receive a 3% discount: 3% of $5,000 = 0.03 × $5,000 = $150; $5,000 − $150 = $4,850.

(b) Since August 15 falls within 20 days of the end of July, the buyer is entitled to a 1% discount: 1% of $5,000 = $50; $5,000 − $50 = $4,950.

(c) Since August 25 falls after the 20-day period starting on July 31, there is no discount. The buyer must pay the full invoice of $5,000.

EXAMPLE 15

The list price of a meat-slicing machine is $780 with a trade discount of 22%. If the terms of the invoice are 2/10, net 30 ROG, how much should the butcher remit if he pays his bill within 10 days of receipt of the machine?

The butcher's trade discount is 22%:

$$22\% \text{ of } \$780 = 0.22 \times 780 = \$171.60$$

so he must pay

$$\$780 - \$171.60 = \$608.40.$$

His discount for prompt payment is

$$2\% \text{ of } \$608.40 = \$12.17$$

so he must pay

$$\$608.40 - \$12.17 = \$596.23.$$

It is a bit more convenient to think of this as a chain discount: 22% followed by 2%. His final payment is then computed:

$$(100\% - 22\%) \times (100\% - 2\%) \times \$780 = 0.78 \times 0.98 \times \$780 = \$596.23$$

SOLVED PROBLEMS

8.13 ABC Supply Company receives a bill for $7,200, dated June 15, with terms 5/10, net 30. How much must they pay if payment is made June 20?

SOLUTION

Since June 20 is within 10 days of the invoice date, they are entitled to a 5% discount:

$$(100\% - 5\%) \times \$7,200 = 0.95 \times \$7,200 = \$6,840$$

8.14 Jemco Plumbing Supply receives an invoice of $7,500 for copper pipe. Terms are 2/10, 1/15, net 25. How much should Jemco pay if they send payment immediately on receipt of the invoice?

SOLUTION

Since they send payment well before 10 days have elapsed, they are entitled to a 2% discount:

$$(100\% - 2\%) \times \$7,500 = 0.98 \times \$7,500 = \$7,350$$

8.15 Jacob's Hardware received an invoice for $1,475 dated October 23 for nails and screws. The price included $25 for delivery. Terms were 4/10, 2/15, 1/20, net 30 EOM. How much should Jacob pay if his payment is received on (a) November 9 and (b) November 19?

SOLUTION

(a)   Although November 9 is more than 10 days past the invoice date, EOM indicates that he has until November 10 to receive a 4% discount. Delivery price is not included in the discount:

$$(100\% - 4\%) \times \$1,450 = 0.96 \times \$1,450 = \$1,392$$
$$\$1,392 + \$25 = \$1,417 \qquad \text{(payment should be \$1,417)}$$

(b)   Since November 19 is within 20 days of the end of October, but more than 15 days, Jacob is entitled to a 1% discount:

$$(100\% - 1\%) \times \$1,450 = 0.99 \times \$1,450 = \$1,435.50$$
$$\$1,435.50 + \$25 = \$1,460.50 \qquad \text{(payment should be \$1,460.50)}$$

8.16 On July 1, AAA Refrigeration Corp. paid two bills dated June 18. The first bill was for $3,000 with terms 3/10, 2/15, net 30 and the second was for $2,500 with terms 2/10, 1/20, net 30. If payment is to be made with one check, what should the payment amount be?

SOLUTION

Since there are 30 days in June, the payment date, July 1, is more than 10, but less than 15 days past the invoice date, June 18. The discount on the first bill is 2%:

$$(100\% - 2\%) \times \$3,000 = 0.98 \times \$3,000 = \$2,940$$

The discount on the second bill is 1%:

$$(100\% - 1\%) \times \$2,500 = 0.99 \times \$2,500 = \$2,475$$

Payment amount = $2,940 + $2,475 = $5,415.

8.17 A carpeting retailer received an invoice in the amount of $6,875 dated September 15 which included $35 for shipping and $15 for special handling. Terms were 5/10, 2/20, net 30 ROG. If the goods were delivered on September 23, and the retailer pays the bill on October 1, how much should the retailer pay?

SOLUTION

Since the payment date of October 1 is within 10 days of delivery, the retailer is entitled to a 5% discount on the cost of the goods only (not shipping or handling). The cost of the goods is $6,875 − $35 − $15 = $6,825:

$$(100\% - 5\%) \times \$6,825 = 0.95 \times \$6,825 = \$6,483.75$$

The delivery and handling ($50 total) must be added to this amount, so the retailer must pay a total of $6,533.75.

8.18 ICT Computer Corp. ordered 15 computers with a list price of $990 each. They are entitled to a trade discount of 15% and an additional discount of 10% for quantity. They receive an invoice dated June 15 with terms 3/15, net 30. How much should they pay if their payment is made before July 1?

SOLUTION

The total price of the order is $15 \times \$990 = \$14{,}850$. The two discounts, applied successively, bring their invoice total to

$$(100\% - 15\%) \times (100\% - 10\%) \times \$14{,}850 = 0.85 \times 0.90 \times \$14{,}850 = \$11{,}360.25$$

Because they pay their bill within 15 days, they are entitled to an additional 3% discount:

$$(100\% - 3\%) \times \$11{,}360.25 = 0.97 \times \$11{,}360.25 = \$11{,}019.44$$

8.4 PARTIAL PAYMENTS

Situations often occur where a buyer wants to pay a bill early in order to receive a discount, but does not have sufficient funds to pay the bill in its entirety. In this case, the buyer will make a partial payment and receive a discount on a portion of the bill. The buyer's account will be credited and the difference will be owed.

To determine how much money to credit the account, we must compute how much of the balance is actually paid off by the discounted payment.

EXAMPLE 16

An invoice of $4,500 is sent to a buyer on July 5 with terms 3/10, net 30. The buyer, unable to pay the full amount within 10 days, makes a partial payment of $2,500 on July 12. What is the balance due on the account after payment is made?

Since the buyer makes the payment within 10 days of the invoice date, she is entitled to a 3% discount. The amount paid, therefore, represents 97% $(100\% - 3\%)$ of the amount to be credited. If we let x represent the amount to be credited to her account, 97% of $x = \$2{,}500$:

$$0.97x = \$2{,}500$$
$$x = \frac{\$2{,}500}{0.97}$$
$$x = \$2{,}577.32$$

Thus $2,577.32 is credited to the buyer's account. The amount owed is $\$4{,}500 - \$2{,}577.32 = \$1{,}922.68$.

EXAMPLE 17

Let us determine how much money the buyer in Example 16 saved by making her partial payment early. Since she paid $2,500 and presumably paid the balance of $1,922.68 within 30 days of the invoice date, she has paid a total of $\$2{,}500.00 + \$1{,}922.68 = \$4{,}422.68$. She has saved $\$4{,}500.00 - \$4{,}422.68 = \$77.32$.

SOLVED PROBLEMS

8.19 Leonard receives a bill for $3,000 with terms 5/10, net 30. How much credit will he receive if he pays half the bill within 10 days?

SOLUTION

Let x represent the credit he will receive. Since he pays $1,500 early, he is entitled to a 5% discount. Since he actually pays 95% $(100\% - 5\%)$ of x, we have

$$0.95x = \$1{,}500$$
$$x = \frac{\$1{,}500}{0.95}$$
$$x = \$1{,}578.95$$

Leonard receives a credit on his account of $1,578.95.

8.20 Betty's Dress Shop usually likes to pay its bills early to take advantage of discounts. On July 1, Betty receives a bill from one of her suppliers for $3,700 with terms 3/10, 2/20, net 30. What will her balance be if she makes a partial payment of $2,000 on (a) July 9 and (b) July 15?

SOLUTION

(a) If Betty pays her bill within 10 days, she is entitled to a 3% discount on the amount paid. We let x represent the amount of the balance to be credited to her account. Since she actually pays only 97% of this amount, we have

$$0.97x = \$2,000$$
$$x = \frac{\$2,000}{0.97}$$
$$x = \$2,061.86$$

Her account is credited $2,061.86. Her balance due is $3,700 − $2,061.86 = $1,638.14.

(b) On July 15, she is only entitled to a 2% discount. Since she pays 98% of the amount due:

$$0.98x = \$2,000$$
$$x = \frac{\$2,000}{0.98}$$
$$x = \$2,040.82$$

Her account is credited $2,040.82. Her balance due is $3,700.00 − $2,040.82 = $1,659.18.

8.21 Peter's Steak House receives a bill dated April 10, from their meat supplier, in the amount of $4,200. Terms are 4/10, 2/20, net 30. On April 15 Peter pays $1,500 and on April 23 he pays another $1,000. How much must he then pay to clear his debt?

SOLUTION

Since he pays the $1,500 before 10 days, he is entitled to a 4% discount. If x represents the credit he will receive on his account, since he pays only 96% of x, we have

$$0.96x = \$1,500$$
$$x = \frac{\$1,500}{0.96}$$
$$x = \$1,562.50$$

His balance due is $4,200 − $1,562.50 = $2,637.50. Now he pays $1,000 but is entitled to only a 2% discount. Let y represent the credit he will receive for that payment:

$$0.98y = \$1,000$$
$$y = \frac{\$1,000}{0.98}$$
$$y = \$1,020.41$$

This further reduces his balance to $2,637.50 − $1,020.41 = $1,617.09. This is the amount due before 30 days.

Supplementary Problems

8.22   (*a*) Compute the discount on a $275 typewriter offered at a 10% discount rate. (*b*) What is the sale price?

8.23   What is the trade discount on a prefabricated fireplace which has a list price of $1,700 given a discount rate of 15%?

8.24   A manufacturer of crystal chandeliers offers a 40% discount to interior decorators and a 15% discount to consumers who visit their retail outlet. If a particular chandelier has a list price of $1,300, how much will it cost (*a*) an interior decorator and (*b*) a consumer?

8.25   A shipment of books had a list price of $2,140 but was sold to a bookseller for $1,819. What was the trade discount rate?

8.26   A sofa with a list price of $575 is offered to a decorator for $460. What was the discount rate?

8.27   An armoire had a sale price of $280. If it was discounted 30%, what was its original list price?

8.28   Don paid $333.75 for a new VCR and three videotapes. The VCR was on sale at a discount of 15%, but the videotapes were not. If each videotape cost $5.00, what was the list price of the VCR?

8.29   A new automobile has a price of $24,500. Of this amount $2,800 are options which were added on by the dealer. If the dealer discounts the base price of the car by 20%, but not the options, what is the sale price of the automobile?

8.30   Which costs less: a wool suit which lists for $450 but is put on sale at an 18% discount or a cotton blend which lists for $500 but is given a 22% discount?

8.31   Macy's sells a men's suit for $450 less 25%. Saks sells the identical suit for $475 less discounts of 20% and 10%. Which store has the suit for a lower price?

8.32   Chicken feed sells for $1.50 a pound. Farmer Gray buys 750 lb of chicken feed. How much must he pay if he is given a 7% farm cooperative discount and a 5% discount for quantity?

8.33   A liquor store discounts its entire stock by 20%. Furthermore, if you buy a case of wine, you receive an additional 10% discount. How much will a case (12 bottles) of Chardonnay, which lists for $12 a bottle, cost?

8.34   What is the net price of a bowling ball which lists for $95, is put on sale for 10% off, and then put on clearance for an additional 20% off?

8.35   A piano originally costs $5,000. It is given successive discounts of 30 and 45%. Verify that the final selling price is the same regardless of the order in which the discounts are taken.

8.36   A snowblower is sold at a discount store at 15% off list price. On March 1, the store manager puts it on sale for an additional 20% off. What is the single equivalent discount for the snowblower?

8.37   Which will lead to a lower price for the consumer?

   (*a*)   A 10% discount followed by a 40% discount

   (*b*)   A 20% discount followed by a 30% discount

   (*c*)   Two successive 25% discounts

8.38   What is the single equivalent discount for a tennis racket which is given successive discounts of 10% and 20%?

8.39   A-1 Home Improvements received a delivery of aluminum siding listing for $1,750. The company receives a 15% trade discount and, because they are such a good customer, an additional 10% discount for quantity. Furthermore, they pay their bill within 5 days, so they receive an additional 5% off. How much money should A-1 pay their supplier?

8.40   What is the single equivalent discount of successive 10%, 15%, and 20% discounts?

8.41   The Swiss Ski Shop pays $2,422.50 after receiving successive discounts of 15% and 25% for an order of ski equipment. What was the list price of the equipment received?

8.42   An invoice of $470 dated October 17 has terms 2/10, 1/20, net 30. How much would a buyer be expected to pay if the bill is paid on (*a*) October 22 and (*b*) November 1?

8.43   A delicatessen received a bill for $1,700 from its food supplier dated May 27. Its terms were 4/10, 2/20, net 30 EOM. How much would the owner have to pay if the bill is paid on (*a*) June 5, (*b*) June 15, and (*c*) June 28?

8.44   A shipment of furniture is sent from a North Carolina factory to the Empire Furniture Store on May 10. The invoice of $12,000 with terms 5/10, 3/20, net 30 ROG arrives on May 13, but the furniture is not received until May 20. If the furniture dealer pays the bill on May 25, how much money must he pay the factory?

8.45   A businesswoman decides to pay her bill early and receive a discount only if her discount amounts to $50 or more. She receives a bill for $1,700 with terms $2\frac{1}{2}$/10, net 30. Should she pay the bill within 10 days?

8.46   A health club buys a new rowing machine which has a list price of $2,500. Because they are a good customer, the club receives a 12% trade discount. The terms of the invoice are 2/15, net 30. How much must the club pay for the machine if they pay the bill within 12 days of receipt?

8.47   An invoice of $7,000 is sent to Beverly's Beauty Shop on August 1 with terms 5/10, net 30. Beverly pays $3,000 on August 6.

   (*a*)   How much must she pay at the end of the month?

   (*b*)   How much did Beverly save by making an early partial payment?

8.48   Barney is having business trouble, so when he receives a $15,000 bill on July 10 with terms 2/15, net 30, he decides to pay one-third of the bill on July 20 and the balance on July 30. How much must he send on July 30?

8.49   Melissa receives an invoice for $3,000 with terms 2/10, net 30. How much money will Melissa save if she pays $1,200 within 10 days and the balance 20 days later?

8.50   Crazy Harry's Electronics store receives an invoice on February 1 for $17,000 worth of TVs. Terms are 5/5, 3/15, net 30. Harry makes a payment of $5,000 on February 5 and another $5,000 payment on February 15. If he wants to pay his balance in full on February 28, how much money must he send?

8.51   Which payment sequence is most advantageous for a building supply retailer who receives a bill on April 1 for $60,000 with terms 4/10, 2/15, net 30?

   (*a*)   Pay $30,000 on April 15 and the balance on April 30

   (*b*)   Pay $20,000 on April 10, $20,000 on April 15, and the balance on April 30

   (*c*)   Pay the bill in full on April 15

Answers to Supplementary Problems

8.22 (*a*) $27.50, (*b*) $247.50

8.23 $255

8.24 (*a*) $780, (*b*) $1,105

8.25 15%

8.26 20%

8.27 $400

8.28 $375

8.29 $20,160

8.30 The wool suit

8.31 Macy's

8.32 $993.94

8.33 $103.68

8.34 $68.40

8.35 Either way, the price is $1,925

8.36 32%

8.37 (*a*)

8.38 28%

8.39 $1,271.81

8.40 38.8%

8.41 $3,800

8.42 (*a*) $460.60, (*b*) $465.30

8.43 (*a*) $1,632, (*b*) $1,666, (*c*) $1,700

8.44 $11,400

8.45 No; her savings are only $42.50

8.46 $2,156

8.47 (*a*) $3,842.11, (*b*) $157.89

8.48 $9,897.96

8.49 $24.49

8.50 $6,582.20

8.51 (*b*)

CHAPTER 9

Selling

9.1 MARKUP IN GENERAL

In order to make a profit, each company must sell its products for more than the products cost the company to make or buy. The difference between a product's cost and selling price is referred to as *markup*.

EXAMPLE 1

A washing machine selling for $300 costs the seller $200. The markup is

$$\text{Selling price} - \text{cost} = \text{markup}$$
$$\$300 - \$200 = \$100$$

SOLVED PROBLEMS

9.1 Find the markup if (*a*) cost is $15 and selling price is $27, (*b*) cost is $30 and selling price is $42.65, and (*c*) cost is $21.50 and selling price is $52.87.

SOLUTION

(*a*)
$$\text{Selling price} - \text{cost} = \text{markup}$$
$$\$27 - \$15 = \$12$$

(*b*)
$$\text{Selling price} - \text{cost} = \text{markup}$$
$$\$42.65 - \$30 = \$12.65$$

(*c*)
$$\text{Selling price} - \text{cost} = \text{markup}$$
$$\$52.87 - \$21.50 = \$31.37$$

9.2 If Johnson Sporting Goods, Ltd. sells a tent for $89.99 and their cost is $52.40, what is the markup?

SOLUTION

$$\text{Selling price} - \text{cost} = \text{markup}$$
$$\$89.99 - \$52.40 = \$37.59$$

9.3 Reed Stereo purchased cassette tapes for $2.95 each. If they sell them for $7.95, what is the markup?

SOLUTION

$$\text{Selling price} - \text{cost} = \text{markup}$$
$$\$7.95 - \$2.95 = \$5$$

9.4	What is the markup on an automobile that sells for $7,958 and costs the dealer $4,621.98?

SOLUTION

$$\text{Selling price} - \text{cost} = \text{markup}$$
$$\$7,958 - \$4,621.98 = \$3,336.02$$

9.5	Shim. Inc. decides to sell lawn chairs for $28.47. They paid $15.25 for each chair. What is the markup?

SOLUTION

$$\text{Selling price} - \text{cost} = \text{markup}$$
$$\$28.47 - \$15.25 = \$13.22$$

9.2 PERCENT MARKUP

Markup is generally expressed in terms of a percent:

$$\text{Percent} = \frac{\text{percentage}}{\text{base}} \times 100$$

where	percent		= markup percent

percentage = markup

base		= selling price or cost

By substitution, we have

$$\% \text{ Markup} = \frac{\text{markup}}{\text{selling price or cost}} \times 100$$

9.3 SELLING PRICE AS THE BASE

EXAMPLE 2

A book selling for $8 cost the seller $6. What is the percent markup based on selling price?

$$\text{Markup} = \text{selling price} - \text{cost}$$
$$= \$8 - \$6 = 2$$

$$\% \text{ Markup} = \frac{\text{markup}}{\text{selling price}} \times 100$$
$$= \frac{\$2}{\$8} \times 100 = 25\%$$

We can use the percent markup to compute either the cost or the selling price.

EXAMPLE 3

A book selling for $8 has a markup of 25% of retail (i.e., selling price). What is the cost?

$$\% \text{ Markup} = \frac{\text{markup}}{\text{selling price}} \times 100$$

$$25\% = \frac{\text{markup}}{\$8} \times 100$$

$$\$8 \times 0.25 = \text{markup}$$

$$\$2 =$$

$$\text{Markup} = \text{selling price} - \text{cost}$$

$$\$2 = \$8 - \text{cost}$$

$$\$8 - \$2 = \text{cost}$$

$$\$6 =$$

EXAMPLE 4

A book has a markup of $2, which is 25% of the selling price. What is the selling price?

$$\% \text{ Markup} = \frac{\text{markup}}{\text{selling price}} \times 100$$

$$25\% = \frac{\$2}{\text{selling price}} \times 100$$

$$\text{Selling price} = \frac{\$2}{0.25} = \$8$$

SOLVED PROBLEMS

9.6   Find the percent markup of retail (i.e., based on selling price) when (*a*) retail = $23.40 and cost = $17.20, (*b*) retail = $46.41 and cost = $21.25, and (*c*) retail = $164.60 and cost = $126.

SOLUTION

(*a*)

$$\text{Selling price} - \text{cost} = \text{markup}$$
$$\$23.40 - \$17.20 = \$6.20$$

$$\% \text{ Markup} = \frac{\text{markup}}{\text{selling price}} \times 100$$

$$= \frac{\$6.20}{\$23.40} \times 100 = 26.5\%$$

(*b*)

$$\text{Selling price} - \text{cost} = \text{markup}$$
$$\$46.41 - \$21.25 = \$25.16$$

$$\% \text{ Markup} = \frac{\text{markup}}{\text{selling price}} \times 100$$

$$= \frac{\$25.16}{\$46.41} \times 100 = 54.21\%$$

(c)

$$\text{Selling price} - \text{cost} = \text{markup}$$
$$\$164.60 - \$126 = \$38.60$$

$$\% \text{ Markup} = \frac{\text{markup}}{\text{selling price}} \times 100$$

$$= \frac{\$38.60}{\$126} \times 100 = 23.45\%$$

9.7 If the markup is \$7 on a pair of jeans which costs Jones Bros. \$18, what is the percent markup based on retail?

SOLUTION

$$\text{Selling price} - \text{cost} = \text{markup}$$
$$\text{Selling price} = \text{markup} + \text{cost}$$
$$= \$7 + \$18 = \$25$$

$$\% \text{ Markup} = \frac{\text{markup}}{\text{selling price}} \times 100$$

$$= \frac{\$7}{\$25} \times 100 = 28\%$$

9.8 Dancin' Shoes has a markup of \$7.59 on a pair of shoes they sell for \$19.25. Find (a) the cost and (b) the percent markup based on retail.

SOLUTION

(a)

$$\text{Selling price} - \text{cost} = \text{markup}$$
$$\text{Cost} = \text{selling price} - \text{markup}$$
$$= \$19.25 - \$7.59 = \$11.66$$

(b)

$$\% \text{ Markup} = \frac{\text{markup}}{\text{selling price}} \times 100$$

$$= \frac{\$7.59}{\$19.25} \times 100$$

$$= 39.43\%$$

9.9 If an item costs \$0.79 and sells for \$1.25, find (a) the markup and (b) percent markup based on retail.

SOLUTION

(a)

$$\text{Selling price} - \text{cost} = \text{markup}$$
$$\$1.25 - \$0.79 = \$0.46$$

(b)

$$\% \text{ Markup} = \frac{\text{markup}}{\text{selling price}} \times 100$$

$$= \frac{\$0.46}{\$1.25} = 36.8\%$$

9.10 Nature's Way, a sporting goods store, buys snow shoes for $26.50 a pair and sells them for $79.27. What is (a) the markup and (b) the percent markup based on retail?

SOLUTION

(a)

$$\text{Markup} = \text{selling price} - \text{cost}$$
$$\$52.77 = \$79.27 - \$26.50$$

(b)

$$\% \text{ Markup} = \frac{\text{markup}}{\text{selling price}} \times 100$$
$$= \frac{\$52.77}{\$79.27} \times 100 = 66.57\%$$

9.4   COST AS THE BASE

When cost is used as the base for markup percent, it is sometimes referred to as "markon." It has the advantage of expressing clearly the fact that the price increase is directly added to the base (cost).

$$\% \text{ Markup} = \frac{\text{markup}}{\text{cost}} \times 100$$

EXAMPLE 5

A record album that sells for $6 costs $4. What is the percent markup based on cost?

$$\text{Selling price} - \text{cost} = \text{markup}$$
$$\$6 - \$4 = \$2$$

$$\% \text{ Markup} = \frac{\text{markup}}{\text{cost}} \times 100$$

$$= \frac{\$2}{\$4} \times 100 = 50\%$$

To calculate the cost from the percent markup and the selling price, we solve the preceding formula for cost as follows:

$$\% \text{ Markup} = \frac{\text{markup}}{\text{cost}} \times 100$$

Since markup = selling price − cost, by substitution we have

$$\% \text{ Markup} = \frac{\text{selling price} - \text{cost}}{\text{cost}} \times 100$$

$$\frac{\% \text{ Markup}}{100} = \frac{\text{selling price}}{\text{cost}} - 1$$

$$\frac{\% \text{ Markup}}{100} + 1 = \frac{\text{selling price}}{\text{cost}}$$

$$\text{Cost} = \frac{\text{selling price}}{(\% \text{ markup}/100) + 1}$$

Note that the denominator of this equation [(% markup/100) ÷ 1] is simply 1 plus the percent markup expressed as a decimal.

EXAMPLE 6

If an item selling for $72 has a 20% markup on cost, what is the cost?

$$\text{Cost} = \frac{\text{selling price}}{(\%\ \text{markup}/100) + 1}$$

$$= \frac{\$72}{\dfrac{20\%}{100} + 1} = \frac{\$72}{0.20 + 1}$$

$$= \frac{\$72}{1.20} = \$60$$

To calculate selling price from cost and percent markup, we restate the formula

$$\text{Selling price} - \text{cost} = \text{markup}$$

as

$$\text{Selling price} = \text{cost} + \text{markup}$$

Since

$$\%\ \text{markup} = \frac{\text{markup}}{\text{cost}} \times 100$$

then

$$\frac{\%\ \text{Markup}}{100} \times \text{cost} = \text{markup}$$

By substitution we have

$$\text{Selling price} = \text{cost} + \left(\frac{\%\ \text{markup}}{100} \times \text{cost} \right)$$

Note that % markup/100 is simply the percent expressed as a decimal.

EXAMPLE 7

If a sweater which costs $10 has a markup of 30% on cost, what is the selling price?

$$\text{Selling price} = \text{cost} + \left(\frac{\%\ \text{markup}}{100} \times \text{cost} \right)$$

$$= \$10 + (0.30)(\$10) = \$10 + \$3 = \$13$$

Alternative solution:

If we let cost = 100%, then

$$\text{Selling price} = \text{cost} + \text{markup}$$
$$= 100\% + 30\% = 130\% \text{ of cost}$$
$$\text{Selling price} = 130\% \times \text{cost}$$
$$= 1.3 \times \$10 = \$13$$

SOLVED PROBLEMS

9.11 Jones Company purchases radios at $150 each. Their markup based on cost is 25%. What is the selling price?

  SOLUTION

$$\text{Selling price} = \text{cost} + \left(\frac{\%\ \text{markup}}{100} + \text{cost} \right)$$

$$= \$150 + (0.25 \times \$150) = \$150 + \$37.50 = \$187.50$$

9.12   Calvin Jenks purchases designer jeans at $17.95 a pair. The markup based on cost is 41%. What is the selling price?

SOLUTION

$$\text{Selling price} = \$17.95 + (0.41 \times 17.95) = \$17.95 + \$7.36 = \$25.31$$

9.13   Nail polish is sold by the manufacturer at $2.50. The dealer's markup is 35% on retail. What is the selling price?

SOLUTION

$$
\begin{aligned}
\text{Cost} &= \text{selling price} - \text{markup} \\
&= 100\% - 35\% \\
&= 65\% \text{ of retail}
\end{aligned}
$$

$$
\begin{aligned}
\text{Cost} &= 65\% \times \text{selling price} \\
\$2.50 &= 65\% \times \text{selling price} \\
\frac{\$2.50}{0.65} &= \text{selling price} \\
&= \$3.85
\end{aligned}
$$

9.14   Hondor, Inc. purchased a microwave oven for $295.71 and wants to mark up 40% on retail. What must the selling price be?

SOLUTION

$$
\begin{aligned}
\text{Cost} &= \text{selling price} - \text{markup} \\
&= 100\% - 40\% = 60\% \text{ of retail}
\end{aligned}
$$

$$
\begin{aligned}
\text{Cost} &= 60\% \times \text{selling price} \\
\$295.71 &= 60\% \times \text{selling price} \\
\frac{\$295.71}{0.60} &= \text{selling price} \\
&= \$492.85
\end{aligned}
$$

9.15   A boutique buys handbags for $19.28 and wants a markup of 56% on retail. Find the selling price.

SOLUTION

$$
\begin{aligned}
\text{Cost} &= \text{selling price} - \text{markup} \\
&= 100\% - 56\% = 44\% \text{ of retail}
\end{aligned}
$$

$$
\begin{aligned}
\text{Cost} &= 44\% \times \text{selling price} \\
\$19.28 &= 44\% \times \text{selling price} \\
\frac{\$19.28}{0.44} &= \text{selling price} \\
&= \$43.82
\end{aligned}
$$

9.16 June's Boutique plans to sell an ascot for $9.59. Her markup on cost is 75%. What is her cost?

SOLUTION

$$\text{Cost} = \frac{\text{selling price}}{\dfrac{\%\ \text{markup}}{100} + 1}$$

$$= \frac{\$9.59}{\dfrac{75\%}{100} + 1} = \frac{\$9.59}{1.75} = \$5.48$$

Alternative solution:

$$\text{Selling price} = \text{cost} + \text{markup}$$
$$= 100\% + 75\% = 175\% \text{ of cost}$$

$$\text{Selling price} = 175\% \times \text{cost}$$
$$\$9.59 = 175\% \times \text{cost}$$

$$\frac{\$9.59}{1.75} = \text{cost}$$
$$= \$5.48$$

9.17 Solco TV & Appliances sells television sets for $674. Their markup on cost is 92%. Find their cost.

SOLUTION

$$\text{Cost} = \frac{\text{selling price}}{\dfrac{\%\ \text{markup}}{100} + 1}$$

$$= \frac{\$674}{\dfrac{92\%}{100} + 1} = \frac{\$674}{0.92 + 1}$$

$$= \frac{\$674}{1.92} = \$351.04$$

9.18 Jones, Ltd. sells a recliner for $479.57. If their markup is 40% on retail, what is their cost?

SOLUTION

$$\text{Cost} = \text{selling price} - \text{markup}$$
$$= 100\% - 40\% = 60\% \text{ of retail}$$
$$\text{Cost} = 60\% \times \text{selling price}$$
$$= 0.60 \times \$479.57 = \$287.74$$

9.19 A retailer sells a pair of shoes for $52.79. If his markup is 67% of retail, what is his cost?

SOLUTION

$$\text{Cost} = \text{selling price} - \text{markup}$$
$$= 100\% - 67\% = 33\% \text{ of retail}$$
$$\text{Cost} = 33\% \times \text{selling price}$$
$$= 0.33 \times \$52.79 = \$17.42$$

9.20   A suit sells for \$249.50 and carries a markup of 42% on retail. Find the cost of the suit.

SOLUTION

$$\begin{aligned}
\text{Cost} &= \text{selling price} - \text{markup} \\
&= 100\% - 42\% = 58\% \text{ of retail} \\
\text{Cost} &= 58\% \times \text{selling price} \\
&= 0.58 \times \$249.50 = \$144.71
\end{aligned}$$

9.5 MARKUP CONVERSIONS

Conversions between percent markups based on retail and cost are often necessary in business. We can convert percent markup based on retail (selling price) to a cost base by using the following formula:

$$\% \text{ Markup on cost} = \frac{\% \text{ markup on retail}}{\text{complement of } \% \text{ markup on retail}} \times 100$$

Note that the denominator is the cost expressed in terms of percent of retail:

$$\begin{aligned}
\text{Cost} &= \text{selling price} - \% \text{ markup on selling price} \\
&= 100\% - \% \text{ markup on selling price} \\
&= \text{complement of } \% \text{ markup on selling price}
\end{aligned}$$

EXAMPLE 8

What is the percent markup on cost if the markup on retail is 63%?

$$\% \text{ Markup on cost} = \frac{\% \text{ markup on retail}}{\text{complement of } \% \text{ markup on retail}} \times 100$$

$$= \frac{63\%}{(100\% - 63\%)} \times 100 = \frac{63\%}{37\%} \times 100 = 170.27\%$$

The percent markup on retail can be calculated from the markup on cost by using the following formula:

$$\% \text{ Markup on retail} = \frac{\% \text{ markup on cost}}{\text{selling price (stated as percent of cost)}} \times 100$$

EXAMPLE 9

What is the percent markup on retail if the markup on cost is 45%?

$$\begin{aligned}
\text{Cost} + \text{markup} &= \text{selling price} \\
100\% + 45\% &= \\
145\% &=
\end{aligned}$$

$$\% \text{ Markup on retail} = \frac{\% \text{ markup on cost}}{\text{selling price (as percent of cost)}} \times 100$$

$$= \frac{45\%}{145\%} \times 100 = 31\%$$

SOLVED PROBLEMS

9.21 What is the percent markup on cost if the percent markup on retail is 50%?

SOLUTION

$$\% \text{ Markup on cost} = \frac{\% \text{ markup on retail}}{\text{complement of } \% \text{ markup on retail}} \times 100$$

$$= \frac{50\%}{100\% - 50\%} \times 100 = \frac{50\%}{50\%} \times 100 = 100\%$$

9.22 What is the percent markup on cost if the percent markup on retail is 64%?

SOLUTION

$$\% \text{ Markup on cost} = \frac{\% \text{ markup on retail}}{\text{complement of } \% \text{ markup on retail}} \times 100$$

$$= \frac{64\%}{(100\% - 64\%)} \times 100 = \frac{64\%}{36\%} \times 100 = 177.78\%$$

9.23 What is the percent markup on cost if the percent markup on retail is 37%?

SOLUTION

$$\% \text{ Markup on cost} = \frac{\% \text{ markup on retail}}{\text{complement of } \% \text{ markup on retail}} \times 100$$

$$= \frac{37\%}{(100\% - 37\%)} \times 100 = \frac{37\%}{63\%} \times 100 = 58.73\%$$

9.24 Find the percent markup on retail if the markup on cost is 125%.

SOLUTION

$$\text{Cost} + \text{markup} = \text{selling price}$$
$$100\% + 125\% =$$
$$225\% =$$

$$\% \text{ Markup on retail} = \frac{\% \text{ markup on cost}}{\text{selling price (as percent of cost)}} \times 100$$

$$= \frac{125\%}{225\%} \times 100 = 55.56\%$$

9.25 Find the percent markup on retail if percent markup on cost is 27%.

SOLUTION

$$\text{Cost} + \text{markup} = \text{selling price}$$
$$100\% + 27\% =$$
$$127\% =$$

$$\% \text{ Markup on retail} = \frac{\% \text{ markup on cost}}{\text{selling price (as percent of cost)}} \times 100$$

$$= \frac{27\%}{127\%} \times 100 = 21.26\%$$

9.6 INVENTORY

In a mercantile business, inventory is merchandise that is held for resale. As such, it will ordinarily be converted into cash in less than a year and is thus a current asset. In a manufacturing business, there will usually be inventories of raw materials and goods in process in addition to an inventory of finished goods.

The *retail method* is one approach to costing inventory. This method of periodic inventory costing is used mostly by department stores and is based on the relationship between merchandise available for sale and the retail price of the same merchandise. Retail inventory is determined by subtracting retail sales from the retail price of goods available for that period. This retail inventory is changed to cost by means of the ratio of cost to selling price.

EXAMPLE 10

	Cost	Retail
Merchandise inventory, Dec. 1	$25,000	$35,000
Purchases	42,200	61,000
Goods available for sale	$67,200	$96,000
Sales for Dec.		81,000
Merchandise inventory, Dec. 31		$15,000
Merchandise inventory, Dec. 31	$10,500*	

$$\text{Ratio: } \frac{\$67,200 \text{ cost}}{\$96,000 \text{ retail}} = 70\%$$

*$15,000 \times 70\% = \$10,500$

Two advantages of this system are

1. It provides merchandise figures for interim statements.
2. It aids in disclosing inventory shortages.

SOLVED PROBLEMS

9.26 Find the estimated inventory cost on April 30 from the following data:

		Cost	Retail
Apr. 1	Merchandise inventory	$350,000	$420,000
Apr. 1–30	Net purchases	400,000	830,000
Apr. 1–30	Net sales	0	410,000

SOLUTION

	Cost	Retail
Merchandise inventory, Apr. 1	$350,000	$ 420,000
Plus: net purchases	400,000	830,000
Merchandise available for sale	$750,000	$1,250,000
Less: net sales		410,000
Merchandise inventory @ retail		$ 840,000

Cost ÷ retail = $750,000 ÷ $1,250,000 = 60%

$0.6 \times \$840,000 = \underline{\$504,000}$ est. inv. @ cost

9.27 Estimate the cost of inventory for GAP, Inc. using the following information.

	Cost	Retail
Merchandise inventory, Sept. 1	$240,000	$420,000
Purchases	124,000	210,000
Purchases returns & allowances	2,400	0
Sales	0	205,000
Sales returns	0	1,500

SOLUTION

	Cost	Retail
Merchandise inventory, Sept 1	$240,000	$420,000
Plus: purchases	124,000	210,000
	$364,000	
Less: purchases returns & allowances	2,400	
Merchandise available for sale	$361,600	$630,000
Less: sales & sales returns		206,500
Merchandise inventory @ retail, Sept. 30		$423,500

$$\$361,000 \div \$630,000 = 0.57 = 57\%$$
$$0.57 \times \$423,500 = \$241,395 \text{ merchandise inv. @ cost}$$

9.28 Figure the inventory at retail and at cost on October 31 for Gibson, Inc. using the following information:

	Cost	Retail
Merchandise inventory, Oct. 1	$221,000	$450,000
Purchases	122,000	246,000
Transportation	1,000	0
Purchases returns	1,500	2,000
Markups	0	2,500
Markdowns	0	1,200
Sales	0	321,500

SOLUTION

	Cost	Retail
Merchandise inventory, Oct. 1	$221,000	$450,000
Plus: purchases	122,000	246,000
transportation	1,000	0
	$344,000	$696,000
Less: purchases returns	1,500	2,000
		$694,000
Plus: markups		2,500
Merchandise available for sale	$342,500	$696,500
Less: sales & markdowns		322,700
Merchandise inventory @ retail		$373,800

$$\$342,500 \div \$696,500 = 49\%$$
$$0.49 \times \$373,800 = \$183,162 \text{ merchandise inv. @ cost}$$

9.29 Determine by the retail method the estimated cost of the December 31 inventory.

	Cost	Retail
Dec. 1, inventory	$280,000	$400,000
Dec. 1–31 purchases	110,000	180,000
Merchandise available for sale	$390,000	$580,000
Sales for Dec.		340,000

SOLUTION

	Cost	Retail
Dec. 1, inventory	$280,000	$400,000
Dec. 1–31 purchases	110,000	180,000
Merchandise available for sale	$390,000	$580,000
Sales for month		340,000
Dec. 31 inventory @ retail		$240,000
Inventory @ estimated cost ($240,000 × 67%*)	$160,800	

*Cost ratio 67% ($390,000 ÷ $580,000)

9.30 Estimate the cost of inventory of May 31 by the retail method.

	Cost	Retail
May 1 merchandise	$18,000	$24,000
May 1 purchases	34,000	41,000
Sales for May		37,000

SOLUTION

	Cost	Retail
May 1 merchandise	$18,000	$24,000
May purchases	34,000	41,000
Merchandise available for sale	$52,000	$65,000
Sales for May		37,000
May 31 inventory @ retail		$28,000
May 31 inventory @ estimated cost ($28,000 × 80%*)	$22,400	

*Cost ratio 80% ($52,000 ÷ $65,000)

9.31 From the following data, determine the inventory cost at March 31 by the retail method:

	Cost	Retail
Inventory, Mar. 1	$39,700	$63,000
Purchases in Mar. (net)	24,000	31,600
Sales for Mar.		56,000

SOLUTION

	Cost	Retail
Inventory	$39,700	$63,000
Purchases in March	24,000	31,600
Merchandise available for sale	$63,700	$94,600
Less: Sales		56,000
Inventory Mar. 31, @ retail		$38,600
Inventory Mar. 31, @ cost ($38,600 × 67%*)	$25,862	

_____

*Cost ratio 67% ($63,700 ÷ $94,600)

Supplementary Problems

9.32 Find the markup when

 (a)   Cost = $24 and selling price = $51

 (b)   Selling price = $22.95 and cost = $10.50

 (c)   Cost = $14.79 and selling price = $21.50

9.33 If Jones Bros. sells a microwave oven for $679 and their cost is $226.29, what is the markup?

9.34 Facials Ltd. purchased cold cream for $1.75 a jar. If they sell it for $4.50, what is the markup?

9.35 What is the markup on a ski suit that sells for $159.60 and costs the retailer $79.41?

9.36 GAP, Inc. sells picnic tables for $75 each. They paid $25.79. What is the markup?

9.37 Find (a) percent markup based on cost and (b) percent markup based on retail when

 (1)   Retail = $26.90 and cost = $15.60

 (2)   Retail = $36.50 and cost = $19.48

 (3)   Retail = $150 and cost = $96.45

9.38 If the markup on a pair of shoes is $9.50, and the shoes cost the retailer $15, what is the percent markup on cost?

9.39 Jones Bros. has a markup of $15.50 on a pair of designer jeans that sells for $31.97. Find (a) the cost, (b) the percent markup on cost, and (c) the percent markup on retail.

9.40 If an item costs $1.21 and we sell it for $3.17, what is the (a) markup, (b) percent markup on cost, and (c) percent markup on retail?

9.41 A stereo center buys a tape deck for $27.50 and sells it for $42.49. What is the (a) markup and (b) percent markup based on retail?

9.42 What is the percent markup on cost if the markup on retail is 65%?

9.43 Find the percent markup on cost if the markup on retail is 38%.

9.44   Percent markup on retail is 42%. What is the percent markup on cost?

9.45   Find the percent markup on retail if the markup on cost is 121%.

9.46   The percent markup on cost is 48%. What is the percent markup on retail?

9.47   GAP, Inc. purchased doghouses at $75 each. Their markup based on cost is 35%. What is the selling price?

9.48   Rinkle Electronics purchased videotapes at $10.97 each. The markup based on cost is 53%. Find the selling price.

9.49   Karol's Kandle Shop buys a candelabrum for $19.59. Her markup is 67% on retail. What is the selling price?

9.50   Curly's Modern Kitchens purchases a dishwasher for $159.67 and wants a markup of 52% on retail. What must the selling price be?

9.51   Johnson Co. buys card tables for $25 and wants a markup of 48% on retail. Find the selling price.

9.52   Jan's Boutique sells handbags for $39.87 each. Her markup on cost is 70%. Find her cost.

9.53   Willie's TV Service sells color television sets for $957.69 each. The markup on cost is 87%. Find the cost.

9.54   GAP, Inc. sells a tea cart for $249. If their markup is 40% on retail, what is their cost?

9.55   A retailer sells a suit for $197.50. If the markup is 52% on retail, what is the cost?

9.56   An automobile sells for $7,595 and carries a markup of 67% on retail. What is the dealer's cost?

9.57   Given the following information, use the retail method to find the estimated inventory cost on May 31.

	Cost	Retail
Merchandise inventory, May 1	$200,000	$390,000
Net purchases, May 1–31	150,000	250,000
Sales, May 1–31	0	410,000

9.58   Using the retail method, estimate the cost of inventory for Jones, Ltd. from the following information:

	Cost	Retail
Merchandise inventory	$300,000	$475,000
Purchases	125,000	300,000
Purchases returns & allowances	1,500	0
Sales	0	325,000
Sales returns	0	850

Answers to Supplementary Problems

9.32 (a) $27, (b) $12.45, (c) $6.71

9.33 $452.71

9.34 $2.75

9.35 $80.19

9.36 $49.21

9.37 1(a) 72.44%, (b) 42%; 2(a) 87.37%, (b) 46.63%; 3(a) 55.52%, (b) 35.7%

9.38 $63\frac{1}{3}$%

9.39 (a) $16.47, (b) 94.11%, (c) 48.48%

9.40 (a) $1.96, (b) 161.98%, (c) 61.83%

9.41 (a) $14.99, (b) 35.28%

9.42 185.71%

9.43 61.29%

9.44 72.41%

9.45 54.75%

9.46 32.43%

9.47 $101.25

9.48 $16.78

9.49 $59.36

9.50 $332.65

9.51 $48.08

9.52 $23.45

9.53 $512.13

9.54 $149.40

9.55 $94.80

9.56 $2,506.35

9.57 $126,500

9.58 $247,032.50

CHAPTER 10

Insurance

10.1   THE NEED FOR INSURANCE

Suppose that you own a small business valued, say, at $100,000. If a fire or other disaster should occur, your business will be ruined and you will suffer financially. If someone would step in and write you a check for $100,000, you could rebuild your business and start over.

Of course, nobody will do this for you out of the goodness of their heart. But if there were some financial incentive, such a scenario might be possible.

This is the basic idea behind the concept of *insurance*.

Suppose, hypothetically, that you pay a $1,000 premium for the promise that you will receive $100,000 should a disaster occur. Since you pay relatively little for the assurance that you will be protected, you gladly agree to pay the money. Why would an insurance company agree to such an arrangement? The answer to this question is based on a little bit of common business sense and mathematical reasoning.

The likelihood of a disaster occurring to your business is small—but not impossible. Insurance companies estimate this likelihood and adjust your *premium*, the amount of money you pay for protection, accordingly. For example, suppose that it is estimated that 1 in every 200 businesses will have a $100,000 loss in a given year. If 200 insurance policies are sold for premiums of $1,000 each, the insurance company will collect $200 \times \$1,000 = \$200,000$. There will be enough money to pay the affected business $100,000, and the insurance company will have a hefty profit.

Of course, it is possible that two or more businesses will have disasters and the insurance company will have to pay each $100,000. However, if a *large* number of policies are sold, *actuaries*, using the mathematical theory of probability, together with data from past experience, can predict, with remarkable accuracy, the percentage that will result in catastrophe. The premium can then be adjusted accordingly.

There are many different types of insurance available to meet different requirements. A few examples are fire insurance, liability insurance, health insurance, accident insurance, theft insurance, and life insurance. Some policies, such as homeowner's and automobile policies, offer combinations of coverage tailored to meet specific needs.

10.2   INSURANCE PREMIUMS

The amount of money you pay for insurance is called the *premium*. The amount of protection you purchase is called the *coverage* or *face value* of the policy. Premiums are usually stated as rates, that is, the amount of money you must pay per \$100 or \$1,000 unit of coverage. In general

$$\boxed{\text{Premium} = \text{rate} \times \text{number of units of coverage}}$$

EXAMPLE 1

The annual premium for a fire insurance policy is \$0.58 per \$100 of coverage. To compute the premium for a \$50,000 policy, we first compute the number of \$100 units in \$50,000:

$$\frac{\$50{,}000}{\$100} = 500 \text{ units}$$

Since the insurance rate is \$0.58 per \$100 unit, the premium is

$$0.58 \times 500 = \$290$$

An insurance premium is generally paid in advance. If you purchase a fire insurance policy but fail to adhere to fire codes, or if you purchase an automobile policy but failed to list your traffic violations, the insurance company may cancel your policy before the end of its term. In this case you will be sent a refund proportional to the number of unused days in your policy. The premium you used for protection before cancellation took effect is called the *short premium*.

$$\boxed{\begin{array}{c} \text{Short premium} = \dfrac{\text{number of days policy is in force}}{365} \times \text{annual premium} \\[2mm] \text{Refund} = \text{annual premium} - \text{short premium} \end{array}}$$

EXAMPLE 2

Suppose that the policy in Example 1 was effective March 1 and was canceled by the insurance company on May 15. The number of days the policy was in force is 76. Therefore

$$\text{Short premium} = \frac{76}{365} \times 290 = \$60.38$$
$$\text{Refund} = \$290 - \$60.38 = \$229.62$$

If the insured cancels the policy before the end of its term, the calculation is just a bit different. As a penalty, you may be charged a higher rate per day than the annual rate. This rate varies with the number of days the policy is in force.

EXAMPLE 3

Suppose that the short rate for policies canceled after 30 days in example 2 is 12% of the annual rate. To determine the short premium and subsequent refund in example 1, we multiply the annual premium by 12%:

$$12\% \times \$290 = \$34.80$$
$$\text{Refund} = \$290 - \$34.80 = \$255.20$$

Note that the short premium is somewhat larger than 1/12th of the annual premium.

SOLVED PROBLEMS

10.1   The annual premium for a life insurance policy for a 25-year-old male who does not smoke is $23 per $1,000 of coverage. How much should a $50,000 policy cost?

SOLUTION

Each unit of coverage is $1,000:

$$\frac{\$50,000}{\$1,000} = 50 \text{ units}$$

$$\text{Premium} = \text{rate} \times \text{number of units of coverage} = \$23 \times 50 = \$1,150$$

10.2   If liability insurance costs $41.20 per $10,000 of coverage, how much would the premium be for a policy whose face value is $250,000?

SOLUTION

$$\frac{\$250,000}{\$10,000} = 25$$

$$\text{premium} = \text{rate} \times \text{number of units of coverage} = \$41.20 \times 25 = \$1,030$$

10.3   A $250,000 fire insurance policy written on June 15, whose annual premium is $672, was canceled by the insurance company at midnight June 30 because the sprinkler system was found to be inoperative. How much refund is due?

SOLUTION

The policy was in force for 15 days. Therefore

$$\text{Short premium} = \frac{\text{number of days policy is in force}}{365} \times \text{annual premium}$$

$$= \frac{15}{365} \times \$672$$

$$= \$27.62$$

$$\text{Refund} = \$672.00 - \$27.62 = \$644.38$$

10.4   Continental Insurance Company issued a $300,000 insurance policy to Ace Paper Company for protection against fire and theft. The annual premium was $11.50 per $1,000 of coverage. Their short rate for one month is 10% of the annual rate. How much refund is due to Ace Paper if

(a)   Continental cancels the policy after one month (30 days)?

(b)   Ace cancels the policy after one month?

SOLUTION

The number of $1,000 units of coverage = $300,000/$1,000 = 300 units. The premium paid = rate × number of units of coverage = $11.50 × 300 = $3,450.

(a) If Continental cancels the policy:

$$\text{Short premium} = \frac{\text{number of days policy is in force}}{365} \times \text{annual premium}$$

$$= \frac{30}{365} \times \$3,450 = \$283.56$$

Refund = annual premium − short premium
= \$3,450 − \$283.56
= \$3,166.44

(b) If Ace cancels:

Short premium = 10% × annual premium = 0.10 × \$3,450 = \$345
Refund = annual premium − short premium
= \$3,450 − \$345
= \$3,105

10.5 ABCO Tool and Die Company took out a \$500,000 liability policy which had an annual premium of \$3.40 per \$1,000 of insurance. After 6 months they canceled their policy. If the insurance company's short rate for 6 months is 55% of their annual rate, how much refund should ABCO receive?

SOLUTION

$$\frac{\$500,000}{\$1,000} = 500 \text{ units}$$

Annual premium = rate × number of units = \$3.40 × 500 = \$1,700
Short premium = 55% × annual premium = 0.55 × \$1,700 = \$935
Refund = \$1,700 − \$935 = \$765

10.3 PROPERTY INSURANCE

To ensure that you have an appropriate amount of coverage for personal property, insurance policies include an *indemnity* clause which states that if you have a loss, the amount you will receive under the policy will not exceed the value of the property. Consequently, if you overinsure your property, you will be paying additional premiums, but will not be able to obtain excessive benefits.

Deductibles are used to eliminate trivial claims and also make the insured bear a part of the loss. The amount of the deductible is subtracted from the amount of loss before any benefit calculation is made.

EXAMPLE 4

Mr. Jones has a \$500 deductible on the theft portion of his homeowner's insurance. If Mr. Jones has a robbery and suffers a \$4,000 loss, he will receive \$3,500 from his insurance company.

Most insurance claims are not total losses. If your property is worth, say, \$100,000, experience shows that it is unlikely that you will have a full \$100,000 loss. To deter property owners from underinsuring their properties, most policies contain a *coinsurance* clause.

Let us say your coinsurance rate is 80%, which is typical of many policies. If your insurance coverage is at least 80% of the replacement value of your property, the insurance company will pay to replace what was destroyed, up to the face value of your policy. If you are insured for less than 80% of replacement value, however, and have a partial loss, your benefit will be proportional to the ratio of your policy limit to 80% of the replacement value of the property.

$$\text{Insurance benefit} = \frac{\text{face value of policy}}{\text{amount of insurance required}} \times \text{loss}$$

$$= \frac{\text{face value of policy}}{80\% \times \text{property replacement value}} \times \text{loss}$$

EXAMPLE 5

Bob Allen's TV repair shop is worth $50,000. However, it is underinsured for only $30,000, and his policy has an 80% coinsurance clause. One day a heavy rain causes a flood and does $4,000 worth of damage. Bob will receive only $3,000 from the insurance company.

$$\frac{\text{Face value of policy}}{80\% \times \text{property replacement value}} \times \text{loss} = \frac{\$30,000}{80\% \times \$50,000} \times \$4,000$$

$$= \frac{\$30,000}{\$40,000} \times \$4,000$$

$$= 0.75 \times \$4,000$$

$$= \$3,000$$

If Bob had a policy whose face value was $40,000, he would have received the full $4,000.

EXAMPLE 6

Suppose that Bob (see Example 5) has a $500 deductible in his policy. The deductible is always applied first so the insurance company will compute his settlement on the basis of $3,500.

$$\frac{\text{Face value of policy}}{80\% \times \text{property replacement value}} \times \text{loss} = \frac{\$30,000}{80\% \times \$50,000} \times \$3,500$$

$$= \frac{\$30,000}{\$40,000} \times \$3,500$$

$$= 0.75 \times \$3,500$$

$$= \$2,625$$

SOLVED PROBLEMS

10.6   Samuel has a property damage policy which has a deductible of $500. During a storm, a tree falls on his house and does $2,250 worth of damage. Assuming that he has sufficient coverage for his property, how much will he receive from the insurance company?

SOLUTION

He will receive a benefit of $2,250 − $500 = $1,750.

10.7   Bill Sawyer's home has a replacement value of $350,000. When he purchased the home 5 years ago, he insured it for $200,000 and never updated his policy. His policy has an 80% coinsurance clause. One day, a pipe burst and caused $22,000 worth of water damage. How much will Bill collect on his policy?

SOLUTION

Since his policy has a face value of less than 80% of his home's replacement value, Bill cannot collect his full damages.

$$\text{Insurance benefit} = \frac{\text{face value of policy}}{\text{amount of insurance required}} \times \text{loss}$$

$$= \frac{\text{face value of policy}}{80\% \times \text{property replacement value}} \times \text{loss}$$

$$= \frac{\$200,000}{80\% \times \$350,000} \times \$22,000$$

$$= \frac{\$200,000}{\$280,000} \times \$22,000$$

$$= \$15,714.28$$

10.8   When a car drove through Jim and Emma Brown's summer home, the cost of repairs was $14,200. The replacement value of the home is $140,000, and they carried an insurance policy of $120,000 with a $500 deductible and an 80% coinsurance clause. How much will the insurance company pay toward repairs?

SOLUTION

Since their $120,000 policy was in excess of 80% of the $140,000 replacement cost of the home, the insurance company will pay for the repairs in full, less the deductible amount. Therefore the Browns will get a check for $14,200 − $500 = $13,700.

10.9   Jacque owns a French restaurant whose value is $400,000. The restaurant has a fire which does $60,000 worth of damage. How much will Jacque receive if

(a)   He has insurance in the amount of $350,000 with a $2,000 deductible?

(b)   He has insurance in the amount of $300,000 with a $2,000 deductible?

SOLUTION

(a)   Since the face value of the policy exceeds 80% of the value of his restaurant (80% of $400,000 = $320,000), Jacque will receive $60,000 less the $2,000 deductible from the insurance company. His total benefit will be $58,000.

(b)   Now Jacque is underinsured. The deductible is applied first so the insurance company will compute his benefit on the basis of a loss of $60,000 − $2,000 = $58,000.

$$\text{Insurance benefit} = \frac{\text{face value of policy}}{\text{amount of insurance required}} \times \text{loss}$$

$$= \frac{\text{face value of policy}}{80\% \times \text{property replacement value}} \times \text{loss}$$

$$= \frac{\$300,000}{80\% \times \$400,000} \times \$58,000$$

$$= \frac{\$300,000}{\$320,000} \times \$58,000$$

$$= \$54,375$$

10.4 MAJOR MEDICAL INSURANCE

Most major medical insurance policies have both an annual deductible and a coinsurance clause. Unlike property insurance, the major medical deductible accumulates. It is not applied separately to each medical visit. Once satisfied, the annual deductible will not apply for the remainder of the year.

Since your health has no real monetary value, coinsurance works differently from property insurance. It serves to limit the amount of money an insurance company will pay to a fixed percentage of the claim.

Suppose that a policy has an 80% coinsurance clause. After applying any deductibles that may be applicable, the insurance company will pay 80% of the claim and the patient will be responsible for the difference. Because the patient pays 20% of the claim, this amount is called a 20% *copayment*.

EXAMPLE 7

Jennifer has a health insurance policy which has a $250 deductible and a 20% copayment. Jennifer goes skiing and breaks a leg and incurs $3,000 worth of medical bills. Her insurance company will pay 80% of the amount in excess of the deductible.

$$\$3,000 - \$250 = \$2,750$$
$$80\% \text{ of } \$2,750 = 0.80 \times 2,750 = \$2,200$$

The insurance company will pay $2,200 and Jennifer will have to pay $800.

After the deductible is satisfied, the insured pays 20% of the medical bill. This amount is known as an "out-of-pocket expense." Many insurance policies have an upper limit on the out-of-pocket expenses an insured is required to pay. After your deductible has been satisfied and your out-of-pocket maximum has been reached, the insurance company pays 100% of the claim.

EXAMPLE 8

Suppose that Harold Weiss had $68,000 worth of medical expenses last year. His insurance policy has a $300 deductible, a 20% copayment, and an out-of-pocket maximum of $1,500. To compute Mr. Weiss' insurance benefit, we first apply the deductible to his medical bill:

$$\$68,000 - \$300 = \$67,700$$

Then we apply the coinsurance to compute the benefit:

$$80\% \text{ of } \$67,700 = 0.8 \times \$67,700 = \boxed{\$54,160}$$

The difference, $67,700 − $54,160 = $13,540, is his out-of-pocket expense. Since the maximum out-of-pocket expense under this policy is $1,500, Harold is entitled to an additional reimbursement of

$$\$13,540 - \$1,500 = \boxed{\$12,040}$$

The <u>total</u> benefit under the policy is then $54,160 + $12,040 = $66,200.

To avoid excessive and unrealistic claims, major medical insurance companies use *reasonable and customary* benefit schedules. These represent average fees doctors charge for medical procedures performed in a certain locality. These schedules determine the maximum benefits that can be considered, regardless of actual charges, before any benefit calculation is performed.

EXAMPLE 9

Mrs. White needs hip surgery. Her orthopedic surgeon wants to charge her $20,000 for the operation. Her major medical policy has a $500 deductible and a 20% copayment. Reasonable and customary charges for the procedure she requires are $17,500 for the city she lives in.

We shall assume that Mrs. White had no other insurance claims that year. (Deductibles are cumulative within a calendar year, for all insurance claims that year.) Even though her surgeon is charging her $20,000, the maximum fee the insurance company will allow is $17,500. After subtracting the deductible, the insurance company will pay 80% of the difference:

$$\$17,500 - \$500 = \$17,000$$
$$80\% \times \$17,000 = \$13,600$$

The insurance company will pay $13,600 and Mrs. White will have to pay the difference, $6,400.

EXAMPLE 10

Suppose that Mrs. White's policy (see Example 9) stipulates that her maximum out-of-pocket expense is $1,000. How much additional will the insurance company allow?

The only part of the medical bill that qualifies as out-of-pocket expense is the 20% of the $17,000 that the insurance company did not pay:

$$20\% \times \$17,000 = \$3,400$$

Since her maximum out-of-pocket expense is $1,000, the insurance company will pay an additional $2,400.

SOLVED PROBLEMS

10.10 Julio received medical treatment totaling $2,700 in 2000. His insurance policy has a $250 deductible and a 20% copayment. His out-of-pocket maximum is $1,000. How much will Julio receive from his insurance company?

SOLUTION

$$\$2,700 - \$250 = \$2,450$$
$$80\% \text{ of } \$2,450 = 0.80 \times \$2,450 = \$1,960$$

Since his out-of-pocket expenses are $2,450 - $1,960 = $490, Julio has not reached his out-of-pocket maximum. He will receive $1,960.

10.11 Jeremy Jenkins fell and broke his collarbone. His medical bills totaled $17,000. How much of the bill is he personally responsible for if his major medical policy has a $750 deductible, a 20% copayment, and a $2,000 maximum out-of-pocket expense?

SOLUTION

$$\$17,000 - \$750 = \$16,250$$
$$20\% \times \$16,250 = \$3,250 \quad \text{(out-of-pocket expense)}$$

Since this exceeds $2,000 he is responsible for only

$$\$2,000 \quad \text{(out of pocket)} + \$750 \quad \text{(deductible)} = \$2,750$$

10.12 Marty had a medical procedure performed, for which his physician charged $3,000. His insurance policy has a $250 deductible and a 20% copayment. He received, however, only $1,560 from his insurance company. What were the reasonable and customary charges allowed for his procedure?

SOLUTION

Let x represent the reasonable and customary charges *after* the deductible is applied:

$$80\% \text{ of } x = \$1,560$$
$$0.80x = \$1,560$$
$$x = \frac{\$1,560}{0.80} = \$1,950$$

The allowed charge was $\$1,950 + \$250 = \$2,200$.

10.13 In 2000, Steve had a series of medical procedures performed:

Procedure	Cost	Reasonable and Customary Charges
Medical checkup by primary physician	$ 100	$ 75
Specialist consultation	250	400
CAT scan	1,375	1,100
Surgery	15,000	12,000
Anesthesiologist	2,500	2,000
Postoperative care	4,000	5,000

His major medical policy has a $750 deductible and a 20% copayment with $1,500 maximum out-of-pocket expense. How much will Steve collect from his insurance company?

SOLUTION

For each procedure, Steve will collect the smaller of (*a*) the actual cost or (*b*) reasonable and customary charges. Thus the insurance company will consider

$$\$75 + \$250 + \$1,100 + \$12,000 + \$2,000 + \$4,000 = \$19,425$$

From this we subtract the deductible: $\$19,425 - \$750 = \$18,675$

Next we apply coinsurance: 80% of $\$18,675 = \boxed{\$14,940}$. The difference, $\$18,675 - \$14,940 = \$3,735$, is Steve's out-of-pocket expense. Since the maximum out-of-pocket expense under Steve's policy is $1,500, the insurance company will pay an additional $\$3,735 - \$1,500 = \boxed{\$2,235}$. Steve's total benefit under his policy is $\$14,940 + \$2,235 = \$17,175$.

10.5 LIFE INSURANCE

Life insurance is designed to protect a person's family or loved ones in the event of their death. The insured enters into a contract with an insurance company that promises to provide a certain amount of money upon his or her death. In return, the insured makes periodic payments, known as *premiums*, to the insurance company. The *insured* is the person receiving the coverage and the *beneficiary* is the person who will receive the benefits when the insured dies.

There are many different types of life insurance available, including the following:

1. A *term life* insurance policy pays the face amount of the policy to the beneficiary if the insured dies during the term of the policy. The term may be 1, 5, 10 years, etc. Insurance is in effect only during the term of the policy; once the term ends, there is no protection. In contrast to other types of policies which "lock in" a fixed premium for the life of the policy, term life

insurance premiums increase as the age of the insured increases. Term insurance is initially cheaper than other types of insurance for the same amount of protection and, therefore, can give the largest immediate coverage for the dollar. For this reason, it is useful for consumers who need large amounts of coverage for known periods of time, such as home buyers, parents of young children, or people with high debt obligations.

2. A *straight* or *whole life* policy combines the protection of life insurance with a built-in cash value. As long as premiums are paid, the policy accumulates value on a tax-deferred basis and can be sold back to the company in return for a lump-sum payment or for an annuity, say, for retirement. While you are accumulating value, you are still protected for the full face value in the event of your death. Most straight life policies allow you to borrow against its cash value without surrendering the policy. Interest rates are usually less than bank rates for borrowing money. The premium for a straight life policy is constant for the life of the policy, but is higher than a term policy premium because it accumulates savings.

3. A *limited payment* life insurance policy is similar to a straight life policy except that payments are made over a fixed period rather than for the rest of your life. However, because of the limited number of payments made, each premium is somewhat higher than a straight life premium for a comparable policy. Twenty-year terms are quite popular.

4. An *endowment* policy is like a term policy with a cash value after a fixed number of years. During the payment period you make payments annually and are fully protected up to the face value of the policy. After the payment period, your life insurance ends and you receive the face value of the policy, either as a lump sum or as an annuity. During the payment period, however, premiums are high. An endowment policy is the most expensive policy you can buy. Twenty-year terms are common for this type of policy.

5. A *universal life* insurance policy is similar to a straight life policy except that its premiums are tied to variable factors such as the prime interest rate, stock market indices, etc. If interest rates fall, for example, the policyholder may be forced to pay higher premiums or accept reduced benefits. Although somewhat cheaper than straight life, it is somewhat riskier.

For problems in this chapter, we will use the hypothetical premium chart shown in Table 10.1 for nonsmoking males. Premiums for women are generally lower, and premiums for smokers are higher. These numbers are not meant to be representative, as rates vary between insurance companies, but only to illustrate the difference in premiums for different types of insurance.

Table 10.1   Annual Premiums per $1,000 for Nonsmoking Males

Age at Time of Purchase	5-Year Term Insurance	Straight Life	20-Year Limited Payment	20-Year Endowment
20	1.93	5.75	8.30	13.95
25	1.93	7.22	10.05	17.30
30	2.05	8.95	12.25	21.10
35	2.27	11.25	15.10	26.50
40	3.50	14.65	18.70	34.00
45	4.65	18.05	22.45	41.10

SOLVED PROBLEMS

10.14 Jim Brown is 35 years old and wants to purchase $50,000 of straight life insurance. What will be his annual premium?

SOLUTION

$$\frac{\$50,000}{\$1,000} = 50$$

$$50 \times \$11.25 = \$562.50$$

His annual premium will be $562.50.

10.15 Bill Murphy is 25 years old. He needs $150,000 worth of life insurance. How much will his premium increase when he reaches age 45 if he purchases (*a*) term life insurance or (*b*) straight life insurance?

SOLUTION

(*a*)   Per $1,000 the difference in premium for term life insurance between ages 25 and 45 is $4.65 − $1.93 = $2.72. The difference in annual premium for a $150,000 policy is

$$150 \times \$2.72 = \$408.00$$

(*b*)   His premium will *not* increase. The premiums for straight life depend only on the age at time of purchase and are fixed for the term of the policy.

10.16 Abe Sanders, age 30, has budgeted $750 a year to purchase life insurance. How much coverage can he get if he purchases (*a*) a 5-year term, (*b*) straight life, (*c*) 20 payment life, or (*d*) 20-year endowment? Assume that insurance can only be purchased in $1,000 increments.

SOLUTION

Since premium = rate × number of units, it follows that premium/rate = number of units.

(*a*)   750/2.05 = 365.85:   He can purchase 365 × $1,000 = $365,000 worth of insurance.

(*b*)   750/8.95 = 83.8:   He can buy 83 × $1000 = $83,000 worth of insurance.

(*c*)   750/12.25 = 61.22:   He can afford 61 × $1,000 = $61,000 worth of insurance.

(*d*)   750/21.10 = 35.55:   He can purchase 35 × $1,000 = $35,000 worth of insurance.

10.17 Scott Murray, age 45, and his son Joseph, age 20, both purchase life insurance policies. Scott buys a $125,000 20-year limited payment policy, and Joseph buys a $200,000 20-year endowment policy. How much more does Scott pay annually than his son?

SOLUTION

Scott pays $22.45 per $1,000 of coverage:

$$\frac{\$125,000}{\$1,000} = 125 \text{ units}$$

$$125 \times \$22.45 = \$2,806.25$$

Joseph pays $13.95 per $1,000 of coverage:

$$\frac{\$200,000}{\$1,000} = 200 \text{ units}$$

$$200 \times \$13.95 = \$2,790.00$$

The difference in annual premium is $2,806.25 − $2,790.00 = $16.25. Note that Joseph gets more coverage and a more valuable policy for less money because of his younger age.

10.6 AUTOMOBILE INSURANCE

A standard automobile policy consists of many different types of coverage. Although requirements vary from state to state, some basic types are:

1. *Bodily injury* liability, which protects you if you injure or kill someone while operating your vehicle. This is coverage you want to keep at a constant level, even as your vehicle ages and declines in value. In the event of a serious accident, you want enough insurance to protect assets that may become subject to a lawsuit. The level of protection is expressed as two numbers indicating the maximum coverage per person and the maximum coverage per accident, respectively, in thousands of dollars. For example, 50/100 means that your insurance company will pay up to $50,000 per person injured in an accident up to a maximum of $100,000 for the accident. Other common limitations are 100/100, 100/300, and 300/300.

2. *Property damage* liability, which protects you in the event that you damage someone else's property. Limitations on this type of coverage are generally lower than bodily injury liability; $50,000 to $100,000 is typical coverage.

3. *Medical payments* and *personal injury protection* (PIP), which pays for the medical expenses of the driver and passengers in your car in the event of an accident.

4. *Collision* insurance, which will pay for damage done to your car in an accident. There is generally a deductible for this coverage, ranging typically from $100 to $1,000. Because you accept a larger part of the risk, premiums are lower for larger deductibles. The maximum protection is limited by the *book value* of your automobile; if it costs more to repair your car than the car is worth, the insurance company will render it a total loss and pay only the book value amount. For this reason many people elect not to take this coverage for older, less valuable, automobiles and trucks.

5. *Comprehensive* coverage, which pays for damage due to vandalism, flood, fire, and theft (but not the theft of contents of your vehicle). A deductible is usually associated with this coverage, although it may be different than your collision deductible. As with collision, the insurance company will pay up to the book value of your vehicle, so comprehensive coverage may not be desirable if your automobile is old and has lost its value.

Insurance premiums vary substantially from state to state and from locality to locality. Areas with high incidence of auto theft, for example, will have high comprehensive premiums. Similarly, collision premiums will vary according to the make, model, and year of your vehicle, and liability rates, as well as collision rates, will depend heavily on your age, sex, and driving record.

EXAMPLE 11

Billy Williams has an automobile insurance policy with 50/100 bodily injury liability protection, $50,000 property damage liability, and collision coverage with $500 deductible. When Billy had an accident, he sustained $2,500 worth of damage to his automobile, $1,500 worth of damage to the other automobile, and the driver of the other car was awarded $57,000 for medical expenses and lost wages. How much did Billy's policy pay?

Payment for damage to Billy's car ($2,500 − $500 deductible):	$2,000
Payment for damage to other car (deductible does not apply):	1,500
Liability for other driver's injuries (maximum policy benefit = $50,000):	50,000
Total:	$53,500

Often an accident is not entirely the fault of one driver, but is attributable to both drivers, although perhaps not equally. In this case, after an investigation, the insurance company will assign a certain percentage of the fault to each driver. Each insurance company will pay benefits to the other driver proportional to the percentage of fault of their insured.[1]

---

[1] Some states have *no-fault laws*, in which case each insurance company pays their own insured regardless of who is at fault.

EXAMPLE 12

One day Mrs. Kelly was driving home from shopping and skidded on ice and hit another car. Mrs. Kelly's car sustained $800 worth of damage. Neither driver had collision coverage, but both had sufficient liability coverage.

Even though Mrs. Kelly had the right-of-way, the insurance investigator attributed 30% of the fault to her because she was traveling too fast, considering the weather, and should have been able to stop in time. The percentage of fault given the other driver was $100\% - 30\% = 70\%$. Mrs. Kelly was awarded $70\% \times \$800 = \$560$ by the other driver's insurance company.

Suppose that the other car had $1,200 in damage. Then Mrs. Kelly's insurance company would pay 30% of $1,200 = \$360$ to the driver of the other car.

A driver who has collision coverage and shares responsibility for an accident will receive full payment for damages less a proportionate part of the deductible.

EXAMPLE 13

If Mrs. Kelly (see Example 12) had collision coverage with a $500 deductible, she would be entitled to receive her *full* damages, $800, less 30% of her deductible.

$$\$800 - 30\% \text{ of } \$500 = \$800 - 0.30 \times \$500$$
$$= \$800 - \$150$$
$$= \$650$$

SOLVED PROBLEMS

10.18 Bernard had an accident in which three people were injured. They sued in court and were awarded $30,000 and $40,000 and $50,000, respectively. If Bernard had a liability policy with 50/100 coverage, how much will he have to pay from his own pocket?

SOLUTION

Even though none of the injured people was awarded damages in excess of $50,000, the maximum coverage for the accident is limited to $100,000. Therefore Bernard will have to pay $20,000.

10.19 Allison had an accident and injured two people. Their medical bills and other costs amounted to $25,000 and $30,000, respectively. If Allison's collision coverage was 20/60, how much of the claim is Allison responsible for?

SOLUTION

Even though the maximum coverage for the accident is $60,000, the maximum coverage for *any one* injured person is $20,000. Therefore Allison is responsible for $5,000 for the first person's injuries and $10,000 for the second person's, for a total of $15,000.

10.20 While driving by himself, Joel had an automobile accident which was, admittedly, his fault. He has an automobile policy which provides for 50/100 liability coverage, $500 deductible collision coverage, and $50,000 personal injury protection. The financial story is

Damage to Joel's automobile:	$ 2,300
Damage to the other automobile:	4,500
Personal injury to Joel:	12,000
Personal injury to driver of other car:	60,000
Personal injury to passenger of other car:	30,000

How much will Joel collect from the insurance company?

SOLUTION

Damage to Joel's automobile is covered for $2,300 less the $500 deductible	$ 1,800
Damage to the other automobile is covered in full; the deductible does not apply.	4,500
Personal injury to Joel is covered under personal injury protection and does not exceed policy limit	12,000
Personal injury to driver of other car is limited to $50,000	50,000
Personal injury to passenger of other car does not exceed policy limits	30,000
Total Payment	$98,300

10.21 While talking on his cell phone, Donald collided with another car. Because of the circumstances of the accident, an insurance investigator assigned him 65% of the blame. Neither driver had collision coverage.

(a) If he sustained $900 in damage, how much money should Donald receive from the other insurance company?

(b) If the other car had $1,600 in damage, how much money should the other driver receive from Donald's insurance company?

SOLUTION

(a) Since Donald was deemed 65% at fault for the accident, the other driver received 35%. The other insurance company must pay Donald 35% of his damages:

$$35\% \text{ of } \$900 = 0.35 \times \$900 = \$315$$

(b) Since Donald received 65% of the blame for the accident, his insurance company must pay the other driver 65% of his damages, $1,600:

$$65\% \text{ of } \$1,600 = 0.65 \times \$1,600 = \$1,040$$

10.22 Suppose that both drivers in the problem 10.21 have collision coverage with $1,000 deductible. How much would each receive?

SOLUTION

(a) Since Donald has collision coverage, he will receive full payment for his damage less 65% of his deductible:

$$\$900 - 65\% \text{ of } \$1,000 = \$900 - 0.65 \times \$1,000 = \$900 - \$650 = \$250$$

(b) The other driver will receive full payment for his damage less 35% of his deductible:

$$\$1,600 - 35\% \text{ of } \$1,000 = \$1,600 - 0.35 \times \$1,000 = \$1,600 - \$350 = \$1,250$$

10.23 Ed Brady has an automobile insurance policy with $1,000 deductible collision coverage. One day Ed has a small "fender bender" with another car and sustains $2,300 in damages. How much money will Ed receive if

(a) The accident is Ed's fault?

(b) The accident is the other driver's fault?

(c) Both drivers are equally at fault?

SOLUTION

(a) If the accident is Ed's fault, his insurance company will pay $2,300 less the $1,000 deductible. Ed will receive $1,300.

(b) If the accident is not Ed's fault, Ed will receive his full damages of $2,300 from the other driver's insurance company. [Typically, Ed's insurance company will pay $1,300 as in part (a) and then *subrogate*, i.e., collect the full amount of damages from the other insurance company. If they are successful, Ed will then be paid his deductible.]

(c) If both drivers are equally at fault, Ed will receive full damages less 50% of his deductible from *his* insurance company:

$$\$2,350 - 50\% \times \$1,000 = \$2,350 - \$500 = \$1,850$$

10.24 Marcia has an insurance policy with comprehensive coverage subject to a $250 deductible. One day her car was vandalized and she had to replace her windshield at a cost of $275, her driver's side door lock at a cost of $75, and her radio at a cost of $125. Furthermore, $350 worth of merchandise, which she had just purchased at a local mall, was stolen from her car. How much will her insurance company pay?

SOLUTION

The windshield, door lock, and radio are covered under her comprehensive policy. Unfortunately, the contents of the car are not covered, so she receives nothing for her packages.

Covered damages: $275 + $75 + $125 = $475
Less deductible: $475 − $250 = $225

She will receive $225 from her insurance company.

Supplementary Problems

10.25 How much must a business pay for a fire insurance policy with a face value $750,000, if the annual premium rate is $0.23 per $1,000?

10.26 The annual rate for a term life insurance policy is $1.95 per $1,000 of coverage. If Jimmy wants to purchase $50,000 of term life insurance, what will his yearly premium be?

10.27 How much liability insurance can Allen buy for $200 if the rate for such insurance is $2.67 per $1,000 of coverage? Assume that this insurance can be purchased only in $1,000 increments.

10.28 If Edward purchases $150 worth of casualty insurance at $1.25 per $1,000 of coverage, how much coverage does he have?

10.29 If it costs $4.25 per $1,000 to insure the structure of a factory and $3.25 per $1,000 to insure its contents, how much will it cost to insure a factory whose replacement value is $225,000 if its contents are worth $50,000?

10.30   It costs $2.50 per $1,000 to purchase liability insurance and $3.75 per $1,000 to purchase fire insurance. If a businessman needs $250,000 of liability protection and $150,000 of fire protection for his office, how much will a policy cost?

10.31   A homeowner's policy from the RESTEZ Insurance Company costs $3.50 per unit of coverage. Each unit consists of $1,000 for the structure of the house and $200 for contents. Each additional $100 of contents coverage costs $0.25 to insure. How much will it cost to insure a house worth $150,000 if its contents are worth $40,000?

10.32   Samantha purchased a $100,000 fire insurance policy for her boutique at a rate of $4.50 per $1,000. After 15 days the insurance company canceled her policy because she received a citation from the fire department. How much refund should Samantha receive?

10.33   Juan Rodriguez purchased a $250,000 liability policy for his grocery store, effective July 1 at a rate of $1.75 per $1,000 of coverage. Because of a building code violation, the insurance company canceled his policy effective August 1. How much refund should Juan receive?

10.34   Adam purchased a $300,000 theft insurance policy for $275. Fifteen days later he canceled the policy because he obtained a cheaper rate elsewhere. It is the company's policy to charge 110% of the normal 15-day premium for the period that insurance was in effect. How much refund will Adam be receiving?

10.35   Charles bought $150,000 of fire insurance on April 1 for $2.43 per $1,000 of coverage. On May 1 he went out of business and canceled the policy. If the insurance company charges a short premium of 10% of the annual premium for policies in effect one month or less, how much money will Charles be receiving from the insurance company?

10.36   Raymond's business has a replacement value of $180,000 but is insured for $126,000 with an insurance policy containing an 80% coinsurance clause. How much money will Raymond receive if he has a $10,000 loss?

10.37   Mark and Mindy just purchased a $300,000 restaurant. Their fire insurance policy has an 80% coinsurance clause. Suppose that they have a $15,000 loss. How much money will they receive if their restaurant is insured for (a) $200,000, (b) $240,000, or (c) $300,000?

10.38   Adrienne has a home worth $150,000. She purchases a $120,000 property damage policy with a $500 deductible and an 80% coinsurance clause. How much will Adrienne receive from the insurance company if she has (a) a $12,000 loss or (b) a total loss?

10.39   Repeat Prob. 10.38 assuming that Adrienne purchases a $100,000 policy.

10.40   A fire damages a warehouse to the extent of $28,000. The building, whose replacement value is $75,000, is insured for $50,000 by a policy with an 80% coinsurance clause and a $1,000 deductible. How much will the owners collect?

10.41   Anne has a major medical policy with a 20% copayment and a $100 annual deductible.

   (a)   If Anne's first medical bill for the year was $150, how much was she reimbursed?

   (b)   If Anne's second medical bill for the year is $150, how much will she be reimbursed?

10.42   If Warren has a major medical policy with a 15% copayment and an annual deductible of $100, how much will he be reimbursed for a $325 stress test if he has previously satisfied $75 of his deductible?

10.43   How much will Benjamin be reimbursed for an appendectomy which leaves him with $12,000 in medical bills? He has a major medical policy with a $250 deductible, a 20% copayment, and an out-of-pocket maximum of $1,500. All physicians' fees fall into the "reasonable and customary" guidelines.

10.44 Darlene and Tom are going to have a baby. The cost for delivery will be $3,000. They have a major medical policy, which has not yet been used this year, which has a $150 deductible and a 30% copayment. How much will the baby cost them?

10.45 Marilyn has a major medical policy which has a $500 deductible, 20% copayment, and $1,000 maximum out-of-pocket expense. She previously satisfied her deductible for the year, and her out-of-pocket expenses thus far have been $900. She is scheduled for a gynecological procedure for which she will be charged $750. How much will Marilyn be reimbursed from her insurance carrier?

10.46 Casper has a major medical policy with a 20% copayment. He had medical bills totaling $7,000 and received $5,200 in benefits. What is his annual deductible?

10.47 If an insurance policy with no deductible pays $600 for an $800 series of medical tests, what is the patient's copayment?

10.48 If an insurance policy with a 10% copayment pays $360 for a $500 medical procedure, what is the policy's deductible?

10.49 How much will Susan be reimbursed for the year if she has a major medical policy with an annual deductible of $250, a 20% copayment, and a $1,000 out-of-pocket maximum?

Visit Number	Date	Amount Paid	Reasonable and Customary Fees
1	Jan. 7	$125	$150
2	Mar. 3	75	60
3	Apr. 11	275	200
4	July 11	300	325
5	Nov. 7	110	100

10.50 What would the annual premium be for a 35-year-old male, nonsmoker on a 20-year endowment policy whose face value is $90,000? (Refer to Table 10.1.)

10.51 If a 25-year-old nonsmoking male buys a $50,000 straight life policy, how much will his annual premium be (a) today and (b) in 5 years? (See Table 10.1.)

10.52 Franco is 20 years old and does not smoke, drink, or gamble. How much (a) 5-year term insurance and (b) straight life insurance can he purchase for $500 a year? Assume that policies are available only in $1,000 increments. (Refer to Table 10.1.)

10.53 Jack and Joe are twin brothers, 30 years of age. Neither of them smoke. They both purchase $60,000 worth of life insurance. What will be the difference in their annual premium if Jack purchases a 20-year limited payment life and Joe purchases a 20-year endowment policy? (See Table 10.1.)

10.54 Brenda hits a telephone pole and does $650 worth of damage to her car. How much will she be reimbursed from her insurance company if her collision coverage has a (a) $250 deductible, (b) $500 deductible, (c) $1,000 deductible?

10.55 If Dick has an accident with another car, and the driver and two passengers sustain injuries of $40,000, $30,000 and $40,000, respectively, how much will Dick be liable for if his liability coverage is (a) 50/100, (b) 30/150, and (c) 100/200?

10.56   George has the following coverage on his automobile insurance policy:

Liability:	50/100
Property damage:	$25,000
Personal injury protection:	$60,000
Collision:	$250 deductible
Comprehensive:	$250 deductible

George had an accident and is liable for the following amounts:

Damage to George's car:	$1,750
Damage to other car:	$3,600
Medical bills for George:	$8,000
Medical bills for driver of other car:	$12,500
Medical bills for passenger #1 of other car:	$62,750
Medical bills for passenger #2 of other car:	$17,500

Assuming that George was 100% at fault, how much money will he have to pay?

10.57   Ida had an automobile accident on her way home from work. Neither she nor the other driver had collision coverage on their automobiles. Ida's car sustained $3,500 in damages and the other car, $4,500. An investigation of the accident determined that Ida was 75% responsible for the accident. Assuming that neither driver was hurt

   (*a*)   How much did the other driver receive from Ida's insurance company in settlement of the claim?

   (*b*)   How much did Ida receive from the other driver's insurance company?

10.58   Victor has collision coverage on his automobile with a $250 deductible. If Victor has an accident with damages totaling $2,750, for which he is 80% responsible, how much will his insurance company pay toward repair of his car?

10.59   Peter and Paul have an automobile accident. Each driver has sufficient liability insurance, and each car sustains $1,800 in damage. An investigation of the accident puts each driver equally at fault. If Peter has $500 deductible collision coverage but Paul has no collision coverage, how much of a settlement will each driver receive from insurance?

10.60   Marge and Harriet collide with one another in a shopping-mall parking-lot. Each driver has 100/300 liability insurance, but Marge has collision coverage with a $500 deductible while Harriet has only $1,000 deductible collision coverage. Marge's car had $600 in damage, and Harriet has to pay $1,400 to have her car repaired. If Marge was determined to be 70% at fault, how much will each receive from her insurance company?

10.61   Henry's car caught fire on the expressway last night. Thankfully, Henry was not hurt but his car, whose book value is $14,000, will cost $10,000 to be restored. Furthermore, Henry's violin, valued at $2,300, was ruined in the fire. If Henry's comprehensive insurance has a $250 deductible, how much should Henry expect to receive from his insurance company?

10.62   Roger's car was broken into and vandalized. The following is a list of damage to his car:

Item to be Repaired or Replaced	Cost
Cracked passenger window	$375
Stolen car radio with cd player	850
Damaged steering column/lock	650
Stolen airbag	990
Stolen golf clubs	675
Damaged trunk lock	85

If Roger has comprehensive coverage with $500 deductible, how much will his insurance company pay him?

Answers to Supplementary Problems

10.25 $172.50

10.26 $97.50

10.27 $74,000

10.28 $120,000

10.29 $1,118.75

10.30 $1,187.50

10.31 $550

10.32 $431.51

10.33 $400.34

10.34 $262.57

10.35 $328.05

10.36 $8,750

10.37   (a) $9,583.33, (b) $15,000, (c) $15,000

10.38   (a) $11,500, (b) $119,500

10.39   (a) $9,500, (b) $99,500

10.40 $22,500

10.41   (a) $40, (b) $120

10.42 $255

10.43 $10,250

10.44 $1,005

10.45 $650

10.46 $500

10.47   25%

10.48 $100

10.49 $428

10.50 $2,385

10.51 (*a*) $361, (*b*) $361

10.52 (*a*) $259,000, (*b*) $86,000

10.53 $531

10.54 (*a*) $400, (*b*) $150, (*c*) $0

10.55 (*a*) $10,000, (*b*) $20,000, (*c*) $0

10.56 $13,000

10.57 (*a*) $3,375, (*b*) $875

10.58 $2,550

10.59 Peter, $1,550; Paul, $900

10.60 Marge, $250; Harriet, $1,100

10.61 $9,750

10.62 $2,450

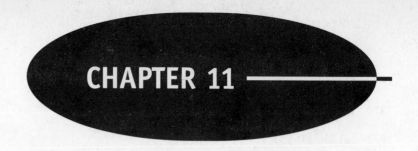

CHAPTER 11

Introduction to Statistics

11.1 UNGROUPED DATA

The results of experimentation often yield vast amounts of data. For example, if we wanted to analyze the distribution of income of blue collar workers within a major urban population, we might have several hundred thousand numbers to contend with, each one representing the income of an individual worker. *Descriptive statistics* is the branch of mathematics which deals with the problem of summarizing data into just a few numbers so that the essence of their behavior can be quickly and easily interpreted.

11.2 THE MEAN

The *mean* is a number which measures the "center" of a large collection of numbers called the *population*. Many people are familiar with the mean as a simple average. It is computed by adding up all the numbers and dividing by their quantity. The Greek letter μ (pronounced "mu") is used to represent the mean of a population.

$$\mu = \frac{x_1 + x_2 + \cdots + x_N}{N}$$

where $x_1, x_2, \ldots, x_N$ represent the values of the data in the population.

EXAMPLE 1

To compute the mean of the five numbers 36, 74, 99, 11, and 65 we add them up and divide by 5:

$$\mu = \frac{36 + 74 + 99 + 11 + 65}{5} = \frac{285}{5} = 57$$

SOLVED PROBLEMS

11.1   Compute the mean of the numbers 153, 287, 248, 101, 65, and 94.

SOLUTION

There are six numbers in the population:

$$\mu = \frac{153 + 287 + 248 + 101 + 65 + 94}{6} = \frac{948}{6} = 158$$

11.2   The annual income of eight families in a small community are \$65,000, \$74,000, \$98,250, \$88,500, \$57,500, \$102,000, \$55,350, and \$77,000. Compute the mean family income for this community.

SOLUTION

$$\mu = \frac{65,000 + 74,000 + 98,250 + 88,500 + 57,500 + 102,000 + 55,350 + 77,000}{8}$$

$$= \frac{617,600}{8}$$

$$= 77,200$$

The mean family income is \$77,200.

11.3   During one trading week the Dow Jones Average closed at 9,139, 9,150, 9,235, 8,911, and 9,050. Compute the mean closing Dow Jones averages for the week.

SOLUTION

$$\mu = \frac{9,139 + 9,150 + 9,235 + 8,911 + 9,050}{5} = \frac{45,485}{5} = 9,097$$

11.4   Frank filled his Cadillac up with gasoline 5 times during January. The number of gallons he required was 15.2, 13.7, 16.1, 14.9, 16.1.
Compute the mean number of gallons of gasoline his car required.

SOLUTION

$$\mu = \frac{15.2 + 13.7 + 16.1 + 14.9 + 16.1}{5} = \frac{76.0}{5} = 15.2 \text{ gal}$$

11.5   A college professor teaches four classes. The number of students in each of her classes is 28, 32, 26, 35.
Her contract with the university states that she must not have a mean class size of more than 30 students. Was this legal under the terms of her contract?

SOLUTION

The mean class size for her four classes is

$$\frac{28 + 32 + 26 + 35}{4} = \frac{121}{4} = 30.25$$

Since this number exceeds 30, her contract was violated.

11.6 A truck driver is entitled to a bonus if the mean number of miles he travels in a week exceeds 100. Rocco traveled the following distances last week:

Monday	111
Tuesday	102
Wednesday	93
Thursday	99
Friday	105
Saturday	100
	610

Is Rocco entitled to his bonus?

SOLUTION

The mean number of miles driven is 610/6 = 101.67. Since this exceeds 100 mi, he should get his bonus.

11.7 Don's delicatessen is open 7 days a week. His gross sales for the first week in February were

Sunday	$10,237
Monday	12,615
Tuesday	11,257
Wednesday	12,193
Thursday	13,012
Friday	10,518
Saturday	9,680
	$79,512

What were his mean gross sales for the week?

SOLUTION

His mean gross sales for the week were $79,512/7 = $11,358.86.

11.3 THE MEDIAN

If we were told that the mean of a set of numbers was *large*, we would probably expect the numbers in the set to be large. The next example shows that this may not be the case at all.

EXAMPLE 2

Consider the set of numbers 5, 1, 3, 8, 7, 2, 6, 5, 3, 960. The mean of these 10 numbers is

$$\frac{5+1+3+8+7+2+6+5+3+960}{10} = \frac{1,000}{10} = 100$$

The mean is 100, yet 9 out of 10 of the numbers are less than 10.

Although the mean is an excellent measure of central tendency, it does have one deficiency—its value can be dramatically influenced by the presence of *extreme values*.

If we were given only the mean, we would be given a misleading representation of the data <u>as a whole</u>. Clearly most of the numbers are small (all except one of them are less than 10), yet the mean has a value of 100.

To allow for a more accurate summary, the *median* is often given, along with the mean and standard deviation, to describe the data. The median is not affected by the presence of extreme values and can help give a much more realistic picture of the situation.

To compute the median, we first reorder the data, smallest number first and largest last. If the data consist of an *odd* number of values, the median is the middle value. If the data have an *even* number of values, we take the two middle values and compute their average. Whether we have an odd or an even number of values, there are always just as many numbers above the median as below it.

EXAMPLE 3

Let's compute the median of the numbers 4, 1, 7, 5, 157. If we reorder (rearrange) the numbers, we get 1, 4, 5, 7, 157.

Since we have an odd number of values, we take the middle value. The median is 5. Note how little an effect the extreme value 157 has on the median.

EXAMPLE 4

Consider the numbers 7, 4, 4, 2, 6, 100. Reordering, we get 2, 4, 4, 6, 7, 100.
The two middle numbers are 4 and 6. Their average is $(4+6)/2 = 5$. The median is 5.

For a large set of numbers, finding the middle number(s) is easy if we first compute its (their) position(s). Suppose that N represents the size of the data set:

If N is odd, the middle number will have position $(N+1)/2$.

If N is even, the middle two numbers will have positions $N/2$ and $N/2 + 1$.

Always remember to reorder the numbers first!

EXAMPLE 5

Compute the median of the data sets

(a)   3, 1, 8, 2, 7, 5, 8, 10, 3, 5, 7, 8, 11, 4, 5, 7, 1

(b)   7, 9, 4, 11, 5, 9, 12, 14, 5, 8, 11, 12, 50, 13

Data set (a) has 17 values, an odd number ($N = 17$). Reordering them, we get 1, 1, 2, 3, 3, 4, 5, 5, 5, 7, 7, 7, 8, 8, 8, 10, 11. The center position is $(N+1)/2 = (17+1)/2 = 9$. The median is the 9th value, 5.

Data set (b) has 14 values, an even number ($N = 14$). Reordering, we get 4, 5, 5, 7, 8, 9, 9, 11, 11, 12, 12, 13, 14, 50. The two middle positions are $N/2 = 14/2 = 7$ and $N/2 + 1 = 14/2 + 1 = 8$. The corresponding data values are 9 and 11. The median is the average of these two values, which is 10. Note that the median is not necessarily a value of the data set. However, it is the middle number, in the sense that there is an equal number of values above and below it.

SOLVED PROBLEMS

11.8   The heights of six people who work for the same boss are (in inches) 68, 71, 66, 69, 73, and 72. Find their median height.

SOLUTION

Reordering the data, we get 66, 68, 69, 71, 72, 73. The two middle values are 69 and 71. Their average is $(69+71)/2 = 70$. The median height is 70 in.

11.9   The duration of nine telephone calls made from a certain telephone one day was:

1 min, 7 s	2 min, 11 s	1 min, 37 s
3 min, 11 s	2 min, 5 s	3 min, 30 s
2 min, 6 s	2 min, 26 s	0 min, 50 s

Compute the mean and median telephone call duration.

SOLUTION

First, we convert the times to seconds. Since there are 60 seconds in a minute, the call times, in seconds, are 67, 131, 97, 191, 125, 210, 126, 146, 50. The mean is

$$\mu = \frac{67 + 131 + 97 + 191 + 125 + 210 + 126 + 146 + 50}{9} = \frac{1{,}143}{9} = 127 \text{ s}$$

To compute the median, we must reorder the data: 50, 67, 97, 125, 126, 131, 146, 191, 210.
The middle value is the fifth $[(9 + 1)/2 = 5]$, so the median call length is 126 s. Note that the median is fairly close to the mean.

11.10   Suppose that an additional telephone call of duration 20 min is added to the calls in Prob. 11.9. What are the new mean and median?

SOLUTION

The mean is now

$$\mu = \frac{67 + 131 + 97 + 191 + 125 + 210 + 126 + 146 + 50 + 1{,}200}{10} = \frac{2{,}343}{10} = 234.3 \text{ s}$$

The reordered list of times now reads 50, 67, 97, 125, 126, 131, 146, 191, 210, 1,200. The middle two positions are the fifth (10/2) and sixth (10/2 + 1). Their corresponding values are 126 and 131. The median call length is now $(126 + 131)/2 = 128.5$. Note how one abnormally large value changes the mean significantly but does not have much effect on the median (compare with Prob. 11.9).

11.11   What would you say about a set of data which has

(a)   A mean of 200 and a median of 20?

(b)   A mean of 20 and a median of 200?

SOLUTION

(a)   The data probably have one or more abnormally large values.

(b)   The data probably have one or more abnormally small values.

11.12   Eight bags of sugar are sitting on a shelf. Their weights are

1 lb 6 oz	2 lb 7 oz
1 lb 1 oz	1 lb 14 oz
2 lb 2 oz	1 lb 5 oz
1 lb	1 lb 9 oz

(a)   What is their mean weight?

(b)   What is their median weight?

SOLUTION

The weights of the eight bags in ounces are 22, 39, 17, 30, 34, 21, 16, 25. The mean weight of the bags is

$$\frac{22 + 39 + 17 + 30 + 34 + 21 + 16 + 25}{8} = \frac{204}{8} = 25.5 \text{ oz}$$

To compute the median weight, we must reorder their weights: 16, 17, 21, 22, 25, 30, 34, 39. The median is the average of the two middlemost weights, 22 and 25:

$$\frac{22 + 25}{2} = \frac{47}{2} = 23.5 \text{ oz}$$

11.13 Compute the median for each of the following data sets:

(a)   41, 54, 42, 53, 49, 51, 37

(b)   41, 54, 42, 53, 49, 51, 37, 75

SOLUTION

(a)   We reorder the numbers: 37, 41, 42, 49, 51, 53, 54. Since there is an odd number of values $N = 7$, the middle value is in position $(N + 1)/2 = 8/2 = 4$. The median is the fourth number in the list, 49.

(b)   Now there is an even number of values in the list, $N = 8$. The middle two positions are $N/2 = 4$ and $N/2 + 1 = 5$, i.e., the fourth and fifth positions. The numbers corresponding to these positions are 49 and 51, so the median is $(49 + 51)/2 = 50$.

11.4 THE MODE

The *mode* is the value in a set of data that occurs most frequently. There is no mathematical calculation necessary to compute the mode—just look over the data and select the one that appears most often. It often helps to reorder the data first.

EXAMPLE 6

To find the mode of the data 15, 12, 17, 15, 21, 17, 15, 27, 9, 15, 18, 17, 19, 15, 11, we first reorder the numbers: 9, 11, 12, 15, 15, 15, 15, 15, 17, 17, 17, 18, 19, 21, 27.

It is clear that the most common number is 15 (repeated 5 times), so the mode = 15.

SOLVED PROBLEMS

11.14 A class of 15 took an exam and received the following grades:

$$
\begin{array}{ccccc}
75 & 97 & 52 & 75 & 90 \\
53 & 86 & 69 & 82 & 80 \\
92 & 75 & 80 & 85 & 78 \\
\end{array}
$$

What is the median and the mode of this set of data?

SOLUTION

We reorder the data: 52, 53, 69, 75, 75, 75, 78, 80, 80, 82, 85, 86, 90, 92, 97. There are 15 (an odd number) scores: $(15 + 1)/2 = 8$. The eighth score, 80, is the median. The most frequently occurring value is 75. The mode is 75.

11.15 Determine the median and mode of a payroll consisting of 10 salary checks:

$2,150 $1,975 $2,050 $1,900 $2,150
$1,875 $1,750 $1,925 $2,100 $2,175

SOLUTION

Reordering the data gives

$1,750 $1,875 $1,900 $1,925 $1,975 $2,050 $2,100 $2,150 $2,150 $2,175

There are 10 (an even number) payroll amounts: $10/2 = 5$ and $10/2 + 1 = 6$. The average of the fifth and sixth values is $(1,975 + 2,050)/2 = 4,025/2 = 2,012.50$. The median is $2,012.50. The most common payroll figure is $2,150 (repeated twice). The mode is $2,150.

11.16 Find the median and mode for the following times that it takes a commuter to get from home to the office (all times are in minutes): 24, 36, 22, 24, 28, 30, 32, 24, 22, 26.

SOLUTION

Reordering the data is crucial for computing the median and is a convenience for computing the mode: 22, 22, 24, 24, 24, 26, 28, 30, 32, 36. Here, $N = 10$. Since N is even, we determine the two middlemost values: positions $N/2 = 5$ and $N/2 + 1 = 6$. The numbers in the fifth and sixth positions are 24 and 26. The median is the average of these two numbers: $(24 + 26)/2 = 50/2 = 25$ minutes. The most common value is 24 (repeated 3 times). The mode is 24 minutes.

11.5   THE STANDARD DEVIATION

The mean gives an excellent indication of the "center" of a collection of numbers, but gives no information as to how far apart they are spread. Both are necessary if we are to have an accurate summary of the data they represent.

If μ is the mean of the set of numbers $x_1, x_2, \ldots, x_N$, then $x_i - \mu$[1] is called the *deviation from the mean*. It tells us how far the number x_i is from the mean, and on which side of the mean x_i lies. The deviation $x_i - \mu$ is positive if x_i is greater than μ and negative if x_i is less than μ.

The number $(x_i - \mu)^2$ is called the *squared* deviation from the mean. It can never be negative. The average of the squared deviations is called the *variance* of the data, and is represented by V.

$$V = \frac{(x_1 - \mu)^2 + (x_2 - \mu)^2 + \cdots + (x_N - \mu)^2}{N}$$

The purpose of squaring is to eliminate negative deviations. If we did not square, the positive and negative deviations would always add to 0. Unfortunately, squaring also exaggerates the values of the deviations, making the variance an unrealistic measure. We compensate by taking the square root of the variance. This number is called the *standard deviation* and is represented by the Greek letter σ (sigma). (You can easily calculate square roots using the $\sqrt{}$ key on your calculator.)

$$\sigma = \sqrt{V}$$

---

[1] The use of x_i is standard mathematical notation. i is a "dummy" variable which can be any number from 1 to N, so x_i represents any of the numbers $x_1, x_2, \ldots, x_N$. Using this device, we can discuss the data more conveniently.

EXAMPLE 7

Compute the standard deviation of the sets of numbers (a) 3, 5, 7, 9, 11; (b) 1, 3, 7, 10, 14; and (c) 7, 7, 7, 7, 7.

(a) The mean must first be computed:

$$\mu = \frac{3 + 5 + 7 + 9 + 11}{5} = \frac{35}{5} = 7.$$

Next the variance:

$$V = \frac{(3 - 7)^2 + (5 - 7)^2 + (7 - 7)^2 + (9 - 7)^2 + (11 - 7)^2}{5}$$

$$= \frac{(-4)^2 + (-2)^2 + 0^2 + 2^2 + 4^2}{5}$$

$$= \frac{16 + 4 + 0 + 4 + 16}{5}$$

$$= \frac{40}{5} = 8$$

Finally the standard deviation: $\sigma = \sqrt{V} = \sqrt{8} = 2.828$.

(b)
$$\mu = \frac{1 + 3 + 7 + 10 + 14}{5} = \frac{35}{5} = 7$$

$$V = \frac{(1 - 7)^2 + (3 - 7)^2 + (7 - 7)^2 + (10 - 7)^2 + (14 - 7)^2}{5}$$

$$= \frac{(-6)^2 + (-4)^2 + 0^2 + 3^2 + 7^2}{5}$$

$$= \frac{36 + 16 + 0 + 9 + 49}{5}$$

$$= \frac{110}{5} = 22$$

$$\mu = \sqrt{22} = 4.690$$

Even though the mean in parts (a) and (b) are both 7, the standard deviation in (b) is much larger than in (a). This is because the numbers in (b) are farther from the mean, so that the individual squared deviations are larger.

(c)
$$\mu = \frac{7 + 7 + 7 + 7 + 7}{5} = \frac{35}{5} = 7$$

$$V = \frac{(7 - 7)^2 + (7 - 7)^2 + (7 - 7)^2 + (7 - 7)^2 + (7 - 7)^2}{5}$$

$$= \frac{0^2 + 0^2 + 0^2 + 0^2 + 0^2}{5}$$

$$= \frac{0 + 0 + 0 + 0 + 0}{5}$$

$$= \frac{0}{5} = 0$$

$$\sigma = \sqrt{0} = 0$$

Note once again that the mean is 7. The standard deviation is 0 because all the numbers are equal and identical to the mean; 0 is the smallest value that the standard deviation can ever be. This can happen only when all the numbers are the same.

There is another way to compute the variance, which is a little more convenient, especially when the mean is not a "round" number. The following alternate formula can be shown to be mathematically equivalent to the formula for variance given previously:

$$V = \frac{x_1^2 + x_2^2 + \cdots + x_N^2}{N} - \mu^2$$

EXAMPLE 8

To show that this formula is an alternate way of computing the variance, we apply it to the data set of Example 7, part (b). The numbers are 1, 3, 7, 10, 14. We have already seen that $\mu = 7$.

$$V = \frac{x_1^2 + x_2^2 + \cdots + x_N^2}{N} - \mu^2$$

$$= \frac{1^2 + 3^2 + 7^2 + 10^2 + 14^2}{5} - 7^2$$

$$= \frac{1 + 9 + 49 + 100 + 196}{5} - 49$$

$$= \frac{355}{5} - 49$$

$$= 71 - 49$$

$$= 22 \quad \text{[compare with Example 7(b)]}$$

$$\sigma = \sqrt{22} = 4.690$$

It is sometimes convenient to compute the standard deviation using a *tabular* format. The next example illustrates how this is done.

EXAMPLE 9

To compute the mean and standard deviation for the data in Example 7, part (b) using a tabular format, we form a table with two columns. The first column represents the data and the second column the square of the data. Then we add the two columns:

x	x^2
1	1
3	9
7	49
10	100
14	196
35	355

$$\mu = \frac{35}{5} = 7$$

$$V = \frac{355}{5} - 7^2 = 71 - 49 = 22$$

$$\sigma = \sqrt{22} = 4.690$$

SOLVED PROBLEMS

11.17 Compute the mean, variance, and standard deviation of the data 2, 5, 8, 10, 12, 14, 19.

SOLUTION

There are seven numbers:

$$\mu = \frac{2 + 5 + 8 + 10 + 12 + 14 + 19}{7} = 10$$

$$V = \frac{(2 - 10)^2 + (5 - 10)^2 + (8 - 10)^2 + (12 - 10)^2 + (14 - 10)^2 + (19 - 10)^2}{7}$$

$$= \frac{(-8)^2 + (-5)^2 + (-2)^2 + 2^2 + 4^2 + 9^2}{7}$$

$$= \frac{64 + 25 + 4 + 4 + 16 + 81}{7}$$

$$= \frac{194}{7}$$

$$= 27.7143$$

$$\sigma = \sqrt{V} = \sqrt{27.7143} = 5.26$$

11.18 Use the alternate formula illustrated in Example 8 to compute the variance and standard deviation of the data in Prob. 11.17.

SOLUTION

As in Prob. 11.17, $\mu = 10$.

$$V = \frac{x_1^2 + x_2^2 + \cdots + x_N^2}{N} - \mu^2$$

$$= \frac{2^2 + 5^2 + 8^2 + 10^2 + 12^2 + 14^2 + 19^2}{7} - 10^2$$

$$= \frac{4 + 25 + 64 + 100 + 144 + 196 + 361}{7} - 100$$

$$= \frac{894}{7} - 100$$

$$= 127.7143 - 100$$

$$= 27.7143$$

$$\sigma = \sqrt{27.7143} = 5.26$$

11.19 Compute the mean and standard deviation of the data in Prob. 11.17 using a tabular format.

SOLUTION

x	x^2
2	4
5	25
8	64
10	100
12	144
14	196
19	361
70	894

$$\mu = \frac{70}{7} = 10$$

$$V = \frac{894}{7} - 10^2 = 127.7143 - 100 = 27.7143$$

$$\sigma = \sqrt{27.7143} = 5.26$$

11.20 The annual salaries (in thousands of dollars) for a group of college professors from eight universities are 65, 57, 60, 75, 76, 72, 64, and 69. Compute their mean income and standard deviation.

SOLUTION

x	x^2
65	4,225
57	3,249
60	3,600
75	5,625
76	5,776
72	5,184
64	4,096
69	4,761
538	36,516

$$\mu = \frac{538}{8} = 67.25$$

$$V = \frac{36,516}{8} - 67.25^2 = 4,564.5 - 4,522.5625 = 41.9375$$

$$\sigma = \sqrt{41.9375} = 6.476$$

Their mean income is $67,250. The standard deviation is $6,476.

11.21 What is the mean and standard deviation of the set of data 13, 13, 13, 13, 13, 13, 13, 13, 13, 13, 13.

SOLUTION

Since the data values are identical, their mean is 13 and the standard deviation is 0.

11.22 A donut machine produces the following quantities of donuts during a 5-hour test. Compute the mean and standard deviation of the numbers of donuts made.

Hours	Number of Donuts
1	156
2	173
3	144
4	150
5	158

SOLUTION

x	x^2
156	24,336
173	29,929
144	20,736
150	22,500
158	24,964
781	122,465

$$\mu = \frac{781}{5} = 156.2 \text{ donuts}$$

$$V = \frac{122,465}{5} - 156.2^2 = 24,493 - 24,398.44 = 94.56$$

$$\sigma = \sqrt{94.56} = 9.72 \text{ donuts}$$

11.23 Without performing any calculation, which data set has the larger (*a*) mean and (*b*) standard deviation?

Data set 1:   35   40   45   50   55   60   65
Data set 2:   20   30   40   50   60   70   80

SOLUTION

(*a*)   50 is the mean of data set 1. (Observe that each number to the left of 50 is "counterbalanced" by a number equally as far to the right of 50.) Similarly, data set 2 has a mean of 50. Both sets have the same mean.

(*b*)   Since the numbers in data set 2 are farther from the mean than the numbers in data set 1, data set 2 has a larger standard deviation.

11.24 Confirm your suspicions in Prob. 11.23 by doing the actual calculations.

Data Set 1

x	x^2
35	1,225
40	1,600
45	2,025
50	2,500
55	3,025
60	3,600
65	4,225
350	18,200

Data Set 2

x	x^2
20	400
30	900
40	1,600
50	2,500
60	3,600
70	4,900
80	6,400
350	20,300

$$\mu = \frac{350}{7} = 50 \qquad\qquad \mu = \frac{350}{7} = 50$$

$$V = \frac{18,200}{7} - 50^2 = 2,600 - 2,500 \qquad V = \frac{20,300}{7} - 50^2 = 2,900 - 2,500$$

$$= 100 \qquad\qquad\qquad\qquad\qquad = 400$$

$$\sigma = \sqrt{100} = 10 \qquad\qquad\qquad \sigma = \sqrt{400} = 20$$

Observe that the means of both data sets are the same. The standard deviation of data set 2 is precisely double that of data set 1. (Can you see why?)

11.6 GROUPED DATA

Computing the mean and standard deviation of large groups of data can be difficult. Often, data sets have repetitive values and the formulas for μ and σ can be modified to take advantage of this.

Suppose that the value x is repeated 3 times. Instead of adding $x + x + x$, it is simpler to multiply x by 3 to get $3x$.

More generally, if x is repeated f times (f is called the *frequency* of x), the value equivalent to $\underbrace{x + x + \cdots + x}_{f \text{ times}}$ is fx or xf.

The mean of a set of numbers can be written

$$\boxed{\mu = \frac{x_1 f_1 + x_2 f_2 + \cdots + x_n f_n}{N}}$$

Here, n represents the number of <u>different</u> values in the set and N represents the total number of values. Note that $N = f_1 + f_2 + \cdots + f_n$. N is called the *total frequency*.

The mean can be conveniently computed in a tabular format.

EXAMPLE 10

Compute the mean of the set of numbers 2, 2, 3, 3, 3, 3, 4, 4, 4, 5. First we list the values of x and their corresponding frequencies:

x_i	f_i	$x_i f_i$
2	2	4
3	4	12
4	3	12
5	1	5
	$N = 10$	33

$$\mu = \frac{x_1 f_1 + x_2 f_2 + x_3 f_3 + x_4 f_4}{N} = \frac{33}{10} = 3.3$$

The variance and standard deviation can be computed in similar fashion. Since it is easily adapted to tabular calculation, the most convenient formula to use is

$$V = \frac{x_1^2 f_1 + x_2^2 f_2 + \cdots + x_n^2 f_n}{N} - \mu^2$$

$$\sigma = \sqrt{V}$$

EXAMPLE 11

Compute the variance and standard deviation for the data of Example 10. Recall that $\mu = 3.3$.

x_i	x_i^2	f_i	$x_i^2 f_i$
2	4	2	8
3	9	4	36
4	16	3	48
5	25	1	25
		$N = 10$	117

$$V = \frac{x_1^2 f_1 + x_2^2 f_2 + x_3^2 f_3 + x_4^2 f_4}{N} - \mu^2$$

$$= \frac{117}{10} - 3.3^2$$

$$= 11.7 - 10.89$$

$$= 0.81$$

$$\sigma = \sqrt{0.81} = 0.9$$

When a data set consists of a large number of values, it is convenient to group them into classes. The upper and lower endpoints of each class are called the *class limits*. The number of values that fall within each class is called the *class frequency*. The midpoint of each class, called the *class mark*, may be used together with the class frequency to obtain accurate approximations of the mean and standard deviation.

EXAMPLE 12

A sample of 50 students showed the following grades on a college entrance exam:

$$
\begin{array}{cccccccccc}
65 & 72 & 87 & 78 & 66 & 85 & 77 & 94 & 62 & 55 \\
75 & 84 & 76 & 88 & 57 & 63 & 88 & 92 & 92 & 87 \\
51 & 66 & 69 & 88 & 97 & 43 & 59 & 77 & 62 & 48 \\
44 & 58 & 68 & 79 & 62 & 55 & 51 & 49 & 57 & 67 \\
52 & 55 & 76 & 88 & 99 & 44 & 56 & 79 & 87 & 59
\end{array}
$$

First we group the data into classes of width 10 starting with a lower class limit of 40. The class mark is the average of the lower and upper class limits. The frequency is the number of values which fall in each class.

Lower Class Limit	Upper Class Limit	Class Mark x_i	Squared Class Mark x_i^2	Frequency f_i	$x_i f_i$	$x_i^2 f_i$
40	49	44.5	1,980.25	5	222.5	9,901.25
50	59	54.5	2,970.25	12	654.0	35,643.00
60	69	64.5	4.160.25	10	645.0	41,602.50
70	79	74.5	5,550.25	9	670.5	49,952.25
80	89	84.5	7,140.25	9	760.5	64,262.25
90	99	94.5	8,930.25	5	472.5	44,651.25
				50	3,425.0	246,012.50

$$\mu = \frac{x_1 f_1 + x_2 f_2 + x_3 f_3 + x_4 f_4 + x_5 f_5 + x_6 f_6}{N} = \frac{3,425.0}{50} = 68.5$$

$$V = \frac{x_1^2 f_1 + x_2^2 f_2 + x_3^2 f_3 + x_4^2 f_4 + x_5^2 f_5 + x_6^2 f_6}{N} - \mu^2$$

$$= \frac{246,012.50}{50} - 68.5^2$$

$$= 4,920.25 - 4,692.25$$

$$= 228.0$$

$$\sigma = \sqrt{228.0} = 15.1$$

SOLVED PROBLEMS

11.25 Find the mean and standard deviation of the following data:

x_i	30	40	50	60
f_i	12	17	16	5

SOLUTION

x_i	x_i^2	f_i	$x_i f_i$	$x_i^2 f_i$
30	900	12	360	10,800
40	1,600	17	680	27,200
50	2,500	16	800	40,000
60	3,600	5	300	18,000
		$N = 50$	2,140	96,000

$$\mu = \frac{x_1 f_1 + x_2 f_2 + x_3 f_3 + x_4 f_4}{N} = \frac{2,140}{50} = 42.8$$

$$V = \frac{x_1^2 f_1 + x_2^2 f_2 + x_3^2 f_3 + x_4^2 f_4}{N} - \mu^2$$

$$= \frac{96,000}{50} - 42.8^2$$

$$= 1,920 - 1,831.84$$

$$= 88.16$$

$$\sigma = \sqrt{88.16} = 9.39$$

11.26 One hundred tires were driven until their tread wore out. The number of miles driven, to the nearest 5,000, was determined and tabulated:

Number of Miles (Thousands)	Number of Tires
30	10
35	16
40	36
45	22
50	10
55	6

Compute the mean and the standard deviation for the number of miles driven on these tires.

SOLUTION

x_i	x_i^2	f_i	$x_i f_i$	$x_i^2 f_i$
30	900	10	300	9,000
35	1,225	16	560	19,600
40	1,600	36	1,440	57,600
45	2,025	22	990	44,550
50	2,500	10	500	25,000
55	3,025	6	330	18,150
		$N = 100$	4,120	173,900

$$\mu = \frac{x_1 f_1 + x_2 f_2 + x_3 f_3 + x_4 f_4 + x_5 f_5 + x_6 f_6}{N}$$

$$= \frac{4,120}{100}$$

$$= 41.2 \quad \text{(thousands)}$$

The mean number of miles driven is 41,200.

$$V = \frac{x_1^2 f_1 + x_2^2 f_2 + x_3^2 f_3 + x_4^2 f_4 + x_5^2 f_5 + x_6^2 f_6}{N} - \mu^2$$

$$= \frac{173,900}{100} - 41.2^2$$

$$= 1,739 - 1,697.44$$

$$= 41.56$$

$$\sigma = \sqrt{41.56} = 6.447 \quad \text{(thousands)}$$

The standard deviation is 6,447 mi.

11.27 A survey of the ages women marry yielded the following data:

25	22	30	19	21	22	29	31
21	23	25	31	30	22	27	24
23	25	20	18	22	34	23	31
22	21	22	20	19	30	32	23
31	33	32	21	22	37	28	27

(a) Starting with a lower class limit of 18, group the data into five classes of width 3.
(b) Compute the mean.
(c) Compute the variance and the standard deviation.

SOLUTION

(a)

Lower Class Limit	Upper Class Limit	Class Mark x_i	Squared Class Mark x_i^2	Frequency f_i	$x_i f_i$	$x_i^2 f_i$
18	20	19	361	5	95	1,805
21	23	22	484	15	330	7,260
24	26	25	625	4	100	2,500
27	29	28	784	4	112	3,136
30	32	31	961	9	279	8,649
33	35	34	1,156	2	68	2,312
36	38	37	1,369	1	37	1,369
				40	1,021	27,031

(b)
$$\mu = \frac{x_1 f_1 + x_2 f_2 + x_3 f_3 + x_4 f_4 + x_5 f_5 + x_6 f_6 + x_7 f_7}{N}$$

$$= \frac{1,021}{40}$$

$$= 25.525$$

(c)
$$V = \frac{x_1^2 f_1 + x_2^2 f_2 + x_3^2 f_3 + x_4^2 f_4 + x_5^2 f_5 + x_6^2 f_6 + x_7^2 f_7}{N} - \mu^2$$

$$= \frac{27,031}{40} - 25.525^2$$

$$= 675.775 - 651.525$$

$$= 24.25$$

$$\sigma = \sqrt{24.25} = 4.92$$

Supplementary Problems

11.28 Compute the mean of the seven numbers 123, 235, 342, 411, 252, 373, 399.

11.29 The annual gross income for the Jones family is

Mr. Jones:	$75,624
Mrs. Jones:	$56,121
Tommy Jones:	$41,437
Terry Jones:	$31,234

Compute the mean annual gross income for the Jones family.

11.30 Compute the mean high temperature for the week given the following daily high temperatures (in degrees Fahrenheit): 70, 72, 62, 79, 69, 70, 75.

11.31 To compute the gas mileage on his new car, Jeremy filled it up 5 times with a measured gallon of gasoline and drove it each time until he ran out of gas. The numbers of miles he traveled were 16.3, 16.9, 16.8, 16.8, and 16.4. What was the mean number of miles Jeremy's car traveled on a gallon of gas?

11.32 If a salesman travels 157 mi on Monday, 143 mi on Tuesday, 211 mi on Wednesday, 120 mi on Thursday, and 146 mi on Friday, what is his mean distance traveled for the week?

11.33 Mrs. Martin had sextuplets (6 babies). Their weights were 3 lb 6 oz, 3 lb 1 oz, 3 lb 8 oz, 3 lb 7 oz, 2 lb 10 oz, and 3 lb 2 oz. What is the mean weight of Mrs. Martin's babies?

11.34 The heights of 5 men are 6 ft 0 in, 6 ft 1 in, 5 ft 10 in, 6 ft 0 in, and 5 ft 11 in. Compute the mean, median, and standard deviation of their heights.

11.35 The men in Prob. 11.34 married, respectively, women whose heights are 5 ft 6 in, 5 ft 9 in, 5 ft 7 in, 5 ft 10 in, and 5 ft 11 in. Compute the mean, median, and standard deviation of their heights.

11.36 Compute the mean, median, and standard deviation of the *difference* in heights between the spouses of problems 11.34 and 11.35.

11.37 What can be said about a set of data whose mean is 149 and whose standard deviation is 0?

11.38 The following three sets of numbers each have mean 60. Which has the largest standard deviation? Which has the smallest standard deviation? (Do not perform any calculation.)

Set A: 52, 56, 60, 64, 68
Set B: 50, 55, 60, 65, 70
Set C: 40, 50, 60, 70, 80

11.39 Compute the standard deviation for each of the data sets of Prob. 11.38 to confirm your previous answer.

11.40 What would happen to the mean of a set of data if each value were increased by 5?

11.41 What would happen to the variance and standard deviation of a set of data if each value were increased by 5?

11.42 A count of the number of cashew nuts in 10 cans of mixed nuts yielded the following data:

Number of cashews: 27, 30, 28, 24, 22, 28, 30, 28, 25, 29

Compute the mean, median, mode, and standard deviation of the number of cashews found.

11.43 The number of innings in 10 Major League baseball games on a recent Yankee road trip was 9, 10, 9, $11\frac{1}{2}$, $8\frac{1}{2}$, 9, 10, 10, 9, $10\frac{1}{2}$. Compute the mean, median, and mode.

11.44 The number of 911 calls arriving at a central dispatch switchboard during 5 consecutive hours was 37, 23, 28, 29, and 32. Compute the mean, median, and standard deviation.

11.45 A class of 20 students took an examination in business mathematics and received the following scores:

27	52	76	98	75
87	75	68	90	87
68	82	35	75	69
99	82	58	70	75

Compute the mean, median, and mode.

11.46 Compute the mean, variance, and standard deviation of a set of numbers with the following frequency distribution:

x	f
2	3
3	4
5	5
6	7
7	1

11.47 Twenty-five women were asked to state the age at which they had their first child. The results were put into a frequency table:

Age	f
19	2
20	3
21	5
22	4
23	4
24	3
25	2
26	0
27	1
28	1

Compute the mean age at which each woman's first child was born. Compute the standard deviation.

11.48 In a medical study, the number of days it took to recover from a certain strain of flu was recorded for a group of 50 people. The results were tabulated and put into a frequency table:

Days	f
1	3
2	9
3	20
4	12
5	4
6	2

Compute the mean recovery time. What is the standard deviation?

11.49 A sample of 50 oranges taken from an orange tree was sampled to determine their size.

Diameter, cm	8.8	8.9	9.0	9.1	9.2
Oranges	7	15	20	5	3

Compute the mean, variance, and standard deviation of the sample.

11.50 Professor Lerner will curve his examination if the mean grade of the class is less than 60. The distribution of grades on his most recent exam was

Grade	f
40–49	1
50–59	7
60–69	12
70–79	15
80–89	4
90–99	1

Will Professor Lerner curve his examination? Use the class marks (center of each class) to approximate the mean.

11.51 A survey was taken of the number of pounds 50 people lost while participating in a nationally advertised weight-loss plan.

Pounds Lost

3	7	10	15	8	11	12	3	21	22
7	9	30	22	11	5	6	6	8	7
2	8	5	30	16	8	10	9	1	1
1	2	3	13	14	15	6	9	2	5
5	7	14	13	12	15	4	6	21	12

(a) Organize the data into a frequency distribution using classes 1–5, 6–10, and so forth.

(b) Using the class mark (midpoint of each class), compute the mean, variance, and standard deviation.

11.52 The annual incomes of 40 people randomly selected from the workforce were compiled.

Annual Income (in Thousands of $)

58	65	93	43	50	99	65	78	45	63
37	52	60	81	55	42	29	44	39	62
59	98	66	48	61	36	44	58	71	74
43	25	80	75	68	55	40	37	34	27

(a) Organize the data into a frequency distribution using classes 20–29, 30–39, and so on.

(b) Using the class mark (midpoint of each class), compute the mean, variance, and standard deviation.

Answers to Supplementary Problems

11.28 305

11.29 $51,104

11.30 71°

11.31 16.64 mi

11.32 155.4 mi

11.33 3 lb 3 oz (51 oz)

11.34 Mean = 5 ft 11.6 in (71.6 in), median = 6 ft 0 in (72 in), standard deviation = 1.02 in

11.35 Mean = 5 ft 8.6 in (68.6 in), median = 5 ft 9 in (69 in), standard deviation = 1.85 in

11.36 Mean = 3 in, median = 3 in, standard deviation = 2 in

11.37 All numbers in the data set are 149

11.38 Set C has largest standard deviation; set A has smallest

11.39 Set A, $\sigma = 5.66$; set B, $\sigma = 7.07$; set C, $\sigma = 14.14$

11.40 The mean would increase by 5

11.41 No change in standard deviation since mean increases along with each value of the data; deviation from mean remains unchanged

11.42 $\mu = 27.1$, median $= 28$, mode $= 28$, $\sigma = 2.51$

11.43 $\mu = 9.65$, median $= 9.5$, mode $= 9$

11.44 $\mu = 29.8$, median $= 29$, $\sigma = 4.62$

11.45 $\mu = 72.4$, median $= 75$, mode $= 75$

11.46 $\mu = 4.6$, $V = 2.54$, $\sigma = 1.59$

11.47 $\mu = 22.4$ years, $\sigma = 2.24$ years

11.48 $\mu = 3.22$ days, $\sigma = 1.14$ days

11.49 $\mu = 8.964$ cm, $V = 0.01$, $\sigma = 0.10$ cm

11.50 Class marks $= 44.5, 54.5, 64.5, 74.5, 84.5, 94.5$ using these values, $\mu = 68.75$, so Professor Lerner will not curve the exam

11.51 (*a*)

Class Limits	Class Mark	Frequency
1–5	3	14
6–10	8	17
11–15	13	12
16–20	18	1
21–25	23	4
26–30	28	2

(*b*) $\mu = 10$ lb, $V = 45$, $\sigma = 6.71$ lb

11.52 (*a*)

Class Limits	Class Mark	Frequency
20–29	24.5	3
30–39	34.5	5
40–49	44.5	8
50–59	54.5	7
60–69	64.5	8
70–79	74.5	4
80–89	84.5	2
90–99	94.5	3

(*b*) $\mu = 56.25$ ($\$56{,}250$), $V = 359.44$, $\sigma = 18.959$ ($\$18{,}959$).

INDEX

Accrued bond interest, 158–159
Accumulated value:
  annuity, 123–126
  in interest calculations, 105–106, 115, 116–117
Accumulation factor:
  annuity, 124, 125
  sinking fund, 132–134
Actuaries, 202
Addition:
  algebra, 18–19
  with calculator, 15
  decimal, 11–12
  fraction, 6–7
  order of operations, 10, 16
  whole number, 1–2
Algebra, 17–19
  exponents (powers), 4, 10, 16
  order of operations, 10, 16
  variables, 17–18, 28
Amortization, 137–141
  calculating monthly payments, 137–140
  principal balance, 137
Amortization schedule, 139
Amount (see Maturity value)
Annual yield, stock, 152–153
Annuities, 123–149
  accumulated value, 123–126
  amortization and, 137–141
  annuity due, 123, 124, 126, 127
  defined, 123
  discounted value, 123, 127–129
  formulas for, 124
  ordinary, 123, 124, 127
  present value, 123, 127
  sinking funds, 132–134
  types of, 123
Annuity due, 123–127
  accumulated value of, 125–126
  present value of, 127
Approximate time, 108–109, 112–113
Automobile insurance, 213–214

Bank discount, 116–117
Banker's year, 107
Beneficiary, life insurance, 210
Bodily injury liability insurance, 213
Bond(s), 157–160
  accrued bond interest, 158–159
  defined, 157

Bond(s) (Cont.):
  evaluating investments in, 159–160
  market quotations, 157–158
  semiannual interest payment, 158–159
Bond rate, 157
Book value:
  defined, 69
  in double declining balance method of
    depreciation, 82–83
  for insurance purposes, 213
  of sinking fund debt, 134
  in straight-line depreciation, 69
Buying, 171–185
  cash discounts, 177–179
  chain discounts, 174–176
  partial payments, 181
  terms of purchase, 178–179
  trade discounts, 171–173

Calculators, 15–16
Capital budgeting, 141–143
  compound interest and, 141–143
  evaluating alternatives, 142–143
  future value of money, 142
  present value of money, 142
Capital gains, 152
Cash discounts, 177–179
  defined, 177
  discount periods, 178–179
  terms of, 178–179
Catalog price, trade discount, 171, 172–173
Certain annuity, 123
Chain discounts, 174–176
  complement of, 174–175
  single equivalent discount, 175–176
Class frequency, 235–236
Class limits, 235–236
Class mark, 235–236
Coinsurance clause:
  major medical insurance, 208–209
  property insurance, 205–206
Collision insurance, 213
Commissions:
  brokerage firm, 151–152, 158–159
  on sales, 50–51
Common denominator, 6–7
Common stock, 151
Complement:
  of chain discount, 174–175

245

Complement (*Cont.*):
of trade discount, 172
Compound interest, 141–143
Comprehensive coverage, 213
Contingent annuity, 123
Conversion period, annuity, 123
Cost:
as base in percent markup, 190–191
conversions between retail price and, 194
inventory, determining, 196
Coverage, insurance, 202–203
Cross-multiplication:
defined, 6
fraction, 6, 18
proportion, 29
ratio, 26
Cumulative preferred stock, 151
Current yield, bond, 159–160

Decimals, 11–13
conversion to fractions, 13
percent conversion to, 31
Deductibles:
automobile insurance, 213
major medical insurance, 208–209
property insurance, 205, 206
Deductions, payroll:
defined, 54
Federal Insurance Contributions Act (FICA), 55
Federal Withholding Tax, 54
mandatory, 54–55
Denominator, 5–8, 29
Depreciation, 68–104
defined, 68
double declining balance method, 82–83, 99
salvage value, 68–69, 75–76, 91
straight-line method, 68–69, 99
sum-of-the-years'-digits method, 91, 99
summary, 99
units-of-production method, 75–76, 99
Descriptive statistics, 222
(*See also* Statistics)
Deviation from the mean, 228–230, 235
Difference, 2
Direct proportion, 28–29
Discount(s):
cash, 177–179
chain, 174–176
partial payments and, 181
trade, 171–173
Discount rate:
complement of, 172, 174–175
trade, calculating, 171–172
Discounted value:
annuity, 123, 127–129
bond, 158

Discounted value (*Cont.*):
note, 116–117
Dividends, cash, 150–153
Dividends, in division, 3–4
Division:
algebra, 18
with calculator, 15
decimal, 12–13
fraction, 7–8
order of operations, 10, 16
whole number, 3–4
Double declining balance method of depreciation, 82–83, 99
Double time, 46
Draw, 51

Electronic calculators, 15–16
End of month (EOM), 178, 179
Endowment life insurance, 211
Estimated total gain, 152–153
Exact simple interest, 107–109, 112, 113
Exact time, 108–109, 112
Execution price, 151–152
Exponents (powers), 4
with calculator, 16
order of operations, 10, 16
Extreme values, 225

Face value:
bond, 157
insurance, 202–203, 206
note, 115
Factorization, 4
Federal Insurance Contributions Act (FICA), 55
Federal Withholding Taxes, 54
Fractions, 5–8
addition, 6–7
common denominator, 6–7
conversion to decimals, 13
cross-multiplication, 6, 18
division, 7–8
fundamental principle, 6
improper, 8
mixed numbers, 8
multiplication, 7
order of operations, 10
ratios compared with, 26, 29
reduced to lowest terms, 6
subtraction, 6–7
in sum-of-the-years' digits method of depreciation, 91
Frequency, 234–236
Future value, in capital budgeting, 142

General annuity, 123
Gross pay, 41–42

Grouped data, 234–236

Hourly rate of pay, 43
Hours worked, 43

Improper fractions, 8
Indemnity, property insurance, 205
Insurance, 202–221
    automobile, 213–214
    coverage, 202–203
    life insurance, 210–211
    major medical, 208–209
    need for, 202
    premiums, 202–203
    property, 205–206
Insured, 210
Interest (*see* Compound interest; Simple interest)
Interest-bearing notes, 114–115
Interest rate:
    bond, 157
    promissory note, 115
Inventory, 196
Inverse proportion, 28–29

Least common denominator (LCD), 7
Life insurance, 210–211
Limited payment life insurance, 211
List price, trade discount, 171, 172–173
Lowest terms, fraction, 6

Major medical insurance, 208–209
Maker, promissory note, 114, 115
Mandatory deductions, 54–55
Manufacturer's suggested retail price, 171
Market value:
    bond, 157–158
    stock, 150–151
Markup:
    defined, 186
    generally, 186–187
    percent, 187–188, 190–191, 194
Maturity date:
    bond, 157
    promissory note, 115
Maturity month, 107
Maturity value:
    annuity, 123–126
    in interest calculations, 105–106, 115, 116–117
Mean:
    defined, 222
    deviation from, 228–230, 235
Median, 224–225
Medical payments protection, 213
Medicare deductions, 54
Mixed numbers, 8
Mode, 227

Multiplication:
    algebra, 18
    in calculating percent, 31–33
    with calculator, 15
    cross-, 6, 18, 26, 29
    decimal, 12
    fraction, 7
    order of operations, 10, 16
    repetitive, 4
    whole number, 3, 4

Negotiable notes, 116
Net pay, 54–55
Noncumulative preferred stock, 151
Non-interest-bearing notes, 114, 115–116
Notes, promissory, 114–117
Numerator, 5–8, 29

Odd-lot differential, 151
Odd lots, 151
Old age, survivors, and disability insurance (OASDI) deductions, 55
Order of operations, 10, 16
Ordinary annuities, 123, 124, 127
Ordinary simple interest, 107–109, 112–113
Out-of-pocket expense, major medical insurance, 208, 209
Overtime, 45–46

Par value:
    bond, 157
    stock, 150
Parentheses, order of operations, 10, 16
Partial payments, 181
Payee, promissory note, 114, 115
Payment interval, annuity, 123
Payroll, 41–67
    commission, 50–51
    gross pay, 41–42
    hourly rate, 43
    hours worked, 43
    net pay, 54–55
    overtime, 45–46
    salary, 49
Percent, 31–36
    calculating, 31–33
    in commission calculation, 51
    conversion to decimal, 31
    decrease and, 35
    increase and, 35
    sales tax application, 32–33
Percent markup, 187–188
    conversions, 194
    cost as base, 190–191
    selling price as base, 187–188
Periodic expense of sinking fund, 134

Periodic inventory costing, 196
Personal injury protection (PIP), 213
Population, 222
Powers (exponents), 4
    with calculator, 16
    order of operations, 10, 16
Preferred stock, 151
Premiums, bond, 158
Premiums, insurance, 202–203
    automobile, 213
    life, 210, 211
Present value:
    annuity, 123, 127
    in capital budgeting, 142
Price(s):
    execution, 151–152
    list, 171, 172–173
    selling, 187–188, 194
Prime factorization, 4
Primes, 4
Principal, 105
Principal balance, 137
Probability, 202
Product, 3
Promissory notes, 114–117
Property damage liability insurance, 213
Property insurance, 205–206
Proportion, 28–29
Purchasing (see Buying)

Quotient, 3–4

Ratios, 25–26, 29
Reasonable and customary benefits, 208
Receipt of goods (ROG), 178, 179
Redemption date, 157
Retail method of inventory costing, 196
Round lots, 151

Salary, 49
Sales commissions, 50–51
Sales tax, calculating, 32–33
Salvage value:
    defined, 68
    in straight-line depreciation, 68–69
    in sum-of-the-years' digits method of
        depreciation, 91
    in units-of-production depreciation, 75–76
Selling, 186–201
    inventory in, 196
    markup, generally, 186–187
    percent markup, 187–188, 190–191, 194
    terms of sale, 178–179
Selling price:
    as base in percent markup, 187–188
    conversions between cost and, 194

Shareholders, 150
Short premium, 203
Simple annuity, 123
Simple interest, 105–122
    accrued bond interest, 158–159
    approximate time and, 108–109, 112–113
    bank discount, 116–117
    calculating, 105–106, 112–113
    defined, 105
    due date calculation, 107–109
    exact, 107–109, 112, 113
    exact time and, 108–109, 112
    ordinary, 107–109, 112–113
    promissory note, 114–117
Single equivalent discount, 175–176
Sinking funds, 132–134
Sliding scale commission, 51
Social Security deductions, 54
Squared deviation from the mean, 228
Standard deviation, 228–230, 235
Statistics, 222–243
    grouped data, 234–236
    mean, 222, 228–230, 235
    median, 224–225
    mode, 227
    probability, 202
    standard deviation, 228–230, 235
    ungrouped data, 222
Stock market, 150
Stocks, 150–153
    common, 151–153
    dividends, 150–153
    evaluating investments in, 152–153
    market quotations, 150–151
    par value, 150
    preferred, 151
    trading of, 151–152
Straight commission, 51
Straight life insurance, 211
Straight-line method of depreciation, 68–69, 99
Subtraction:
    algebra, 18
    with calculator, 15
    decimal, 11–12
    fraction, 6–7
    order of operations, 10, 16
    whole number, 2
Sum, 1–2
Sum-of-the-years'-digits method of depreciation,
        91, 99

Taxes:
    Federal Withholding, 54
    sales, calculating, 32–33
Term:
    of annuity, 123

Term (*Cont.*):
  of bond, 157
  of note, 115, 116
Term life insurance, 210–211
Terms of purchase/sale, 178–179
Time-and-a-half, 45
Total frequency, 234
Total gain, 152–153
Trade discounts, 171–173

Ungrouped data, 222
Units-of-production method of depreciation,
  75–76, 99
Universal life insurance, 211

Variable commission, 51

Variables, 17–18, 28
Variance, 228, 235

Whole life insurance, 211
Whole numbers, 1–4
  addition, 1–2
  division, 3–4
  mixed numbers, 8
  multiplication, 3, 4
  primes, 4
  subtraction, 2
Word problems, 19

X (extra) discount, 178

Yield to maturity, bond, 159–160